W9-CDT-935

THE FERGUSON GUIDE

RÉSUMES
AND
JOB-HUNTING
SKILLS

A Step-by-Step Guide to Preparing for Your Job Search

MAURENE J. HINDS, CPRW

Checkmark Books®
An imprint of Facts On File, Inc.

The Ferguson Guide to Résumés and Job-Hunting Skills

Copyright © 2005 by Maurene J. Hinds

Checkmark Books
An imprint of Facts On File, Inc.
132 West 31st Street
New York NY 10001

Library of Congress Cataloging-in-Publication Data
Hinds, Maurene J.
The Ferguson guide to résumés and job-hunting skills: a handbook for recent graduates and those entering the workplace for the first time/Maurene J. Hinds.
    p. cm.
Includes index.
ISBN 0-8160-5792-3 (hc : alk. paper)—ISBN 0-8160-5796-6 (pb : alk. paper)
1. Résumés (Employment) 2. Job hunting. I. Title.
HF5383.H49 2005
650.14—dc22   2004024445

Checkmark Books are available at special discounts when purchased in bulk quantities for businesses, associations, institutions, or sales promotions. Please call our Special Sales Department in New York at (212) 967-8800 or (800) 322-8755.

You can find Facts On File on the World Wide Web at http://www.factsonfile.com

Text design by Mary Susan Ryan-Flynn
Cover design by Pehrsson Design

Printed in the United States of America

VB FOF 10 9 8 7 6 5 4 3 2 1

This book is printed on acid-free paper.

Contents

PART III: **Letters**

PART IV: **Interviewing**

APPENDIX I. **Contributors**

APPENDIX II. **Organizations**

INDEX

Acknowledgments

Many people were involved in the creation of this book. I would like to thank all the professionals who contributed their fine work as samples and those who gave their time in the form of interviews. Special thanks also needs to be given to Frank Fox, Executive Director of the Professional Association of Résumé Writers and Career Coaches (PARW/CC), Linda Matias, President of the National Résumé Writers' Association (NRWA), and Wendy Enelow, former Executive Director of the Career Masters Institute (CMI). I would also like to extend thanks to all the professionals of these organizations who give so generously of their expertise to fellow members and are so dedicated to their clients' successes. And to James Chambers and the staff of Ferguson Publishing, Inc., I give you my thanks for the opportunity to write this book.

Introduction

Whether you are fresh out of high school, in college, or have recently graduated from college, chances are you may be experiencing a variety of feelings when thinking about your future and career. Finding a career path can be exciting, overwhelming, fun, and frightening all at the same time. Most of us, from early childhood on, have thought extensively about what we want to do "when we grow up." For some, the decision may be easy. A child may have answered "a doctor" when posed that question and never waived from that decision. For others, the thought of choosing a career is more difficult. Some people have many interests and do not know how to narrow them down to a career field or find a career that allows them to incorporate as many interests as possible. For some, the choices may seem so immense that they have no idea where to begin. Still others find themselves drawn to a particular field or profession, yet find themselves fighting that impulse for a variety of reasons. Beliefs engrained in such phrases as "the starving artist" or pressures from family may cause someone to veer away from an instinctual but risky or difficult career path and toward something more financially secure or acceptable.

This book is for those seeking a career path.

It is recommended that you read the book through once before beginning your résumé or job search to gain an understanding of how all the components fit together.

Part 1

FINDING A CAREER PATH

Chapter 1

What Do I Want to Do?

Many high schools are underfunded, and career guidance options are limited as a result. Often, the student-to-counselor ratio is so high that guidance counselors do not have adequate time to spend with individual students. A 2002 Fast Response Survey System report showed an average of 249 students for every guidance staff member and 284 students for every guidance counselor, including full- and part-time counselors. This means that those of you in high school facing career and educational choices may feel lost or misdirected. Those who have gone on to college from this situation may find themselves searching for a major, declaring a major that does not feel right, or completing an area of study that is not the right fit. While some school programs do provide excellent vocational guidance, the bottom line in any scenario remains the same: You must take responsibility for your own future. Does this mean that you are completely on your own when it comes to finding a career path and eventually a job? No. It simply means that you must take the helm and carve your own path. Tools and resources are available, but it is ulti-

mately each person's responsibility to determine his or her own way.

What Do I Want to Be When I Grow Up?

If only there were a magic test that could answer this question and tell you what to do, planning a career would be simple. But there is not.

Fortunately, there are a variety of assessment tests and career professionals that can help you identify your interests and values, determine your skills, and match these with different types of jobs. When paired with other tools, assessments can help point you in the right direction. Relying too heavily on one type of assessment or tool can limit your search, so it is a good idea to investigate a few of these methods before jumping headlong into a college major or full-fledged job search. This is your future, after all, and it is worth the time and effort to get to know yourself better (this knowledge will help you later as well, when engaging in other job-related activities such as writing your résumé, cover letters, and conducting interviews). The more you know

3

about yourself, the better you will be able to make an informed decision. And when it comes to selling yourself to a prospective employer, you will be in a much better position. Imagine a salesperson. He or she needs to know a product or service well to sell it to a customer. The same is true in the job search process. You are the "goods." Knowing your product (yourself) will help your marketing efforts tremendously.

Just Because You Are Tall Does Not Mean You Should Play Basketball

At 6'5" Jeremy towered above his classmates. From middle school on, he was surrounded by pressure to go out for the basketball team. Even though he did not like basketball, he caved in to the pressure early on. The thought of becoming a star player could mean benefits like college scholarships. But Jeremy quickly learned that his suspicions were correct—he hated the game, and shortly after starting he quit the team, much to the chagrin of his coaches, parents, and even friends.

Before assessing what might seem like a natural course of action, it is important to gain an understanding of one's interests and values. It is all too easy for a person good with numbers to conclude that he or she should be an accountant. Or that someone with a flair for words should be a creative writing major in college. Not only does college cost a lot of money; students spend an extraordinary amount of time taking classes in their chosen major. And upon entering the workforce, a person will work 40 or more hours per week on the job.

It is worth taking the time to explore your interests and values.

What if you make a mistake? While determining a career path is an important step, take

heart. Many people change jobs and even careers numerous times. Your time working with self-assessment tools can only help you. But making the effort to find a good career match for you has numerous advantages (such as getting an earlier start in your chosen career instead of trying to do it after years of employment). This does not mean that you are stuck with your decision forever. Even if you find that you are about to graduate college with the "wrong" degree, this does not mean that your options are totally limited. Obviously, some jobs require a specific set of skills and education; but this is not the case for many jobs. Lots of people find work in positions outside their field of formal study. So relax and enjoy the journey.

Assessment Tests

Many career counselors and some career coaches use assessment tests to determine a person's interests, values, skills, and goals. All this information put together can paint a picture of what may be a good career choice. Some high schools provide this type of testing through classes or optional programs. College career centers have many of these tests available to students as well. What are these assessment tests like? The following is a list of some of the more common testing methods and what they test for.

If you decide to use assessment tests, keep in mind that no test, no matter how comprehensive, can tell you what you should do with your life. There are no right or wrong answers on these types of tests, and ultimately you make the final decision on what you are going to do next. Even skills assessment tests are not the final word on your capabilities; as you continue to learn and gain more experience in the working world, your skills will change as well.

Common Assessment Methods

Myers-Briggs Type Inventory (MBTI)
(Consulting Psychologists Press Inc., renamed CPP Inc. at http://www.cpp.com)

Myers-Briggs is the gold standard in personality testing and was developed by Isabel Briggs Myers and Katharine C. Briggs. It assesses four areas of personality to determine a unique combination of factors. From these components, 16 personality types are identified. The four main personality components are:

Extraversion–Introversion: Describes where people prefer to focus their attention and get their energy—from the outer world of people and activity or the inner world of ideas and experiences.

Sensing–Intuition: Describes how people prefer to take in information—focused on what is real and actual or on patterns and meanings in data.

Thinking–Feeling: Describes how people prefer to make decisions—based on logical analysis or guided by concern for their impact on others.

Judging–Perceiving: Describes how people prefer to deal with the outer world—in a planned orderly way or in a flexible, spontaneous way.

The MBTI test is the most widely used personality test in history, and as such, it should be relatively easy to find a testing site. MBTI tests vary in the amount of information provided. Many books are based on the principles of the MBTI assessment. *Do What You Are* by Paul D. Tieger and Barbara Barron-Tieger is a well-known book based on the principles of the Myers-Briggs test.

Elevations

Elevations is a card-sort tool that takes the user through a four-part series of exercises to determine values, skills, career interests, and personality themes. The results direct the user to potential career options and help determine which skills may need improvement. The test can also help users gain a better understanding of which skills are transferable between career choices. The assessment also guides the user in how he or she works with other people. The test takes most people two to three hours to complete. The results from the assessment are quite involved; having a career counselor or coach guide the user through the process will help that person get the most out of this assessment tool. An online version is available through Scully & Associates for a cost of around $30. However, local sources may also have access to this tool.

For more information, see Scully & Associates online at http://www.scullycareerassociates.com/p3505.html.

Strong Interest Inventory
(Stanford University Press)

The premise of this test is that people are most happy and productive when working in a job they like. The test takes the user through a variety of questions and links interests to various career fields or college majors. The career/interest match-up was determined by taking interest inventories of people already working in, and enjoying, these careers. The idea is that careers will attract certain people with similar interests.

DISC assessments

These assessments highlight how a person will behave in the workforce. DISC is an acronym for each aspect of the assessment. *D* describes how a person will respond and react to problems. Will the person be decisive and quick to action or mull things over? *I* indicates how a person interacts with others. Is this person people-oriented and outgoing? *S* indicates a person's preferred work pace. Does this person work in a slow, deliberate manner? Does the person prefer to work in the background? *C* gives an idea of how a person will comply with work rules and procedures. Is the person conscientious? Basically, DISC assessments give the user an idea of his or her behavior and communication styles; they help show users what they do and why. How does this help in the job search? If someone uses these assessments and determines that he or she is a people person, that is, very outgoing and needing lots of interaction, this person may want to steer clear of occupations that are very solitary with little interaction with other people.

Holland Code (RIASEC)

The Holland Code is based on the research of Dr. John Holland, who developed a theory about how people choose careers. His idea is that people with certain interests will be drawn to certain types of careers or college majors. The Holland Code compares the user's interests to those of other people to discover what types of professions people with similar interests chose. Over 12,000 occupations and many college majors have been coded into this system. The Code is based around six areas: *Realistic, Investigative, Artistic, Social, Enterprising,* and *Conventional* (RIASEC). For a basic overview of the Holland Code, see http://jobs.utah.gov/wi/Regions/central/holland.pdf. The Code helps people gain a better understanding of occupational types.

Birkman Method

The Birkman Method is often used by corporations to gain a better understanding of how their employees work. It is frequently used by people in career transition, switching from one career to another. It can also be useful for those exploring career options. The Birkman Method is a personality assessment that provides information in four areas: strengths, needs at work, what motivates a person, and how a person reacts in stressful situations. The results can help the user determine what type of working environment he or she is best suited for, his or her interests, how he or she usually behaves, how he or she reacts to stress, and what he or she needs from a job. As with the Holland Code, this information can be used to determine which types of careers and working environments might be a good match for the test-taker.

SCANS

This stands for the *Secretary's Commission on Achieving Necessary Skills,* a U.S. Government project that identified the skills necessary for a high level of job performance. The project began under former U.S. Secretary of Labor Lynn Martin. The results of the project were compiled and published in a 1991 report called "A SCANS Report for America 2000." The list of skills is still used today as a way for students and job seekers to determine which skills they need to improve upon. For more information about SCANS, see http://wdr.doleta.gov/SCANS/

Focus

Focus is a comprehensive assessment process that highlights interests, values, personality, skills, and leisure activities using a variety of methods. The system helps users identify and narrow career matches to their personal profile. For more information, visit http://www.focuscareer.com.

Availability of Assessment Tests

All of these tests, or variations thereof, are available through a number of online sources for a fee, but be sure to check into local possibilities first. Your high school or college may have a given test available for free or for a lower charge than you may find elsewhere. Professional résumé writers and career coaches often have access to these types of tests and can provide additional resources and one-on-one coaching. While the tests are available online in various formats, keep in mind that they vary—some are shorter than others, for example. Some will give a minimal list of results consisting of general career categories; others will provide a more detailed list and/or the option of a consultation with a career counselor. Also look into local possibilities such as job service or career-placement agencies (see page 29 for more discussion on placement agencies and headhunters/recruiters).

Among the websites worth looking into is the Princeton Review, at http://www.princetonreview.com/cte, which allows you to take self-assessment tests and provides information on a variety of careers free of charge. The site also provides a lot of information on job seeking in general. Another good site, especially for students, is Careersmarts.com, which provides a variety of assessment tools.

What If I Flunk?

There are no right or wrong answers to assessment tests. While you can do your own assessment of the results, it may help to meet with a professional if you are still stuck, do not like the results, have conflicting results, or just do not feel that any of the suggested career paths are a good match.

Keep in mind that no assessment, skills, interests, or other test (or group of tests) can tell you what you should do with your life. Furthermore, your interests and skills are bound to change as you move along your career path. Remember, most people change jobs multiple times and even change careers a few times throughout their working lifetimes.

If your results show you are lacking skills for a particular profession now, that does not mean this will always be the case. If you have the desire, chances are you can improve your skills in an area where you may currently be weak. There are, of course, exceptions, but you can always improve capabilities and grow as a person. And there are always alternative positions within a field of work; if one position is unrealistic, another closely related job may be just the thing.

You, not a test or even another person, have the final say in determining your career path. If you are feeling unsure or stuck, consult the services of a career counselor or coach. Sometimes the added information and objectivity that these professionals can provide will be enough to help you move forward. It may consist of further explanation regarding how an assessment test works, what exactly a particular career entails, or simply the go-ahead to pursue your chosen path. If you need help, it is available.

Mining Your Past

Assessment tools are not the only options when it comes to figuring out what direction you want to pursue in life. Your past is also a good indication of where your future may lie. By taking time to review your interests, hobbies, and activities, you can gain great insight into what direction is best. Set aside a large enough chunk of time so that you can gather your thoughts, reflect on your past, and jot down some notes.

While some people prefer to keep their hobbies and work life separate, hobbies and interests can be an indication of what type of work you may be best suited for. An avid fly fisher may also enjoy the detailed and creative work of tying flies. Such a person may enjoy working alone, focusing on details, creating something realistic, and working with his or her hands. These are all traits that can be transferred into the working world. Even more "modern" hobbies such as playing video games, for example, can highlight a person's aptitude and interests. Many games require strategic planning, quick thinking, working as part of an online group to accomplish a task, or the ability to solve puzzles that require the player to think in a creative manner. Such a person may enjoy problem solving or tackling a challenge as part of a team while on the job.

What about your past? Have there been activities or skills that you find yourself repeatedly drawn to, or are there activities that have always seemed to come naturally to you? Have you enjoyed these things? Are they worth exploring in greater detail? Chances are that as you explore your past, you will find activities that have similar attributes or characteristics— these may be a good indicator of the type of work you will find most enjoyable.

Make lists of activities, pastimes, and hobbies that you have taken part in throughout your life. Do the items on your list require similar skills? Do they have similar characteristics such as taking place alone or in a group? Do they require a certain way of thinking about things? Do they require hands-on manipulation, or are they more cerebral in nature? Circle the attributes that are similar, and you may be surprised to find a common theme or trend.

What Not to Do

Just as important as knowing what you want to do is knowing what you do not want to do. While this may seem obvious, it is an often-overlooked area that deserves attention. A person may be certain that he or she wants to work with people; but if that person is not clear about how, the results may not be as intended. Someone in sales, for example, may enjoy the challenge of selling but not the idea of working with the general public. In this case, a more specified selling position, such as medical equipment, might suit this person better.

Knowing that you enjoy teaching can lead you in the wrong path if you do not acknowledge that you do not want to work with high school students. In a case like this, an elementary teaching certificate is more desirable than a secondary teaching certificate, or if you already have a K-12 teaching degree, you can try avoiding positions teaching older students. Obviously, it is impossible to avoid every possible dislike. There are usually aspects of a job that a person prefers over others; however, avoiding general dislikes on a larger scale is important to long-term satisfaction.

My Perfect Day

A common exercise in determining what you are "meant" to do is to use the "perfect day" visualization. Imagine that money is no object. Where would you live? What would your home be like? What would you do first thing when you got out of bed in the morning? How would you spend your day? Whom would you spend it with? Where would you spend your day?

A related exercise is to ask yourself one of the following questions: What would I continue to do even if I weren't getting paid? If I won the lottery, but still had to work, what would I do? In other words, if money were not a factor, what type of work would you pursue? Is the answer to this question different from the career path you are currently considering?

Money can be a difficult issue. We work to pay the bills, put a roof over our heads, and put food on the table. Yet money is not the clear solution to career satisfaction. Considering the amount of time spent at work and the self-identification associated with one's work, it is only natural that other means of satisfaction be derived in order to be happy at work. In your ideal day or lottery-winning workday, what elements of satisfaction are garnered when money is no longer a central factor? These elements are key to your satisfaction at work, which leads to the next area of exploration.

What Do You Want in a Job?

What do you value in a potential job? There are two types of work values to consider: intrinsic and extrinsic. Intrinsic values relate to the actual work and its contributions to society. Extrinsic values relate to external features such as the working environment.

Besides a handsome paycheck, what elements of a potential job are important to you? What types of hours would you like to work? Do you prefer to work during the day or at night? Do you want to work more or less than 40 hours per week? Do you prefer to work alone or as part of a group? Do you see yourself in a leadership or support position? Where would you like to work? Do you prefer the rush of the city or do you prefer a rural setting? Would you rather work for a large corporation or a small, family-owned business? Do you want to start your own business? Do you want to work indoors or out? Do you prefer being active or sitting at a desk?

This is only a sampling of possible questions, but writing down the answers to these and other questions about your preferred working environment will help you determine what you would like to do, where, and with whom.

Dealing with Well-Wishers

Chances are good your parents and friends only want what is best for you. Their opinions about your future, however, may not mesh with your own ideas, interests, or skills. Parents want their children to succeed. They want to see their children have a secure future. As such, parents sometimes misguide or pressure their children into following a career path that may not be the best fit for the child. As the child, it can be difficult to fight this pressure. Take, for instance, the child who does not wish to run the family business or follow in his or her parents' footsteps. It can be a challenge to say no to ideas that may have been engrained from an early age. However, with proper career counseling or coaching, saying no may be the best option. If you find yourself in this situation and need assistance in how to cope with it, consult a career counselor who has experience in this area.

"A career counselor can provide objectivity," says MJ Feld of Careers by Choice Inc., who holds a master's in career counseling (see p. 241 for page numbers of résumé samples). "When young people look into career options, they often first start with what their parents do, and then either accept or reject [that line of work]." Feld says the key components for young people seeking a career path are twofold. The first entails looking at yourself and really thinking about who you are. This is often not done. Second, Feld recommends self-assessment testing because it provides objectivity. This is especially important because "it is hard for young people to make a career decision. They do not have much work experience and it is a big decision." Objectivity when researching careers is particularly important for those majors with a large upfront investment of time and money, such as law or medical school.

Following self-assessment, career counselors can help career seekers investigate many different options and provide choices. This is followed by researching careers of interest. Feld emphasizes that career counselors do not make decisions for people. "Ownership lies with the individual."

Chapter 2

Putting It All Together

Making career choices is hard work. Don't be afraid to ask for help or make use of all the resources that are available to you.

School Programs

If you are in high school or college, take advantage of any career-guidance programs available. The results can be worth the effort as well as time and can be cost effective for you. While some public schools are grossly underfunded, most try to offer as much as they can in terms of career planning. Make an appointment to visit with your school's career counselor. If your school offers a special program or coursework in career planning, add it to your curriculum.

For those in college, check out your school's career guidance center when you are a freshman or sophomore (particularly if you are having trouble deciding on a major). Guidance counselors can assist you with all aspects of career planning and may have special programs in conjunction with the community to assist students in finding internship programs and job placement opportunities.

A Model High School Program We Can All Learn From

Smithtown High School in Smithtown, New York, offers a fabulous career planning program for students called "Career Jump Start." Sue Gubing is the School Industry Coordinator and Mary Pat Grafstein is a career planning teacher. They work with students from grades 10 through 12 on career planning. The program includes comprehensive assessments to determine potential career paths; after taking the classes, students conduct research on their fields of interest. Research includes all aspects of the job, from what is expected on a daily basis to salary ranges and future job prospects for a particular industry. In addition to researching primary interests, students also look into alternative career choices.

Through this process, Gubing reports that about 85–90 percent of students fit into a career path. About 10–15 percent may feel "stuck," but this is often resolved by clarifying the vocabulary used in assessment testing and results. If needed, students will complete additional assessment testing.

Ms. Gubing works with local businesses to help students find opportunities for job shadowing. Determining whom to shadow takes students two to three weeks. They choose about five potential businesses and then narrow the list down to the top choice. Ms. Grafstein sends a letter on behalf of the students to the business, and the students call a few days later to set up an appointment.

The job-shadowing process has proven extremely helpful in allowing students to get a feel for what a given job is really like. The process tends to reinforce a career choice or to make students realize that their preconceived notions of the job were off and that a different choice might be better. Interviewing professionals about their careers is also part of the process. Students write a report of their findings and experiences and present the information to the class.

As part of the program, students must also write a résumé. The creators of the program have developed a great website that provides information on career planning and résumé writing for high school students. In particular, Ms. Gubing developed the "Long Island Résumé," which is specifically geared toward the needs of the younger job seeker. More information can be found at http://www.careersmarts.com and http://www.careerjumpstart.org. (Please note that all information provided on these sites is copyrighted. The links are provided to be used as a general reference.)

By the time the process is complete, many students have a clear idea about the career path they would like to follow. About 95 percent of Smithtown High School's students go on to college. For those who have completed the career-planning program, many have already decided on a major.

Ms. Grafstein says that one of the problems she sees in students planning for college is that they choose a college before a major. This can lead to problems when the school does not offer a program in the chosen field. She recommends deciding on a major and then doing research on schools to see which ones offer the best programs.

Smithtown's program is lucky in that it receives a lot of support from the school, parents, and the local community. While not every school can afford to implement such a program, imagine how many "mistakes" could be avoided if young people had the support and guidance to research and follow their career dreams. (Information on the program's advisory board can be found at http://www.smithtowniab.org.)

So, You Think You Have It Figured Out—Or at Least an Idea

What do you do with all the information you have gathered about yourself? At this point you may have a general idea of the direction you would like to follow, or perhaps you are feeling pretty clear about the whole thing. Or maybe you still do not have a clue.

Really stuck or facing a difficult challenge? Seek the help of a career counselor or coach. Not sure which one you need? Generally speaking, career counselors have degrees in counseling and choose to work in the career fields, or they have specific degrees in career counseling. Career coaches are professionals who work in the careers industry but do not necessarily have a counseling background. Both can be very helpful in the job search process, but one may be a better option for you than another, depending on your situation. If you are feeling stuck or needing some clear direction about discovering and defining your career goals, you will probably want to seek the help of a career counselor. This person will guide you through assessments and other exercises to help you determine your ideal job. Additionally, if you happen to be facing a particularly difficult situation, such as extreme pressure from family to pursue a certain path, or are feeling completely clueless, it may be to your advantage to seek the advice of a career counselor. Some of the issues that could come up in the process may be best suited for someone with training in counseling. Career coaches can be of great assistance for those who feel they are on the right path and already know what area they want to focus on but could use a little guidance. Coaches can help fine-tune the process and help you utilize the best methods to achieve your goals.

The National Career Development Association lists the following on their website to describe the role of career guidance professionals. They:

- Conduct individual and group personal counseling sessions to help clarify life/career goals

- Administer and interpret tests and inventories to assess abilities, interests, and other factors, and to identify career options

- Encourage exploratory activities through assignments and planning experiences

- Utilize career planning systems and occupational information systems to help individuals better understand the world of work

- Provide opportunities for improving decision-making skills

- Assist in developing individualized career plans

- Teach job-hunting strategies and skills and assist in the development of résumés

- Help resolve potential personal conflicts on the job through practice in human relations skills

- Assist in understanding the integration of work and other life roles

- Provide support for persons experiencing job stress, job loss, and career transition

Notice the types of words that stand out: encourage, assist, help, teach, provide. (For more information on career counselors, visit the NCDA website at http://www.ncda.org.)

What should you look for in a career counselor or coach? First and foremost, an honest person who has the education and/or credentials that he or she claims to have. Just as anyone can post a website and claim to be an expert on something, anyone can open a business and claim to have your best interests at heart. Be cautious of anyone or any program that asks for a lot of money upfront, claims to be able to solve all your problems, promises unrealistic results, or wants to tell you what to do rather than guide you. The following are some credentials to look for in a counselor or coach.

The Board for Certified Counselors offers a Nationally Certified Counselor (NCC) credential. Individuals must have an advanced degree in counseling from an accredited college or university, must have completed a certain number of supervised hours in counseling, and must have received a passing score on the National Counselor Examination for Licensure and Certification (NCE). The National Career Development Organization recognizes three different levels of membership, the Master Career Counselor (MCC), the Master Career Development Professional (MCDP), and the Fellow. Other certifications include the Job and Career Transition Coach (JCTC) and the Certified Job Search Trainer (CJST). Both of these certifications are offered through the Career Planning and Adult Development Network. The International Coach Federation offers a number of certifications, including the Associate Certified Coach (ACC), the Professional Certified Coach (PCC), and the Master Certified Coach (MCC). The Career Coach Academy offers a Certified Career Management Coach program (CCMC), and the Career Coach Institute offers a Certified Career Coach (CCC) credential. (For a list of additional organizations that offer career coaching certification, please refer to Appendix II.)

Obviously, there are a number of legitimate credentials a career counselor or coach may hold. The preceding list is by no means exhaustive. What this means for the consumer is that, as with all products and services, some common sense and perhaps a little bit of research may be in order if the qualifications of a career coach are at all questionable. All of the organizations providing legitimate credentials expect those who are certified to follow strict ethical guidelines. (Many of the professionals who contributed sample résumés and cover letters for this book hold counseling and/or coaching credentials. Please refer to Appendix I for more information.)

If you choose to use the services of a professional, ask for an initial meeting to get a feeling for how the person works. This does not have to be a lengthy meeting, should not cost you much, if at all, and can save you a lot of frustration if you decide you are not a good match. It is okay to shop around; after all, you are looking for help making one of the most important deci-

sions you will face. If you decide to work with a professional and have already taken some assessments or done any career research, be sure to take all that information with you to your meeting. Both career counselors and coaches can help you make sense of the results. Just as with testing methods, career professionals cannot tell you what you should do—they guide and coach you, but ultimately it is your decision as to what path you should take. Choosing a career can be scary or intimidating, and while it is tempting to wish for a magic test or someone else to tell you exactly what is best for you, it is not going to happen (if it does, proceed with caution). It is okay to be wary; but taking on the challenge of finding a career path is also an exciting turning point in a person's life.

If you are wading through your assessment results on your own, gather all your information and create charts and lists. Do not rely on only one test; take at least a couple to see if they're showing similar results or something completely different. After taking the assessments, look both for consistencies and inconsistencies. If similar patterns are emerging, do they seem accurate? Do the results point to similar career choices? If not, try to pinpoint where the differences occur. Do you have seemingly conflicting interests in your results? Create a full inventory of your interests, skills, values, and personality type and match this information to career choices. Should you choose to "go it alone," it may be useful to use assessment tests that automatically assign your results to career profiles; otherwise, it may be too overwhelming a task to do on your own.

There is no stigma in seeking the advice of a professional. Your career choice will make a huge impact on your life. It affects your financial comfort, your feelings of self-worth and accomplishment, your feelings of making a unique contribution, and your overall emotional well-being. Taking the time to do it "right" the first time can save you much stress down the road. While it is not impossible to recover from a degree or career that is not the best fit, it can be avoided. This is your life and your dreams we are talking about!

What if you have already done it wrong? The good news is that a lot of knowledge and many skills are transferable. Even some of the more specialized degrees and careers have attributes that can be put to good use elsewhere. With a little help from a counselor or coach and some creative thinking, it is possible to get back on the right track.

Christine Edick of Action Résumés is a career professional who has been in the business for over 13 years and has been coaching since 1995 (see http://www.acareercoach4u.com). She emphasizes that her role as a coach is as a guide—clients have the answers, but they need a little help sometimes or permission to explore possibilities. She works with assessments and also helps clients research potential careers. The clients do the legwork; she gives them guidance. Some of Edick's recommendations include talking to people who work in the business and job shadowing (see information on these topics in the following chapter). If a client is really stuck in determining a career path, her advice is to "keep moving." That is, if a particular exercise or method is not working, she will help the stuck client by suggesting new ideas and assisting that person in finding fresh ways of looking at things.

Chapter 3

Do Not Hit the Pavement Yet

So, you have at least narrowed the field to some specific career areas that interest you. Before jumping headlong into finding a position, though, take some time to learn about the available jobs within your area of interest. You might come across a job that you didn't even know existed, and it could be a good match.

Some jobs are obvious—doctor, lawyer, teacher—but what about other job titles such as reflexologist, biofeedback therapist, aquarist, real-time captioner, or endodontist? How does one learn about positions that may be related to one's interests but are not necessarily jobs that immediately come to mind?

Numerous reference sources exist that list various types of jobs. Most of these references provide information on the working environment, what type of education or credentials are required, typical pay ranges, and employment prospects. One of the best-known and widely used databases is the *Dictionary of Occupational Titles* (DOT), a U.S. Government publication that lists numerous job titles and corresponding information. Visit the local library to review the books; most libraries will keep them shelved in the reference area where they cannot be checked out. O*NET (Occupational Information Network) provides information similar to the DOT in an online version, providing information for over 950 occupations. Information can be researched by job title, job category, skill type, or by using other job classification systems. To visit the O*NET, go to http://www.occupational outlook-handbook.net/index.html. Users can register for free and search the site. The *Occupational Outlook Handbook* is another government reference listing various job titles and related information.

Many other publishers provide similar job-related books. Ferguson's *Encyclopedia of Careers and Vocational Guidance* lists occupational information by job type; the most recent version (the 13th Edition) provides a full range of information for job seekers in the first volume, including sources for determining career interests, writing a résumé, and interviewing.

The *Careers in Focus* and *Career Opportunities* series, also by Ferguson, provide more detailed information on careers within a specific field or area of interest. Other titles, such as *The Big Book of Jobs,* provide similar information.

The reference librarian at your local library can point you to these and other materials to help you in your search. The library also provides free Internet access if you do not have it at home.

Informational Interviews

How does the informational interview differ from the job interview? First and foremost, the informational interview is not conducted with the goal of obtaining a job offer, even though this can, and sometimes does, result.

Informational interviews are conducted by the person seeking a job but are carried out for the purpose of learning more about a particular industry or specific job. If someone is interested in health care but is undecided whether or not to pursue medical school or some other field, he or she may conduct interviews with different types of health care workers. Interviews might include talking with a family physician, an occupational therapist, and an optometrist. All are areas within health care; all require different types of training.

The informational interview can also help a job seeker get a feel for a "day in the life of" a particular occupation much better than simply reading about the job in a book. Really knowing what the day-to-day business is like can help a person determine whether or not he or she is on the right path. Someone who has been convinced that she is destined for writing, for example, may be turned off by the prospect of repeated rejections. Or a very outgoing psychology major may decide that he would be better suited to working in group-therapy set-

tings or treatment centers rather than in a private practice.

Another important benefit of conducting these types of interviews is that they allow the job seeker to learn the lingo of the business and get an insider's view. While this viewpoint will not be as involved as someone's who is already in the business, it will allow the job seeker to feel more comfortable during the job interview process. He or she will have a feel for the job and be better able to speak to why he or she is a better candidate than someone else. And the informational interview will help the candidate use appropriate language, dress, and professional mannerisms better than someone who simply reads about a profession or models him or herself after examples from movies or television. The insider information gathered through informational interviews can be invaluable.

Another benefit of conducting informational interviews is that it gives a person a chance to practice communication skills without the added pressure of competing for a job, as is the case in a job interview. As you become more comfortable meeting professionals in the working world, it will be that much easier when it comes to meeting professionals who are interviewing you for a potential job. Simply realizing that everyone is human, an obvious reality, makes the eventual job interview easier. If informational interviews are conducted with people at all levels of the professional ladder, you will come to realize that everyone started somewhere and that you are no different. Your communication skills will become more refined, you will be getting out into the working world, and you will learn a lot along the way.

If the thought of conducting an informational interview seems intimidating, there are ways to make it easier. Contacting professionals through a letter or e-mail can break the ice and let the person know that you will be contacting him or her by phone later on. Having a script on hand or some basic notes can make that telephone call a little easier. And of course, the more you do this, the easier it will get. Be considerate of the other person's time, and always be polite and professional on the phone. Inquire as to the possibility of meeting with the person, and ask when the best time is to meet within his or her schedule. When you do make an appointment, make sure you arrive on time and are aware of how long the interview should last.

How do you find people to interview? Your school or guidance counselor may have a program in place for setting up informational interviews. If not, counselors know a lot of people in the community and may have suggestions. Friends and family members are also good sources of contacts, as are classmates and colleagues if you are already working. If there is a local company that you would like to get more information about but have no inside contacts, you may need to make a cold call and ask for names of people in management or particular departments.

People like to talk about themselves, their jobs, and how they arrived at their current positions. As such, it may prove easier than you think to find people willing to share some time to discuss their fields and their companies. Just keep in mind the purpose of the interview—to gather information about a profession, a company, and job prospects in general, not to ask for a job. This may come later; it may not. However, informational interviewees, when treated with respect, can become wonderful allies and members of your personal networking group. Keep them informed of your job progress. People like to know when they have been of service and when it has paid off.

Not Sure What Is a Good Fit? Try 'em on for Size

A job may look good on paper, or even sound like the perfect match, but if you are not quite sure, real-world experience can be a great option. Many possibilities exist to try on various jobs for size and fit. Some of those possibilities include:

Job shadowing

Job shadowing is a chance to spend a day or two observing or "shadowing" someone in your prospective career. It can give you an idea what a typical day is like in the profession and an opportunity to ask questions about the job. Following an informational interview, job shadowing is a good way to get more of a hands-on feel for a job. If you are interested in job shadowing, consider asking about it when conducting your informational interviews. Some high school programs offer job-shadowing opportunities as part of the program. For those in college, check with the career center to see if anything is in place for this type of experience. Otherwise, continue your networking and informational interviewing, asking about job-shadowing opportunities when appropriate. Just as with the informational interview, many people are happy to share their knowledge and experiences.

Internships

Internships may be paid or unpaid, depending on circumstances. They are usually obtained through a school program. Internships are often undertaken for school credit and allow students to gain experience working in the "real world" in their chosen profession or in a position closely related. These positions operate just like real jobs and can be a great source for learning about the profession, improving one's skills, proving one's abilities, and making valuable contacts. Ideally, companies providing internships are doing so to help students and to possibly gain future employees. Unfortunately, in some cases, businesses use interns to do the "grunt" work and other tasks not associated with the program's goals. It is vital that these situations be reported to the school and dealt with immediately to maintain the integrity of the programs.

MJ Feld is a career counselor who has extensive experience working with college students and highly recommends students take advantage of internship opportunities. Because many students do not have work experience in their field of study, Feld says, "One of the best things students can do is internships or volunteer work in their area." The other advantage to interning is that students can gain an inside look at their career field and determine if they have made a good choice. It is a short-term commitment and a good way to investigate the career. Following school, it is no longer possible to intern, and students will not be able to "figure it out" through a succession of jobs. A lot of schools have programs to assist students in finding internship opportunities. If you are still in school, take advantage of these programs.

Volunteer positions

Volunteering is a great way to make a contribution to the community, provide valuable services, and learn more about a field of interest. It is also experience that can be put on a résumé; volunteer work is often looked upon admirably by employers. Volunteering is a good way to network and make contacts from all areas of the business community, because volunteering attracts a wide range of personalities. Many communities have volunteer placement agencies. If yours does not, peruse the yellow pages,

talk with a reference librarian, and do some networking to find potential volunteer opportunities. Cold calling a company or organization to offer your services may work as well if you know specifically how you would like to volunteer your time.

Summer jobs

While it can sometimes be difficult to find a summer position in one's desired field, a benefit to summer employment is that it provides valuable work experience, allows you to demonstrate your work ethic, provides a source for additional networking contacts, and helps you develop skills that can be transferable to other positions later on. Naturally, you will want to aim for a position related to your long-term career goals. However, even a job that seems completely unrelated can be of benefit. Take, for example, a position that requires a clear head, quick thinking, and high levels of responsibility. The stereotypical example of the summer lifeguard is one such example. Many skills required of a lifeguard are transferable to other positions. The lifeguard must obtain certification, proving that he or she has the desire and ability to learn and obtain qualifications necessary for the job. The lifeguard must also "multi-task," keeping an eye on the water, the surrounding areas, and everywhere in between. Communication skills are also required, in that the lifeguard often has to inform visitors of the rules and stop any unwanted or unsafe behavior. Additionally, the lifeguard must react quickly and use sound judgment in the face of an emergency. The lifeguard is held to a high level of responsibility: ensuring the safety of all visitors while he or she is on shift. What kinds of employers would not want their employees to possess such skills?

When looking into summer positions, keep in mind that while the job may not be in itself a starter to a career, it can provide many benefits down the road. Keep a list of skills required for the job and any accomplishments made during the time on the job—it will be stuff that good résumés are made of later.

Work study programs

As with summer employment, work study programs can provide valuable work experience while helping to lower your college tuition payments. When you are filling out your financial aid application, there will be a place to indicate if you are interested in work study programs. If it is feasible for you to do so, taking part in these programs can be a good way to gain valuable work experience and help you determine what you do and do not like in a job.

Temping and subcontracting

Temp work is a great way to gain experience and try out a variety of positions. Agencies that place temporary workers may have openings ranging anywhere from one day to a number of months or even a year or more. This type of work can expose you to different industries and companies and may lead to a permanent posi-

tion. At the very least it is an opportunity to learn and hone skills and develop more networking contacts.

The types of jobs offered through temp agencies vary a great deal, from physical work to administrative services to more involved positions with longer placement timeframes. While highly skilled or professional positions are not as likely in this scenario, this does not mean they are never available. Some technical positions can be well-suited to temp work, for example, when a short-term project or issue needs attention.

Similarly, working on a subcontract level is a way to gain exposure to more than one company, although this type of work requires knowledge and preferably experience in a specific field or area. Subcontract work varies anywhere from yard maintenance to highly skilled jobs. Subcontracting work can be more difficult to find, as it often requires self-marketing and word-of-mouth references. However, if you are able to obtain this kind of opportunity, it is a wonderful way to get your foot in the door, meet valuable contacts, and gain experience. After a successful subcontracting experience, you may decide that you prefer to continue in this line of work rather than seek a permanent position.

Chapter 4

Where the Jobs Are: Beyond the Classifieds

Many people automatically turn to the classifieds, either online or in a local newspaper, when beginning a job search. Unfortunately, using the classifieds is not the most effective way to find a job. For one, many companies do not list openings in the first place or do so only as a last resort or to ensure equal opportunity for anyone interested. Online positions usually garner thousands of applications for each opening, and those résumés are typically scanned into a computer system that searches for certain keywords through a special program. If the keywords are not present, or if the résumé does not contain enough of them, the résumé does not even make it through the first cut.

There are two types of job search methods. One is the passive method, in which people send their résumés in response to a classified position and sit back hoping to hear a response. The other is the active method, in which a person treats the process as a job itself, makes regular contact with people who may know of job openings, and takes other initiatives to find a job. In the first method,

job seekers look for positions that may be a good fit, hoping that, if called in for an interview and hired, they can make themselves fit the job. In the second method, job seekers look for positions that match their interests, values, and skills. The difference between the two methods regarding how long it can take to find a position (and not just any position—the right position) can literally be months.

How, then, do companies find employees and employees find well-fitting jobs? The answer is referred to as the "hidden job market." The hidden job market refers to positions found through word of mouth, direct references, and even jobs that did not previously exist until someone saw a need and suggested a new position. The majority of jobs are filled through methods such as these, not through the classifieds. This does not mean that you should never respond to a posted job opening. Smaller communities, for example, are much more likely to have a higher ratio of job postings per actual jobs than a larger city. However, most of your efforts should concentrate on activities that will help you tap into the hidden job market.

Networking

First and foremost, every job seeker should focus on his or her list of networking contacts. Networking is a process of making contacts with people—all kinds of people—who may at some point be able to help you land a job. It is not about using others. Networking is so important that entire books have been devoted to the subject. One of the best is *A Foot in the Door* by Katherine Hansen (Ten Speed Press, 2000), which explores networking in detail and is easy to read. What follows is an overview of the process, with a recommendation that further reading on networking be undertaken by those less familiar with networking or "starting from scratch" where networking is concerned.

The process of networking is a give and take. Even if you feel you have nothing to offer someone else as far as his or her ability to find a job or gather more information, you may surprise yourself. And you may have a lot more to offer down the road, which leads to the next point. Keeping in contact with your network is vital. Even if you land your dream job right away, it is still important to maintain those relationships you worked so hard to build. First, you never know when you may be hit with a layoff or some other unforeseen circumstance, and second, you may be able to help one of your networking contacts who previously helped you. As the saying goes, "What comes around goes around." Keeping in touch with your contacts is a simple courtesy; it shows them you care and is a sign of professionalism and maturity.

With whom should you network? Everyone. Your family, friends, colleagues, classmates, coworkers, faculty—the list goes on. While it may seem like you should always aim high, such as networking with those in management and/or hiring positions, you should aim for a mix of people at various stages and levels in their career paths. The "gatekeepers," as administrative, human resources, and secretarial employees are sometimes called, often have access to the higher-ups who can be difficult to contact. Similarly, these people often know the inner workings of the company the best—they know who is doing what, who is hiring, what departments are down- or upsizing, and many other goings-on at the company. The person who may surprise you the most as far as your networking efforts are concerned may be the last person you would expect to have inside information. Your friend's mom may know the CEO of the local up-and-coming business.

Networking can occur in just about any setting, at any time, anywhere. If you approach the idea of networking as simple communication and making conversation, the process suddenly becomes something you do on a regular basis. You ask questions about the other person and offer information about yourself. The key is to be aware of the other person's time, and if the place seems inappropriate, it may well be. Interrupting someone for a quick conversation in the grocery store is more appropriate than interrupting someone's dinner.

Prepare a few different "speeches" for different situations. These are basic outlines of the main points you want to hit. Use the term "speech" loosely. You do not want to memorize it word for word, but you do want to have an idea of what to say.

The first is commonly referred to as the "elevator" speech because it is short and takes about the amount of time to travel between two floors on an elevator. This is a short, 30-second overview of who you are and what you do. In the case of networking for a potential job, you will want to have a quick speech prepared to convey your background and goals. You do not want to include asking for a job as part of this short speech, but if the conversation takes off from there, you can ask if the other person has any insights, advice, or knowledge of other people you could be talking to.

For situations where a longer conversation is appropriate, have a similar presentation prepared to go into more depth about what you are looking for. This could be a follow-up to the elevator speech, should that conversation continue. Finally, be prepared for an in-depth conversation about your background and goals. This type of presentation is best suited for one-on-one, scheduled meetings, such as the informational interview mentioned earlier.

When working on your presentations, practice in a comfortable situation. You do not want to sound "canned," but you do want to include all the pertinent details. Practice with family or other friends who are in the same situation as you. Your networking skills can be honed with other networkers.

When will you use these prepared speeches? Some organizations set up meetings for this very purpose. The local Chamber of Commerce may offer an after-hours get together, for example, to which members are invited. This is an ideal opportunity to "schmooze" and meet professionals in the community. Some colleges may offer networking groups. Other business-related social events are also possibilities. Keep an eye out for events taking place in your community. Remember, also, that traditional social events are options for networking; just do not overdo it. Social events are meant to be social—if the atmosphere lends itself to talking a little about your career goals, go ahead. If it does not feel quite right, it probably is not.

What about people that others have referred you to or that you do not know but would like to meet? For those that have been referred, the easiest thing to do is call or write, stating that so-and-so recommended you give them a call. Provide the basic reason for your call and ask if they would be agreeable to meeting you. If you are shy about calling or have trouble making your way through voice mail, sending a letter or e-mail ahead of time can help break the ice and give the person a head's up that you will be following up with a phone call.

As for cold calling someone you do not yet know but with whom you would like to schedule an informational interview, your personality may prescribe the best method for you. An outgoing person who is comfortable making cold calls may want to go ahead and make the call, being respectful, as always, of the other person's time. For those who are shy or worry about saying the wrong thing, an introductory letter or e-mail may be best, followed up with a phone call. Be sure to inform the person in the correspondence that you will be calling within a certain amount of time. This can help make the eventual phone call more comfortable. Having a loose script or some notes on hand when you do call can also aid you in staying on track and remembering to say what you intend.

What do you say in the letter or when you call? This depends on the situation. If you were referred by someone, your conversation will be slightly different than if you are making a cold call. In general, you want to state your name, the purpose for your call (to gain information), and whether or not you can schedule an appointment. If you are leaving a message, be sure to include your return phone number. If you are calling on a referral, state the name of the person who referred you. Be sure to reiterate that you are not seeking a job. You are looking for information about that particular career or advice on how to improve your résumé or your job search. When calling, you may want to have some notes on hand to remind you of what to say, but try not to read from a script. You want to allow the conversation to take on a life of its own if that happens, and you also do not want to sound rehearsed. Again, practice on your friends and family beforehand if the idea of calling makes you nervous. *The Savvy Networker* by Ronald and Caryl Krannich (Impact Publications, 2001) provides some samples of what you may say on the phone. Remember, though, that you are selling yourself, and you will want to use a method and words that fit your personality. Trying to be someone else may help you in the short run but can be detrimental down the road when your true personality comes through. Use words and phrases that are comfortable for you.

For those who are uncomfortable beginning with a phone call, e-mail or a letter is a good alternative. Just as in the phone call, state who you are and why you are contacting that particular person; for example, you were referred by someone else, or you are impressed with the person's qualifications or company's success. You may go into a little more detail in your letter about your background, but provide only enough information to give the person a sense of who you are. Remember, you are not asking for a job. Too much information may make the contact feel as though you are asking for one thing (information) but have hidden motives (a job offer). But a little bit about your background may help the person gain a better understanding of what type of information you are looking for.

As a new graduate or someone just entering the workforce, the contact may very well relate to your desire to learn more about a particular field before jumping in. Everyone started some-where, and people like to talk about why they chose their particular profession and how they got to where they are today. People also like to help others, particularly those just starting out. If you are earnest in your approach and are truly seeking information, your contacts will sense this. Many people will appreciate being seen as an adviser and will want to help. Who would not want to have some influence on helping discover the next great thing?

Not everyone will be so inclined, however. Keep in mind that you will face rejections and that this is a normal part of the process. People are busy, and with the recent emphasis and attention put on networking, many people have become put off by the process. Because some people have abused the true meaning of networking, by using other people to get what they want and then abandoning the relationship and showing no appreciation, some people have backed off from engaging in networking activities. If you are rejected, do not take it personally. It may take many calls to obtain a few positive responses. Keep plugging away. The contacts that you do make can prove to be invaluable and are worth the time and effort that you put into them.

When you do obtain that coveted interview, be prepared and act professionally. Some of your interviews may take place over the phone; some will be in person. Some people may even prefer to use e-mail. However your interview is conducted, be sure to have your list of questions on hand, but be prepared to allow the conversation to move into other areas if that happens. If the conversation veers away from the original purpose, gently guide the conversation back by reiterating something said earlier, asking the person to clarify something, or asking your next question. When conducting your interview, ask specific questions about the job, such as:

What is your educational background?

What types of education and skills are needed for this profession?

What is a typical day like for you?

How did you find your first or present job?

What advice do you have for someone like me who is just starting out?

What do you think the future is in this field?

What is the general salary range for this position?

Tailor your questions to your specific needs, but do try to get an overall sense of the job.

Again, always be conscious of the other person's time. Try to have your questions answered in about 30 to 45 minutes, unless the person has indicated that he or she has more time or is obviously willing to continue the discussion. At the close of the interview, ask for any referrals and/or if the person would be willing to take or review a copy of your résumé. Thank them for their time, and ask that they please keep you in mind should they hear of any job openings.

Always follow up with your contacts. If you get a referral from someone and then meet with that referral, thank both parties. Send a note to the first person, thanking them for their referral and letting them know how the interview went. Send another thank-you to the person you interviewed. Let that person know that you appreciated his or her taking the time to speak with you and that you value the information shared, including any further referrals. When you do eventually find a job, send a quick note to everyone who helped you along the way. Let them know that you have found a position, what you are doing, and that you appreciate the valuable advice you received from them. People like to know that their efforts have paid off.

Electronic Networking

Many of the same rules apply to electronic networking that apply to traditional networking. Just because you are not sitting across from the person does not mean that you should not be aware of his or her time. Even though e-mail allows a person to respond at a convenient time, do not bombard your electronic networking contacts with e-mails, jokes, and forwarded messages. When first contacting someone through e-mail, introduce yourself as you would with a phone message. State your name, how you heard of the person, the reason you are contacting him or her, and request further information.

If you use newsgroups, chat rooms, or message boards, get a feel for the communication style of the group by "lurking" for a while before posting a message yourself. Then conduct yourself professionally and offer help to others as often as you are able. Networking is a two-way street. You do not want to make a bad name for yourself by jumping online, gathering as much information from others as you can, and then leaving. Use these sources as they are intended: to offer mutual support. Also be sure to read the guidelines for each group before participating.

Louise Garver of Career Directions, LLC (see page 241 for page numbers of résumé samples), is a career professional who has been in the business for over 17 years. She notes that new graduates in particular have a tendency to "put the cart before the horse" in that they create their résumé and cover letter without first researching the job market. This results in "a generic résumé and cover letter that lack focus and do not show an understanding of the position they are applying for." When working with her clients, Garver uses a variety of tools to help people gain a better understanding of where they are going and potential job targets. This includes assessment testing, reviewing interests and personal history, and job research.

Garver notes that researching jobs is an important element of the job search process. Research allows a client to determine if a potential career matches the client's personal interests and other personal insights he or she has gained through the process. If not, it is time to revise the job search plan. Only after a person has determined a job path should the marketing documents such as the résumé and cover letter be prepared. This approach enables the client to choose a path that is right for him or her and then target the marketing materials to the specific job.

Garver also recommends, and coaches on, building and maintaining networking contacts. Her take is that "networking is a nurturing process that should be life-long." She advises maintaining relationships by keeping in touch with networking contacts.

Professional Organizations and Networking Groups

Professional organizations can be a great way to network, but keep in mind this is not the primary aim of many organizations. While some are designed to act strictly in a networking function, many are designed to help further the goals of the profession (this does not include helping you find a job). That said, joining a professional organization of your trade can be a valuable resource on many levels. For one, you gain an insider's view of the profession, learn its lingo and professional atmosphere, and have an opportunity to get involved and get your name out there. Simply joining an organization will not help you much in your job search (and subsequent career goals). Getting involved, however, shows you have an interest in the profession and are willing to put in the effort. Being a member of the XYZ

Association will not do as much for your résumé or your goals as being the local chairperson for the XYZ Association. Subsequently, this gives you more exposure and access to other professionals, and it increases your network circle without violating the unwritten rules of networking.

To find professional organizations, talk with your local reference librarian. You may also refer to the *National Trade and Professional Associations* or the *Encyclopedia of Associations*. There are also a number of online references. The American Society of Association Executives provides an option to search for associations that operate online by keyword or association name at http://info.asaenet.org/gateway/OnlineAssocSlist.html. The Internet Public Library also offers a search at http://www.ipl.org/div/aon/. A general search on the Web with your industry name and the word "association" may also yield results.

Networking groups specifically designed for this purpose may be worth looking into, if for nothing else than to practice your skills. Depending on what types of people are involved, and whether or not those individuals are interested in developing long-term relationships or are simply looking for the quickest way to land a job, you may have some success with these groups. Check with your local Chamber of Commerce and library to find more information about what is available in your area.

Networking groups also exist online and may be another resource for you, particularly if you are willing to relocate. Online groups attract people from many geographical areas, and making connections with people outside your immediate area can be of use. (Also keep in mind other resources for long-distance networking such as relatives, classmates who have moved, alumni, and the like.) Many of the larger job sites, such as Monster.com, have networking services available.

Job Fairs

If you are in college, take advantage of any job fairs offered. If you do not yet have your résumé prepared, consider taking small cards similar to business cards that highlight your pertinent information. You can give these out as needed.

Spend time talking to recruiters, and remember to ask questions. Just as recruiters are looking for information about students, you can use these opportunities to learn more about companies. Job fairs are also good practice in talking with potential employers, using your elevator speech, and getting a feel for particular industries.

The Classifieds

Even though the majority of job openings may not be listed in the paper or online, this does not mean that you should completely ignore this method for learning of potential job openings. You should, however, take a more active approach than simply putting your résumé in the mail. When answering ads, either locally or online, it pays to do some research on the company. If an ad asks you to send your résumé to the human resources department, for example, call the company and try to get the name of a specific person to contact. And while you are calling, ask about the position in general to see if you can gain any further information. You may be able to find out a little more about the position, how long the company will be accepting applications, and when they plan to begin interviewing. Even before you make the first call, see if you can learn more about the company itself. Check to see if they have a website for further information and ask around to see if any of your network contacts know anything of the company or someone who works there. When you know more about the professional atmos-

phere of the company, you can tailor your application. You may be able to make some adjustments to your résumé, and you definitely want to tailor the cover letter to the position and company when possible.

Job Service

Walk into any job service center, and you will see a number of people filling out applications, a number of people reviewing the job board, and a number of people waiting. Does this mean you should walk out? No. As with the classifieds, the local job service will not have access to every job available in town; in fact, it probably lists only a few. However, some employers will only list positions through the job service and nowhere else. If you are interested in city, county, or government jobs, this is the place to be. These employers must follow certain guidelines when hiring and may only list through the job service.

Take advantage of some of the programming offered through the job service as well; many are free and can provide information that you may not have access to otherwise.

When responding to jobs through the service, be sure to attach your résumé whenever possible. Because the job service screens all candidates through an application, it is not always possible to highlight your best qualities the way you can with a résumé. Do, however, take care to fill out the application thoroughly and with care, reading and following all instructions. You do not want to be screened out because of a mistake or omission on your application.

Cold Calling and Direct Mail Letters

Both of these options entail contacting employers and asking if they have any job openings.

Cold calling requires a bit more aggressiveness than does a direct mail letter, because you will potentially be talking directly to a person with hiring power. When making cold calls, just as with answering ads, try and find the name of the person who makes hiring decisions. Simply talking to a secretary or someone in human resources may not be enough. Chances are you will be told that the company is not hiring. Many will offer to keep your résumé on file, but that does not mean your résumé will ever be read. When making the call, ask for the name of the person in charge of the department you are interested in, and then ask to speak with that person. If you are able to get the person on the phone, briefly tell them your name and your qualifications, and inquire if there are any positions available. Talking to the person with hiring power will not necessarily increase your chances, but you never know. This type of calling will result in many rejections, so be prepared. With enough calls and persistence, it could result in an offer to submit your résumé or possibly an interview.

The direct mail letter operates in the same vein, but because it is a letter and not a phone call, it feels less risky but is also less effective than other means of learning about job openings. The direct mail letter is sent out to many employers in the hopes that someone has an opening. As with the phone call, the letter will inform the reader who you are and give some information about you as a person. Unlike a cold call, you automatically send your résumé along with the broadcast letter. Like the cold call, this type of job search results in many rejections (in the form of not hearing back) and requires many submissions before you get a hit. Because the direct mail letter is less targeted (and requires a more generic résumé), any hits you receive may not be exactly what you are looking for. But as with everything else, there is no way of knowing what may happen, and it could result in an interview. Sometimes all it takes is impressing the right person at the right time.

Follow Your Bliss (or Favorite Company)

Perhaps there is a company you have admired for a long time, or type of position that you know is perfect for you. In some cases, simply walking into a business or contacting someone in charge to let them know how impressed you are with their business is enough to get you an interview and potentially a job. If you truly have a passion or intense interest in a particular field or business, it does not hurt to pass that information along. Employers want employees who like their work. Happy employees are much more productive, have fewer sick days, and stay in positions longer. When someone shows a great interest in a particular company, it may be exactly what an employer is looking for. The only rule here is not to fake it just to try and get a job. Your lack of enthusiasm will soon show itself after you have landed the position, and that is not a good situation for anyone.

If following your bliss has nothing to do with a particular company or employment situation, be prepared to look into alternatives while you continue to build your "true" career. This scenario is common to those in artistic fields, such as fine artists, dancers, writers, and actors. It may be necessary to find jobs unrelated to your ideal profession while you continue to hone your skills and market yourself. While it can be risky to follow your true passion, it may also be the only way to find peace with yourself. Denying who you are and trying to mold yourself into a "secure" career can potentially make you miserable. It may be useful to seek the advice of a career counselor or coach on how to best go about this process.

Similarly, those with an entrepreneurial bent may only be happy when self-employed, starting their own business, or working toward some other creative means of making a living. Again, these people may need to work as an employee for someone else while pursing their passions. Learning as much about business as possible, developing strategic goals, and working hard can make these dreams come true.

Create a Job

Suggesting a new position may sound aggressive, and sometimes it is; however, it can lead to a very satisfying career path. If there is a need for a position, and you can show that there is and prove that you are the right person to fill the need, you may find yourself in the enviable position of writing your own job description. There are two primary ways of going about this. One is to research companies that you are interested in working for or ones that you have noticed frequently have classified listings. Of those frequently hiring, chances may be that a company is understaffed. While you may not be interested in any of the positions listed, you can do a little sleuthing to find out where potential problem areas exist and then contact someone within the company to suggest filling the need that you have discovered. This process includes some research and may lend itself well to an informational interview. Your networking con-

tacts may also come in handy to gather more information.

Another method of suggesting a new position occurs when you are already employed but do not want to stay in your current position. If you can identify a need within the company, you already have an "in," know whom to talk to, and hopefully have a good track record to back up your position as a desired employee. For the new graduate, using your soon-to-be or recently obtained degree can help qualify your readiness to move up to the next level. Use any other experience you have obtained along the way to show that you are the ideal person to fill the need.

Placement Agencies and Recruiters

The primary thing to keep in mind when using placement agencies or recruiters is that they are often employed by companies, not you. (But be wary of those who ask for an up-front fee—most independent agencies ask for some type of payment only after they have helped secure you a position.) What this means for the job seeker is that the agency or recruiter has the interests of the company in mind, not yours. That does not mean you should never use these services. Some positions (often higher-level or high-tech) are available only through these methods. What it does mean for you is that you want to be careful of protecting your interests and rights. You should continue your job search on your own as well and make sure that you do not sign any agreements that inhibit your ability to do so.

Chapter 5

The Next Step:
Back to Square One

Here is the part that seems contradictory. Before you begin networking, for example, you will want to create your résumé. But before you write your résumé, you need to know your target audience, that is, know what type of position you are aiming for and who will be reading your marketing materials. Of course, your networking process includes the informational interview, which can help you determine what type of career you want to pursue. So where does this leave you?

You have some options. If you are pretty clear about your career direction, and are conducting informational interviews to confirm your desires, you can create your résumé with that job target in mind and ask your interviewees to review and critique your résumé or keep it on file should they hear of any openings. Review comments you receive from those who critique your résumé and make changes as you see fit. When you feel you have developed the best possible résumé you can, read the chapters on writ-

ing your letters and begin your job search. You will most likely use letters in your networking efforts, so you can read the section on these types of letters and begin writing those as well.

Use every option available for finding positions. Do not limit yourself to your networking contacts, posting your résumé online, or responding to advertisements in the local paper. Follow the tips in this book to gain as many leads as possible. In the meantime, focus on developing your letter-writing skills because, as you will see, this will be an integral part of your job search and subsequent career goals.

If you are at an earlier stage and conducting interviews from the standpoint of wondering whether or not this career is of interest, you can always ask the person if you may send them your résumé at a later time for their review and critique or to keep on hand should they learn of any openings. Write your résumé with the information and direction that you have at this point—it is good practice and it will be easier for you to update it later on if you have a working base to start from. As you take advantage of volunteer or internship activities, you can simply add the experience as you go. By keeping your résumé updated, you are doing yourself a huge favor.

You, too, will want to read the chapters on letter writing and begin a cover letter for your résumé as well as compose letters to your networking contacts. You may also want to send letters out for additional informational interviews or job-shadowing opportunities. The more exposure you get, the clearer your direction will be. An added bonus is that you will gain a clearer understanding of the business world, which will work to your advantage when it comes to interviewing for positions.

If needed, seek the assistance of a career coach or counselor if you have not already done so. A professional in the careers field can help you develop a résumé that you can use to send to your networking contacts and in seeking informational interviews and other information gathering strategies. Then, when you have a better idea of the direction you want to go, you can refocus your résumé to your desired industry. Many people have multiple versions of their résumés depending on the intended use. There is no reason why you cannot do the same.

Do not let the fact that you are unclear about your career direction stop you from moving forward. Keep gathering as much information as possible, allow yourself time to sort things out, and move from there. Taking the time at this point to figure things out will be much easier in the long run. You will be way ahead of others when you hit your career stride and they are realizing that they made a wrong career choice.

Part II

WRITING THE RÉSUMÉ

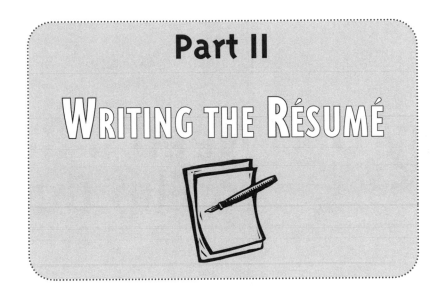

Chapter 6

Why Do I Need a Résumé to Flip Burgers?

A résumé is essentially a document that enables you to sell yourself to an employer; yet, as seen in the previous chapters, it can function in many other ways, too.

Is a résumé a marketing tool or a business document? This is a question under continual debate. And, while it is definitely not a piece of fiction, it is a creative document that can, and should, be adapted to meet differing needs.

There are no rules, and yet there are; but rules can be broken depending on the circumstances.

Is it any wonder so many people find résumé writing to be a difficult process?

You want your résumé to "sing," but not too loudly. While the résumé is an advertisement of sorts, most will not go to the lengths of what we see in ad copy and on television, except perhaps on a résumé for an advertising writer.

On the flip side, you do not want your résumé to evoke yawns from the person reading it. The résumé is a business document and should therefore follow rules of business writing, except that many of the standard rules of

writing, including business writing, do not apply.

What Exactly Is a Résumé?

A résumé is a brief summary of your skills, accomplishments, and history as it relates to a potential job. It is a selling tool used to get an interview. Employers may receive hundreds or even thousands of résumés for a particular job. The résumé may be the first document an employer sees about you. If a job does not require an application, your résumé may be the *only* information an employer sees. And an employer may see that information for a very short time. On average, employers scan résumés for about 20 seconds to determine whether or not candidates are worth a more thorough reading. Twenty seconds! That is not much time in which to make a positive impression.

The good news is that unlike a job application, the résumé highlights only your strengths. Information such as why you left a job or other potentially negative or damaging points are not included. Other good news is that different formats may be used to best highlight a person's experience. The format chosen will be the one best suited to promote your assets. Further good news is that if you follow the steps provided here and the instructions listed, you will have a much better chance of creating a résumé that will get a second look.

Writing a résumé can seem like a huge and difficult task. But once the process is broken down into smaller steps, it can be much easier to face. It is even possible that you may learn some things about yourself! Believe it or not, the writing process can actually be fun. Sure, some issues can be challenging, such as how to show experience if you are a first-time job seeker. But other parts can be very satisfying, such as finding the perfect action words to describe your experience or discovering that you have skills you never thought of as marketable before.

Why Do I Need a Résumé?

You may wonder why you need a résumé, particularly if you are seeking a job that only requires you to fill out an application. There are a few answers to this question.

Even for jobs that ask only for an application, having a résumé on hand will make filling out that application much easier. You will have all the necessary information in front of you on one (or maybe two) pieces of paper; it will help when filling out the section of the application that asks for previous experience.

Having a résumé can also boost your confidence. By walking through the writing process, you may surprise yourself as you come to realize that you have more experience than you thought. Or maybe your list of your skills looks more

impressive on paper than you thought it would. Just knowing that you have put in the effort to write the résumé and see what you have to offer an employer can put you above the competition.

When you walk into your first interview, your experience from writing the résumé will make you much more confident when it comes to answering tough questions. You have already outlined your strengths and accomplishments; now you can elaborate on them. And because your résumé will be targeted to a specific job type, you will be able to gear those interview answers accordingly. Chances of getting taken off guard by a simple question such as, "Why do you want this job?" will be very few—you will be able to give an insightful answer because you will have put in the thought ahead of time. While other candidates may give reasons such as "I want to buy a car," you will be able to answer honestly how that particular job fits your goals and objectives—and how your particular set of skills will benefit that employer.

And why not submit that résumé with the application? Job applications are very specific and limited. A résumé can fill in some blanks, further explain skills and experience, and set you apart as a serious contender for the job. That you care enough about yourself to put in the effort and submit your résumé with an application can demonstrate to an employer that you are serious about your job search and future.

For the recent college grad, a résumé is absolutely essential. In short, nearly everyone needs a résumé.

When Should I Start Writing My Résumé?

Now. The earlier you start working on your résumé, the better. This not only gives you a jump on the job search process (if you haven't officially started yet), but will also make it easier to update as you progress through your educational and working life. A high school student can start by listing coursework and extracurricular activities specifically related to his or her career choice. This information can easily be revised as more coursework is completed or edited as new experience becomes more important (or as career goals change).

A college student may not have a great deal of time to devote to a résumé, but adding a few brief notes along the way will make the refining process that much easier as graduation approaches. Waiting until the last minute or even the last few months before graduation can cause undo stress. Besides, it is impossible to know when an opportunity may come knocking. An unexpected career fair may pop up, a recruiter may pass through town, or, as you practice your networking skills, you may come across the perfect person to give your résumé to—and you will want to be prepared for those moments.

Can I Use My Résumé for More than Looking for a Job?

Absolutely. You will find that your résumé is an invaluable tool, applicable in many situations. For those who are just starting a career or education, the résumé becomes essential.

College applications

When submitting college applications, include a copy of that hard-earned résumé. Many applications will allow students to send additional information that may help admissions officers make decisions when looking at prospective students. Your résumé will not only highlight your best qualities but will also show your initiative.

Once you have been accepted to the school of your choice, you may wonder how you are going to pay for it. Scholarship, grant, and work study program applications may also allow for additional information. Your résumé should be among the list of essentials included in that application packet.

Internships and co-ops

Even though school programs help place students in internship positions, your résumé is still crucial. Make sure that administration and faculty involved in the internship program have a copy on file. Additionally, you will want to send a copy ahead of time to the employer you will be working with or bring it along your first day. Even though as an intern your primary objective is to learn, you still want to present your most professional side to the employer you will be working with. You never know what possibilities may await—ensure that you put your best foot forward!

Work co-ops are another possibility. Unlike internships, co-ops are paid positions that incorporate classroom study and real-world experience. Competition for these positions can be tough. Your résumé should demonstrate why you are the ideal candidate for one of these positions.

Following your internship or work co-op, do not forget to add to your résumé your new skills, responsibilities, and achievements acquired during the program.

Volunteer and community service

Even though volunteer work is not paid, it still requires the amount of responsibility you would show for a "real" job. Many volunteer organizations want and need to know the caliber of their volunteers, particularly if the job entails work with a special population such as children, the elderly, or the disabled. No one can and should expect to walk into a volunteer organization and be given a job on the spot simply because the work is non-paying. Have your résumé on hand when seeking volunteer work. Even if part of your reason for volunteering is to gain work experience, you will still want to bring the best version that you have available.

Help! I Do Not Have Anything to Include on a Résumé!

Some of you, even after reading through the entire résumé section, will feel that you do not have enough experience or credentials to list. Your grades may be less than ideal, or maybe you have not participated in as many activities as you feel you should have. Or maybe your coursework and activities have nothing to do with your chosen field. How do you solve the age-old question, "How can I get experience if I cannot get that first job?" Fortunately, there are ways to gain experience and prove yourself a worthy and reliable employee.

Job-training programs

If you are a high school student, find out if your school has a school-to-work program. (If it does not, why not look into helping get one started? Such initiative would look great on your résumé.) For those who fall in the 16 to 24-year-old category, see if there is a local Job Corps office. This private and government-funded program works with youth to develop and train for career goals. Visit with career counselors or contact the local Job Service to find out what options are available in your area.

Volunteer work

Donating your time is an excellent way to learn new skills and help your community. Volunteer work comes in many forms, from working with children to building a new home. Volunteering can be an excellent way to meet people and, as

you prove yourself, become an excellent means to gain references. And all the work that you do as a volunteer can go on your résumé as opposed to a job application, where space may be too limited—see why it is a good idea to attach that résumé?

How do you find volunteer work? If you are in high school, contact the guidance counselor's office, or if in college, contact the vocational guidance office or general studies office. Chances are that someone there will know of groups actively seeking volunteers. You can also try the local Chamber of Commerce. Other ideas are to contact some of the larger organizations, such as Americorps (http://www.americorps.com) or United Way (http://national.unitedway.org/). Your school or public reference librarian may also have suggestions for volunteer work. Ask around. If you have a particular interest, such as tutoring children, contact local schools. If you have an interest in social work, call the local food bank or Salvation Army. Browse through the yellow pages for organizations that provide services similar to those in which you would like to eventually find work.

Spot and temp jobs

A great way to earn some extra money while looking for a permanent position is to work spot or temporary jobs. Spot jobs are available through the local Job Service (and sometimes employment agencies) and are usually "at the last minute." Once you get yourself on the spot job list, you will be asked to call in on the mornings of days you are available to work. If a position is available, you will be directed where to go and when. These types of jobs often involve physical labor, but they can be an excellent way to improve your skill set and prove your reliability and willingness to work (and get paid to exercise!).

Temps, or temporary jobs, are also available through the Job Service or other employment agencies. These types of positions can also be found through networking (a friend of a friend knows of a company that needs a temporary receptionist while the permanent one is out on maternity leave), the classifieds, recruiters, and other traditional forms of finding work. While these positions are not permanent, they can be a great way to prove yourself, learn new skills, earn references, network, and perhaps work into a permanent position. If you do a great job for the company, they may decide that you are worth keeping around (or refer you to another company looking for someone exactly like you).

Can't I Just Buy Some Software?

Many software programs and websites claim to help you create a fast, easy, yet effective résumé. Prices for these "services" vary quite a bit. One problem with software and "fill in the blanks" Internet programs is that there is little room for variety. The programs use pre-set formats with limited space. While some of the layouts are very attractive, that is only one element of the résumé; content, and using a format that is right for you, is also important—which sometimes requires breaking the rules. It can also be much more difficult to target a résumé when using software—computer programs can be quite rigid. As such, hiring a real person skilled in the art of résumé writing is a much better choice if you ultimately decide you want help.

Hiring Someone to Write Your Résumé

We consider résumé writers to be "advertising agencies for individuals"' which encourages creative freedom and uniqueness rather than conformity . . . if appropriate in meeting a client's career goals and "standing out from the pack."

—Frank Fox, Executive Director,
Professional Association of Résumé Writers
and Career Coaches

A professional résumé writer can help not only write a better résumé but determine what information should be included and what can be left off. A résumé writer can also help target the résumé, give it a professional appearance, and add creative flair. Professional résumé writing services vary in price, but on average, a high school or college grad can expect to pay anywhere from $75 to $150, depending on what is included (résumé only, résumé and cover letter, etc.). Often, a job package will include both hard and electronic copies of the résumé and a cover letter. Depending on your budget, needs, and the services offered, professionals may also provide career coaching, job search assistance, and marketing assistance. Be careful when seeking a professional. The Internet, in particular, is overcrowded with less-than-qualified people offering a variety of job-search services. At a minimum, seek a member of a professional résumé writing organization such as the National Résumé Writers' Association, the Professional Résumé Writing and Research Association, or the Professional Association of Résumé Writers and Career Coaches. All of these organizations offer certifications for writers, and, ideally, a professional that you choose will hold one or more of those certifications. (Information on how to contact these organizations and their certifications can be found in Appendix II.)

Even if you decide to hire a résumé writing professional, it is still a good idea to write at least a draft of your résumé for your own purposes and the reasons already mentioned. Additionally, a résumé-writing professional will ask you a wide variety of questions and/or ask you to fill out a questionnaire. You need to be prepared to answer those questions. Even a professional will be unable to write the best résumé if you do not provide adequate information.

Linda Matias, president of the National Résumé Writers' Association and president of CareerStrides (http://www.careerstrides.com), says that one of the biggest challenges new graduates face today is how to leverage their experience into what an employer is looking for. College students are taking their job search more seriously than their parents did, because the first job out of college sets the tone for their career. As such, students need to know how to relate transferable skills from part-time jobs held during college into full-time career jobs afterwards. Students are making better choices and do not want to get stuck in the wrong type of job.

At the same time, students are realizing that they do not have to remain in the same job as their parents may have. Company loyalty does not exist like it used to, and students look for jobs with this mindset. Students are looking at jobs as opportunities to learn more about their field.

When it comes to job searching, Matias recommends going back to the basics. "The person who will stand out is the one who has done his or her research. It may sound like old advice, but the ones who follow it are the ones who succeed." Candidates need to show an interest in the company, not just the job; that can be the crucial difference.

Matias recommends that students go into the job search emotionally and mentally prepared for the long haul. A degree does not necessarily mean a ticket in the door. Finding the right job can take a while. She suggests that students have a plan in place in case the job search stalls temporarily. This can help deal with the accompanying emotions and help students revisit their job plan if needed.

The Final Word: Honesty

Perhaps the most important thing to keep in mind when writing your résumé is that everything on it must be accurate. Word choices and presentation are geared to truthfully describe your experiences and present them in the best possible way—but not to embellish them. The best wording, descriptions, and formatting mean nothing without honesty.

Now let us dive into the résumé-writing process itself.

Chapter 7

Types of Résumés

Before you begin your résumé, you need to know the different types of résumés and their purposes.

Résumé Formats

In basic terms, there are three general formats: functional, chronological, and a combination of the two. There are other formats, but these are the most common and the most likely to be used by a recent graduate or someone new to the workforce.

Chronological

The chronological résumé is formatted how it sounds—by chronological order, typically listing the most recent position held first. This type of format will often list education toward the bottom of the résumé but not always.

For those who have a steady work history, this format can work very well. Employers also tend to like this format because it is straightforward, easy to understand, and does not leave any timeframe unaccounted for. For the same reasons, however, this format may not be suited

for those who have little or no work history, an inconsistent work history, gaps in employment, or a trend of job-hopping. These "red flag" issues will stand out immediately in a chronological format.

What about those with little or no paid work history? The chronological format can be designed to work with situations challenging for new grads. Volunteer work, internships, and work study programs can all be presented as legitimate work experience in a chronological format. The difficulty with this format for new grads is, of course, that many do not have much work experience, that what they do have is inconsistent (such as seasonal work or various part-time jobs throughout college), or that their work history is very limited. For those people, the functional or combination format may work best.

An outline for a chronological résumé may look something like the example on page 41.

Functional

In the functional format, skills, achievements and other important highlights are presented

---

Name

| Address | Phone |
| City, State | E-mail |

OBJECTIVE OR PROFESSIONAL PROFILE

WORK HISTORY

Position Title, City, State   From - To
Brief Job Description
Accomplishments

Position Title, City, State   From - To
Brief Job Description
Accomplishments

Position Title, City, State   From - To
Brief Job Description
Accomplishments

EDUCATION

Degree, School, City, State   Graduation Date

---

in order of substance, and work history, if any, is either listed toward the bottom or, in some cases, not listed at all. Headings vary according to what the person has done. Possible headings include education and coursework, volunteer work, and related organizational memberships. Education is often listed near the top of the résumé in the functional format because it can be the applicant's best selling point. This is often the case for new graduates.

Because work experience is not highlighted in direct relation to an accompanying position, some employers are wary of the functional for-mat. However, in the case of a new graduate, employers also realize that this population often has little or no paid work experience or that work history may not be directly related to the applicant's college major or current job tar-get. In this case, it would be silly to not high-light one's education, relevant coursework, and affiliations, because these are the items direct-ly related to the current job search. Listing unrelated part-time jobs in a chronological for-mat could actually work against the applicant, even for an employer that typically prefers a functional format.

An outline for a functional résumé for a new graduate with no paid work history could look something like the layout below.

Combined

This format uses elements from both the chronological and functional formats and combines them in the document. For recent grads who have both relevant paid or nonpaid work experience in addition to education, this format could work, although it is best suited for someone with a lengthy career history. The first part of the résumé is dedicated to showing-off career highlights and accomplishments; the following

---

Name

Address	Phone
City, State	E-mail

OBJECTIVE OR SUMMARY

EDUCATION

Degree, School, City, State	Graduation Date

Relevant Coursework:

Course	Course	Course
Course	Course	Course

Special Projects:

Project
Description

Project
Description

SELECTED ACHIEVEMENTS/ACCOMPLISHMENTS

- Accomplishment
- Accomplishment
- Accomplishment

VOLUNTEER WORK

Position, Organization, City, State	Dates volunteered
Brief description of volunteer work	

---

sections outline the candidate's work history. For most recent graduates and people new to the workforce, a variation of the chronological or functional formats will usually suffice; functional is often the format of choice. As you will see in the sample résumés provided, there is much room for creativity and tailoring basic résumé styles into documents that work very well for each candidate. (For an in-depth discussion on résumé formats beyond the scope of this book, refer to *Résumé Magic* by Susan Britton Whitcomb.)

Newsletter

Newsletter résumés, though not one of the primary formats, are just as they sound; formatted to look similar to a newsletter. Typically two or three columns, information is presented in an eye-catching manner and is best suited to more creative-oriented jobs. (Please refer to page 145 to gain a better understanding of this format.) When used appropriately, it can be very effective and help the applicant stand out from the crowd.

CV

The CV, or curriculum vitae, is a style used primarily by those in the education and medical fields. It is a straightforward listing of education, work history, publications, and other relevant material. College graduates with doctorate and possibly master's degrees will sometimes need a CV depending on the position being sought. (Refer to the sample doctorate CV on page 152.)

Most positions are best suited for a résumé that leans more toward the conservative side using a well-known format. There are cases that warrant a more creative approach, but these are typically reserved for those seeking positions in creative fields. Artists and designers, for example, are better suited to using a more creative and riskier approach than someone with an M.B.A. looking for a position on Wall Street. Similarly, those seeking positions in advertising or sales may take a more aggressive approach in their résumé and cover letter than would someone in accounting.

While it can be tempting to create a flashy résumé or presentation, in most cases it is best to err on the conservative side. Even artists can deliver a "traditional" résumé to accompany a portfolio, which will showcase the artist's true talent.

Write for Your Audience

In all forms of writing, including résumés and cover letters, the most important question to ask is, "Who is my audience?" It may seem contradictory, but you are not writing your résumé for yourself; you are writing it for the person who reads it, and you want that person to call you immediately to schedule an interview. Therefore, your résumé needs to catch that person's attention and show how you can meet that person's needs.

Language

Use language appropriate for the field in which you are trying to get a job. If you are unsure of the "speak" of a particular profession, consider joining a professional organization in your field, paying careful attention to how language is used within the community. (For those with e-lists or online discussions, take a month or so to observe how members communicate with each other before posting a message yourself.) Reading trade magazines is another way to get a feel for the types of words and communication styles used within your soon-to-be profession. Also consider perusing want ads for the types of jobs you are considering applying for. Often, job postings will use keywords and phrases typical to the type of job being advertised.

Be cautious of overusing technical terms or acronyms. Even if these terms are commonly used in your field, it does not hurt to spell-out acronyms and use slightly less technical language or a combination of both (for when résumés are electronically scanned). The initial reader of your résumé may be someone in the human resources department who is not as familiar with the jargon as is the person with the ultimate hiring power. You do not want to talk down to your reader, nor do you want to confuse your reader.

Keep it simple

It can be very tempting to use fancy language, verbose sentences, and multi-syllabic words in an attempt to impress your reader. The downside to this approach is that your prose can become bogged down and you may come off sounding more foolish than intelligent. Also remember those few seconds you have in which to impress your reader. Making that person wade through a long sentence will not help your cause; you want to present information in a clear, easy-to-understand format that will quickly tell your reader what you are capable of, not that you are capable of constructing complicated text.

Watch for the potential overuse of action verbs, adverbs, and adjectives. Many résumé books provide lists of action verbs to choose from when describing your experience, and yes, they are important. But they are most effective when used sparingly and in the right context. Action verbs are words such as allocated, initiated, managed, provided, assisted, directed, etc. Adverbs describe verbs (action) and often end in "-ly," such as quickly, rapidly, adroitly, impressively, wholeheartedly, etc.

Adjectives describe nouns. Your keywords will typically be nouns; when using your keywords in sentences (as opposed to a list, which is also acceptable and sometimes more appropriate), the tendency to back-up those nouns with adjectives can be tempting and distracting. Let us say that quality assurance is one of your keywords. Stating that you developed "a comprehensive, all-encompassing, detail-oriented, innovative, structured, and really, really, really impressive quality assurance program" would definitely be overkill. Choosing one hard-hitting adjective may work to your advantage. Trying to drive the point home with excessive adjectives and adverbs will not. (Think of the child who tries to make a point carry more weight by saying that he or she is very, very, very, very, very, very, very, very hungry and really, really, really, really, really, really, REALLY wants ice cream.)

Your résumé is not an exercise in seeing how many different types of fonts, font sizes, and bullet styles you can cram into one page. You may want to use a different font for your name or main headings. You may want to highlight important information with a different bullet style from that used in the rest of your résumé. Limit your fonts and bullets to one or two styles. If using more than one, choose a second one that is complimentary to the first.

For all things résumé, less is generally more.

General Formatting Issues

Place your most important information in the top third of your résumé. Again, employers will do a quick visual scan of your résumé and may not even make it to the bottom of the page. You want to include your best information in the most eye-catching position, the top third, to make your reader want to read the rest of the material. Use the rest of your page space to back-up what you state at the beginning.

Use white space to your advantage. White space is exactly as it sounds—the parts of the page that do not contain type or graphics. Aim for a balance of white space throughout your résumé to make it visually appealing and easy to read. If your résumé is crammed full of type from top to bottom and left to right, it will be difficult to read and will be a turn-off to your reader, no matter how well you have composed the information. Use your formatting wisely to accommodate for white space. You can do this by changing font size (but do not go smaller than 10-point type), using bullets and tabs, creating space before and after headers, and so on. (Keep bulleted lists short; too many bullets are just as distracting as a lot of type.) If needed, use more than one page (see the following).

Use your headers wisely. Your name should be the largest print used. From there, a gradation of heading sizes should follow but not be overdone. More than three sizes of headers will make your résumé look junky. Also avoid excessive use of bolding, italics, and underlining. These enhancements should be used sparingly to highlight only the most important information. Use these features too much, and your reader will be left confused as to what is important and what is not. Worse yet, your reader may determine that you yourself do not know what is most important.

Keep your font size readable. Your name and contact information may be quite large and in a fancier font, but the rest of your document should fall within standard sizes; 10 to 12 point for most of your text. You can play around with your headers to find something attractive that works, but remember to be consistent. You want your headers to grab attention, not leave your reader feeling dizzy.

How many pages?

Your résumé should be as long as it needs to be to convey all the pertinent information while still using sharp, concise writing.

Too vague? Obviously, your résumé will be at least one page and should be formatted in such a way to fill the page without crowding it. For those who have concerns that they do not have enough information to put on a résumé, please refer to the previous chapter.

You may have heard some "hard and fast rules" about page length when it comes to résumés. Some will tell you that someone just entering the workforce or fresh out of high school or college should never have more than one page. Even those within the résumé-writing profession do not always agree on this issue. But to say that a college graduate should ALWAYS have a one-page résumé is akin to saying that an executive should ALWAYS have a two-page or longer résumé. The fact of the matter is that résumés are individualized, creative documents geared toward a particular person's history. Oftentimes that history can be well summarized on one page; sometimes it can not. A general guideline to attempt to keep your résumé to one page is not a bad one to follow, primarily because it forces you to focus on what is most important and keeps you from becoming too wordy. However, if you need additional space, use it; but use it wisely. See the samples on pages 123 and 140 for examples of two-page résumés for high school students.

If your résumé falls onto a second page, you need to use your judgment about whether or not to keep it on two pages or condense it to one. If only a few lines spill over, you need to reformat or cut to make it fit on one page. Any additional pages, whether they are the second, third, or fourth, should have enough information to cover at least half the page, if not most of it.

Who is most likely to need additional pages? Obviously a seasoned worker with a long history will have a greater chance of needing additional pages. For graduates, those with advanced degrees (masters or doctorates) may require additional pages to cover relevant educational experience and/or publications. (These groups will also more likely fall into the category of needing a CV, or curriculum vitae, instead of a résumé.) However, those with significant experience, whether paid or unpaid, or with extensive related activities may also find that two pages are better than one.

I have a heading but not much else

If you have information that you need to include but is not enough to stand on its own under a separate heading, consider combining such information with another category. For example, you may only belong to one professional organization, but it is a crucial one to your field. Listing only one piece of information under a heading is a waste of a heading, can lead to too many headings, and can take up valuable space. Limit your résumé to a few crucial headers and combine as needed. You will notice in the samples that headings have been combined in numerous ways, such as: Activities & Organizations, Affiliations & Activities, Organizations & Volunteer Activities, Honors/Activities, etc.

Built-in templates

Hopefully, the information presented here and the samples given will be enough inspiration to allow you to strike out on your own. The problem with templates that come as part of your word-processing program is the same problem that occurs with using résumé-generating software. It can be too limiting, thereby stifling your creativity, and the auto-formatting functions can be enough to drive you batty if you try to customize your document. Another potential problem is that your résumé will come out looking as though it was generated from a template. You want your résumé to speak to your audience about who you are and why you are unique—not scream, "I used a template!"

If you are uncomfortable with the idea of writing your résumé from scratch, it may help to invest in a good book outlining all the bells and whistles of your particular word-processing program or to enroll in a course. This will help boost your confidence as well as teach you new things. Heck, you can then add it to your list of computer skills on your résumé!

Chapter 8

Step-by-Step

Where to begin? The blank page can be quite intimidating. Take some advice from other writers—you have some options. Many writers start by free writing, that is, they write the initial story quickly, without any regard for formatting, editing, or self-censorship; the goal is to get the main elements on paper. Then they revise, edit, and put things into an order that makes sense.

If this approach sounds too haphazard, try an outline. Many nonfiction writers start this way, with an overall idea of what is to come. The writer then goes back and systematically fills in the various elements. This is also followed by revising and editing and moving information around as needed to best present the information.

Résumé writers have similar systems. Some prefer to jump right in and write as they go. Others create a basic outline and fill in the proper information. Whatever the method, the thing to keep in mind is that, even with an outline, no résumé is "one size fits all." Your résumé is a portrait of your unique history. Using examples from a book (including this one) and trying to make it fit your situation will generally not work, as you may end up using wording that is not your style or personality and does not represent your uniqueness. When résumé professionals work with their clients, they take detailed notes from conversations and/or questionnaires completed by the applicant. This way they can create a unique document tailored to the personality of each client.

Much of the editing and revision for all types of writers involves cutting—finding more succinct ways of saying things and deleting unimportant information and wording. Moving and changing the order of information can also be done in the editing and revising stage to create the best possible document.

Given that the blank page can be intimidating, what follows is an outline approach that will take you through the process step by step. Keep in mind that the format you choose may not be in the exact order as the following sections; similarly, you may not be using each section, depending on your unique circumstances. Feel free to skip around—if you find one section easier to write than another, start with that. This will help you get into the flow of writing and will help build your confidence for the tougher sections.

What You will Need

Remember all that stuff you learned about yourself when taking your interest, values, skills, and aptitude tests? Here is where you get to put some of that to work. As you prepare to write your résumé, you will need a variety of information on hand. Compile or make lists of the following information:

Education   Have a copy of your transcripts handy. Review your coursework to see which are most relevant to the job you are seeking. Compile information on any special projects you completed (particularly senior projects) and how these contribute to your position as a job candidate.

Skills   Make a list of your skills, or refer to any skills assessment tests you completed.

Work history, internships, etc.   Make a list of all the jobs you have held, your job descriptions, and, most important, what you accomplished while on the job. How did you help your employer? Did you contribute to cutting costs or increasing sales or improving service? If you have copies of any performance reviews, look those over as well. (If not, make a mental note to hang on to them in the future so you can update your résumé as you move through your career.)

Volunteer or organizational involvement   Summarize any volunteer positions, community involvement, affiliations, etc. If you hold or held any positions within these organizations, write them down.

Professional memberships, certifications, training, etc.   Make a list of any professional organizations to which you belong. If you have completed any special certification or training beyond your education, make a note of that as well.

Special interests   Do you have any hobbies or special interests directly related to the type of position you are seeking? You may want to add them to your résumé.

Computer and specialized skills   Make a list of all the software you are familiar with and any other special computer or technical knowledge that you have.

Your references   Although you will not be listing your references on your résumé, make a note of who may be willing to serve as a reference. Keep your list limited to professionals. Previous employers, teachers, professors, volunteer leaders, and the like are better choices than your best friend, your pastor, or your mom or dad.

Get ready to begin!

"A real benefit to preparing your résumé is that none of your prep work will go to waste. Every minute you put into it can be used throughout the networking, correspondence, and interview process."

—Susan Britton Whitcomb, quoted from
Résumé Magic

Your Name and Contact Information

This part should be easy. It is usually at the top of the résumé (but not always) and you should know what it is. Include as much contact information about yourself as needed. Make it easy for employers to contact you, but do not overdo it. If you have a home phone, office phone, cell phone, and beeper, you may not want to include all those numbers. You do not want your header to take up most of the top third of your résumé. Pick the phone numbers that will make it the easiest for a potential employer to reach you. You will also want to include your address and possibly your e-mail address and website address if you have one. Your goal is a balanced arrangement of your contact information. Look through the samples in this book for ideas on how to showcase your contact information. You may already have an idea of how you would like it to look. If you are stuck on this, do not fret—you can do final formatting after you have entered all of the vital information on your résumé. Making it pretty is important, but just as important is including all of the relevant information. Play around with some general ideas, but try not to get stuck on this part too long. You can always reformat as needed.

Objective

The objective statement is seen by many as passé, particularly in the way it has been traditionally used. Job seekers have often used the objective statement to state what they are looking for in a job as opposed to how they can benefit an employer. Or, perhaps even more annoying to employers, objective statements have become blanket expressions that tend to all sound alike, such as, "A challenging entry level position in (insert job title) with room for advancement."

The objective statement can still work for many new graduates or those without much or any work history. Because professional profiles or summaries are often used in place of the objective, someone with limited experience may prefer to use an objective. The key is to make it unique to your situation and show how you can be of benefit to the employer. There are many fine examples in the sample résumés to follow.

If you choose to not use an objective but want to say something similar, there are other options. If you are targeting a specific company or type of position, you can include a header that encompasses your expertise or job goal. You will see a variety of ways this is done in the sample résumés. Some use the job title as the header with a line or two afterwards to further describe the expertise. Other headers include Target, Career Goal, and Career Focus.

Summary or profile

A summary or profile is an overview of a candidate's history or expertise. It can be used in conjunction with or in replacement of an objective. Often, a summary or profile will contain keywords; other times it is more of a narrative describing the benefits of the candidate to the employer. The narrative may also include important key words written into the summary rather than presented as a list.

Because the summary or profile is an overview of your expertise, you may want to complete this section after you have written the other sections of your résumé. You will want this section to highlight your capabilities, which will be backed up by specifics in your résumé. It may be easier to do this in reverse, by listing the specifics in the body of the résumé and then completing the profile that summarizes everything else you have included in the document. Otherwise you may feel that you are not sure what you are supposed to be summarizing.

Education

For many recent graduates, education will be given prominent placing on the résumé because it is the candidate's most valuable asset at this time. With limited work experience, an impressive education section can showcase your knowledge, related coursework, and projects completed while in school that are directly related to an employer's needs.

How much information is included about your education will depend on your circumstances and how much other experience you have to include on your résumé. At a minimum, include your degree earned, the school's name, and the city and state of the school. You do not need to include the exact address of the school.

Should you include your GPA? This is a question of considerable debate, even among résumé professionals. As a general rule, anything below a 3.5 should be omitted. For highly technical and competitive fields, you may not want to include it unless it is a 3.8 or above. What if you have a 4.0? Some may feel this is an honor worth noting; it takes a lot of hard work and dedication to achieve this grade level. But keep in mind you may be asked in an interview what you did besides schoolwork. Employers like their employees to be well rounded with skills above and beyond academics. Interpersonal skills can be just as important, if not more so, than academic grades. Again, use your discretion when determining whether or not to include your GPA. What may be appropriate for one person and one field may not be for another. A good rule of thumb: If you are in doubt, leave it off (this applies to everything else on your résumé as well).

Whether or not you include relevant coursework is dependent upon what courses you completed and whether those courses are useful for the job you are seeking. The more specialized your degree is, the better chances that you have relevant coursework. Nursing students, for example, may want to include coursework in specialized subjects that qualify them to work in particular areas of nursing. An engineer with little work experience may want to list coursework that demonstrates a competency in various engineering methods. Conversely, an English major seeking a position in sales need

not include medieval literature as a selling point; it is not relevant.

Special projects completed in school may be included in lieu of real-world working experience. Sometimes these projects require just as much, if not more, work than do their real-world counterparts. Assignments often include challenging parameters that are not likely in the outside world or that could be negotiated in a real-world scenario. It can be helpful to note these challenges and how they were overcome in the project description. Any special skills used to complete the project should be included and, if appropriate, the grade received. If the project has the potential to be completed in the real world, or if this actually happened (such as a landscape design used by a local resident), it can be worth noting. Note positive results whenever possible.

Work experience

As you will notice in the sample résumés, how you list your work experience can take many forms. At the least, you want to include your position title and the company name. While most résumés will somehow show a length of time worked at a particular job, not all will. If dates are not listed, however, it may look suspicious to a potential employer. If you have a solid work history, or worked the same job for a fairly long period of time, you may do well to list years only. If your employment was shorter, or if you are listing an internship, for example, you may want to use both the month and year.

The job, what you did, and how or if it relates to your target position will determine how much and what kind of information you include in the employment section. For positions that have little to do with your target, you may only list the job title and employer. For positions that are similar to your target, or require you to use similar or transferable skills (those applied in a different situation but easily adapted to your new line of work), you may go into more detail.

You may want to list what you did at your previous job. The tendency is to write "responsible for" or "duties included" and then list what you did. Over the years, the words "responsible for" have become overused on résumés, and it is best to avoid using them. Eliminating the "responsible for" and using the rest of the description can work or at least give you a starting point. For example, *Responsible for monitoring cash flow* can be changed to *Monitored cash flow*. Use succinct descriptions and action verbs or nouns when possible. This will keep your copy short and to the point. If you have copies of your job descriptions from previous positions, use them as a reference, but do not use them word for word. If you are currently employed, use present tense when describing your position (manage cash flow). If you are referring to a previous job, use the past tense (managed).

How well did you do your job? Did you go above and beyond? Did you make any special contributions, cut costs, improve sales, provide exceptional customer service or devise a better way of doing things? Any accomplishments you achieved while on the job can and should be listed on your résumé. Ideally, you will be able to quantify your achievements, that is, provide a number detailing money saved or earned for the company, time reduced, etc. The more you can show the results of an activity, the better. Accomplishments can be listed under the job title or, depending on the format, may be set off as a separate heading altogether.

Alternate Headings

Education and work history are probably the two main headings that most people include on a résumé. Many alternate headings can be applied to the résumé. In a functional style, an achieve-ments, highlights, or skills section may be set aside to draw attention to specific details, leaving the work summary section to list the basic information of job title, employer, and dates. You will notice that the samples in this book use a variety of headings to showcase different accomplishments or highlights from a person's background. Also note that not all of the highlighted information is from work-related experience. Experience from volunteer work, internships, and positions within organizations can all contribute to a list of achievements and highlights. Sample headings used to highlight achievement-related activities from the samples in this book include: Selected Leadership Highlights, Telecommunications Highlights, Highlights of Value Offered, Skills Summary, Strengths & Accomplishments, and Experience Summary.

Because the recent high school or college graduate presents a unique set of challenges to résumé writing, many other areas of a person's history may end up on the résumé that probably would not for those who have a few years of work history behind them. These listings are appropriate but should only be used if they help support the goal of the résumé; that is, they should only be listed if they support the candidate's position that he or she is the best person for the job. Listing that you were a member of the football team may not help you if you are seeking a position as a laboratory researcher; but it may help if you are applying for a position that requires a great deal of teamwork. Whatever you decide to put on your résumé, ask yourself if it will help position you as a stronger candidate than your competition. If the answer is no, or even a maybe, leave it off. Unnecessary or weak information can be more detrimental than no information. The following is a list of potential headings frequently used for new graduates or those just entering the workforce. (Refer to the samples for ideas on how alternate headings are used.)

Internships

If you took part in internships and the experience was directly related to your job target, include this as a separate heading. Similarly, if you do not have paid work experience but do have internship experience, this can be used in lieu of the work history.

Certifications/training/ professional training/licenses

Many specialized degrees and related jobs require certification or training above and beyond one's degree. If you hold certifications that add credibility to your standing, include them on the résumé (but only if they support your candidacy—many people have outdated or current certifications that are no longer relevant to the types of positions they are currently pursuing). Similarly, any additional training or licensing beyond your formal education that can set you apart from other candidates should be included, particularly if the training or licensing is challenging or requires prerequisites to obtain. Some jobs require that applicants hold specific certifications or licensing; if this is the case, be sure to include this information. Not doing so can be a reason for immediate disqualification.

Computer skills/technical

In today's workforce, computer literacy is almost always a must. Even listing basic computer knowledge such as Microsoft Office lets the employer know that you are capable of using a computer. (If this is all you know, you may want to combine this information with another related subject so it does not stand out.) For jobs that require an intimate knowledge of advanced or specialized computer software, be sure to include this on your résumé (as long as you are indeed proficient in the use of the program). CAD (computer-aided design) programs are one

such example. If you are seeking programming positions, list all of the languages you know that are still technically relevant.

Professional affiliations/ memberships/organizations

Any involvement in professional organizations related to your target job can be included on your résumé. If you hold any positions or leadership roles within these organizations, mention that on your résumé and what your duties are. Listing your length of time as a member may also serve you well if you have been with the organization for a long time (if you have recently joined, leave this information off). If you are a member of an organization considered "standard" for your field, be sure to include it. This will help demonstrate that you are familiar with the field and its common practices and expectations.

Volunteer/activities/collegiate activities/leadership positions/ community involvement

While these types of activities can be incorporated into a work history, your level of involvement and responsibility may warrant placing this information under a separate heading. If you have limited paid work experience, a section on your activities might highlight your commitment to your field or your community much better than your limited experience in the workforce. Any leadership roles or other positions that you hold or held during your involvement can be included to demonstrate your abilities to work with others and your commitment to getting things accomplished.

Languages

As the world economy continues to change and grow and as employers open offices across the globe, communication is an ever-more important issue. If you are fluent or can communicate in any foreign languages, it may work to your advantage to include this on your résumé. If you are interested in working abroad, definitely include this information. Even within the United States, those who are bilingual or multilingual may have a distinct advantage over their competitors, as businesses, services, and educational facilities are more attuned to the advantages of being able to reach various cultures.

Academic honors/awards

Depending on the honors or awards you may have received, referring to them on your résumé may be to your advantage. Listing academic honors can be particularly useful for those continuing in or entering education fields, although this information may be useful for other fields as well.

High school achievements

High school achievements can be a bit tricky. If you are currently enrolled in or fresh out of high school and seeking work, by all means use your high school achievements to your advantage. For those who are out of college, generally speaking, high school achievements will probably not be necessary unless they are still relevant to your job search and extremely outstanding. Ideally, your activities during college will be more impressive than what you did in high school.

Interests/personal

Including personal information and interests used to be the norm in résumé writing. Now this type of information is typically left off, but as with all aspects of résumé writing, there are exceptions. Personal interests that support your job search may sometimes be included if they have a direct relation to the job you are seeking. If golfing is one of your hobbies and you are seeking a position as the landscaper of a golf course, this information would be relevant. Stating that you like to collect rare comic books would not.

Personal information is also generally left off for a number of reasons. First and foremost, this information could be used to discriminate against you, whether done consciously or not. Purposeful discrimination against a candidate based on personal information such as marital status, religion, race, and age is illegal. However, for those seeking international positions, this type of information may be included if it is standard practice in the country in which you are applying. Many countries routinely include personal information on résumés. If you are intimately familiar with the target country's practices, include whatever information is deemed standard. If you are unsure, seek the help of a professional résumé writer.

Quotes from others

While not a separate heading, including quotes from supervisors, teachers, or other persons in positions to support you can add some pizzazz and credibility to your résumé. Always seek permission from the person being quoted before using the quote.

References

As with personal information, there was a time when references were either added to the résumé or the standard line of "references available upon request" was included toward the bottom. Listing references is no longer a common practice; it is generally assumed that a candidate will be able to provide such a list if necessary.

Chapter 9

Common Mistakes and How to Avoid Them

Employers may receive thousands of résumés for one position. Because of this, they are often looking for any reason to throw out a résumé. While résumé writing is a creative process, allowing writers to "break the rules" when appropriate, some rules should not be broken.

These are the rules pertaining to typos, misspelled words, grammatical errors, and consistency. To quote Frank Fox, Executive Director of the Professional Association of Résumé Writers and Career Coaches, "We have always said that 'in résumé writing, there are no rules . . . except that there should be no typos, misspellings, or grammatical errors.'"

Some broken rules are acceptable, such as the use of sentence fragments to make the writing crisp. But if you are going to break the rules once, do it consistently; a résumé that uses complete sentences in one section and fragments in another can be distracting to the reader. Remember, you are not writing for yourself. You are writing attention-grabbing copy that will show how you can meet the needs of your audi-

ence, such as a potential employer, someone offering an internship, or the admissions personnel for graduate school.

Basic Guidelines

What rules can be broken, and which ones should not?

One of the primary differences between résumé writing and business writing is that the résumé falls somewhere between the "hard sell" of advertising and business writing. Ad copy, for example, frequently uses short, to-the-point wording. Very often, this wording does not come out in the form of a complete sentence. Similarly, résumé writing is compiled of succinct, to-the-point copy that often comes out in the form of sentence fragments or with wording missing typical elements such as articles. Words such as "it," "the," "a," and "an" are articles and are frequently omitted to save space, allow for quick reading (remember how long a résumé reviewer typically spends scanning a résumé), and make the point.

Before you begin your résumé-writing journey, get your hands on a good grammatical reference guide. If you want to go for the best, pick up the latest edition of either the *Gregg Reference Manual* or the *Chicago Manual of Style*. They are a bit pricey but worth it, particularly if you find yourself doing other types of writing as well. Otherwise, there are plenty of good reference guides to choose from.

The following is a general list of some common errors. It is by no means exhaustive. *The Chicago Manual of Style* contains well over 300 pages on grammatical and punctuation issues alone. If you are especially grammatically challenged, ask someone (or a few someones) more comfortable in this area to proofread your résumé for you. Do not rely solely on your computer's grammar and spell check.

Action verbs

Here they are again. Begin your sentences with action verbs or nouns when describing your experience. Show the results of your actions, and then say how you accomplished them. Bear in mind that action verbs are not the same as keywords (discussed later). Keywords are nouns or short phrases. Both keywords and action verbs may be combined into the same sentence, such as:

Implemented project management system; increased production rate by 50 percent.

"Implemented" is an action verb; "project management system" is a keyword phrase.

Active versus passive voice

The active voice shows the subject of the sentence doing the action, as opposed to an action being done upon the subject. Consider the following example:

The bone was eaten by the dog.

This is an example of passive voice. The dog is doing the action (eating), but the subject of the sentence is the bone (bone=noun, was=verb). Written in the active voice, the sentence reads:

The dog ate the bone (dog=noun, ate=verb).

Two things are notable. The subject of the sentence, the dog, is doing the action—eating. Secondly, the resulting sentence is shorter by two words. This equals "tighter" writing, which is what you want to aim for in résumé writing. You want your reader to see the point quickly and efficiently.

While the following is not always the case, one way to look for passive voice is past tense of "to be" verbs. These are "was," "were," "been," and "being." Also watch for "have" or "had."

First person

Most résumés are written in first person but without actually using "I." Third person is when the résumé refers to you as Ms. Jones or by your first name. Some marketing pieces work well in third person, and some résumés do as well (see the sample résumé for Sara Moon on page 114). For most résumés the use of first person is preferable. If you are having trouble with the first person usage, write out your accomplishments first using "I" to ensure that you are staying consistent with your wording, and then go back and cut out the reference to yourself. For example, you might write:

I reduced production costs by 50 percent.
This would then be changed to:

Reduced production costs 50 percent.
You begin with your action and then show the result.

Tense

Remain consistent with your use of tense (past, present, or future). When describing what you did on the job or in school projects, use the past tense. These are again your action verbs that typically end in "-ed": managed, maintained, supervised, etc. Past tense verbs also include words such as oversaw, overcame, ran, etc. When referring to jobs or projects you are currently involved with, use the present tense, but for that particular job or project only. Using the preceding words, they would be listed as: manage, maintain, and supervise, and oversee, overcome, and run.

Use of articles

Articles are "a," "an," and "the" and should be omitted when possible. Why? You do not need to use unnecessary words in your résumé; these take up valuable space. Again, the tighter your writing, the better. Eliminating articles is one of those rules broken for résumé writing. As with all rules, use it consistently. If some sentences use articles, but not all, your résumé will not "flow" and could be distracting to your reader, something you want to avoid at all costs.

Punctuation

Punctuation exists to make reading easier. Otherwise, sentences would run together and the reader would not know when one sentence ends and another begins. Notations such as commas and parenthetical marks also let the reader know when to pause and when information is included as a side thought.

Periods mark the end of a sentence. In résumé writing, incomplete sentences, also called fragments, are used frequently. If these are in a bulleted list, it is up to you to decide whether or not to use a period at the end of each item. There are technical rules regarding lists, but because résumé writing often breaks the rules, they will not be covered here. The pri-

mary issue is to be consistent in your use of periods throughout your document. You may need to use a period with some abbreviations.

Commas denote a slight pause or separate items in a list and are used in compound sentences. A compound sentence joins two main clauses with a conjunction. Conjunctions are "and," "but," "or," "nor," "for," "yet," and "so." For example, the use of a serial comma is an issue under continual debate among experts, so it follows that résumé writers do not agree on the subject either. The serial comma is used following the last item in a list, as in the following sentence:

She went to the store to buy bananas, apples, bread, cheese, and milk.
The serial comma is the one preceding the word "and."

Those who support the use of the serial comma argue that it helps prevent ambiguity, particularly if the list contains grouped items that require the use of "and" as in the following example:

His collection of photographs included prints, slides, black and white, and color. Without the serial comma separating "black and white" from "and color," the sentence could be confusing.

Commas are also used following an introductory phrase of a sentence, such as: Because I'm going to write my résumé tomorrow, I'm going to get a good night's sleep tonight. "I'm going to get a good night's sleep tonight" is a complete sentence. "Because I'm going to write my résumé tomorrow" is an introductory phrase, not a complete sentence on its own.

Semicolons help distinguish complex items in a list; they can also join two separate but related sentences. Semicolons used in a list are most helpful when the listed information contains commas.

Colons anticipate something to follow. *Dashes* look back to something already said. Colons introduce an element or series of elements. When used within a sentence, the word following the colon is not capitalized unless it is a proper name or begins another complete sentence.

Capitalization

Proper nouns and names should be capitalized, such as the names of schools and universities. Headings should be capitalized consistently throughout the document. Do not capitalize a word just because it seems important. If you are unsure about the capitalization of a word, consult a manual.

Numbers

How numbers should be presented is another topic of debate. A generally accepted rule is to write-out numbers one through nine and use digits for 10 and above (pick a rule and stick with it). However, when a number begins a sentence, it must always be written rather than listed numerically. Another argument says that all numbers should be treated the same to allow for consistency throughout the document and to save space.

Whatever you decide to do, do it throughout. Do not decide to write a number below 10 in one section and then list it numerically in others.

Typos and Misspelled Words

What you do not want to be consistent with is typos and misspelled words. Relying on your computer's spelling and grammar check is not enough. Many words can be missed that are spelled correctly but used in the wrong context or with a completely different meaning.

Words Commonly Used Incorrectly

The following is a short list of commonly misused words. Your grammar and spell check will often not pick out these words if they are used wrong, because they will be spelled correctly but used in the wrong context. Keep an eye out for words used incorrectly. Ask someone else to proofread your résumé for you.

Accept/except   To accept is to receive something. She accepted his apology. Except is a preposition that means but or with the exception of. I would use accept, except it is not the correct word.

Affect/effect   To "affect" is to influence or change. He affected her emotions. An "effect" is the result of something, as in cause and effect.

And/or   This usage implies three outcomes, not two. I will write a résumé and/or a cover letter means that the person will either: (1) write a résumé; (2) write a résumé and a cover letter; or (3) write a cover letter.

Assure/ensure/insure   To "assure" is to convince or to guarantee. The administrator assured him that his résumé had been received. "Insure" means to guard against loss. I insured my car. "Ensure" means to make certain. I ensured that I insured my car.

It's/its   This is one of those cases that is an exception to the rule. While the apostrophe typically denotes a possessive, in this case, "it's" means *it is,* and "its" is the possessive.

Their/there/they're   "Their" is a possessive; something belongs to them and it is theirs. "There" is where something is; it is over there.

"They're" is where they are; they're (they are) over there.

Then/than   "Then" is when something will happen and means next or consequently. I will go to the store and then go home. "Than" indicates a difference. Chocolate is better than vanilla.

To/too/two   "To" is a function word indicating an action or process. I want to write my résumé. "Too" indicates an excessive amount of something. I am too tired to write my résumé. "Two" is the number that follows one and precedes three.

Utilize   "Utilized" means use. Use "use."

Whose/who's   "Whose" is a possessive. Whose résumé is it? "Who's" means who is. Who's at the door?

Your/you're   "Your" is a possessive. It is your turn. "You're" means you are. You are correct.

For practice and more commonly misused words, see "Words Commonly Confused" by V. Bell, J. Cheney, P. J. King & M. P. Moore at http://homepage.smc.edu/reading_lab/words_commonly_confused.htm or do an online search for "commonly confused words" and you will find plenty of results to choose from.

Parallel Structure

Words, formatting, and grammar should be parallel. That is, they should be consistent. If you have a list of bolded achievements and the first one begins with an action verb, every item in your list should begin with an action verb. If you begin with a noun or noun phrase, all items in the list should begin with a noun or noun phrase.

Similarly, you should keep your writing parallel within your sentence structure. Use of adjectives and nouns must be parallel in structure. Consider the following examples:

Correct:
The program was motivating and thrilling.
Incorrect:
The program was motivating and a thrill.

Sentence Fragments

Sentence fragments lack a noun or verb to make a sentence complete. These will sometimes find their way into a résumé. Consider the following:

Oversaw all aspects of inventory control.

The preceding statement is a fragment because it is missing the subject "I" at the beginning.

Maintained personnel and public safety.

This is a fragment for the same reason as the previous sentence.

Fragments end up in résumés as a result of the "telegraphic" style of writing often used. While you do not want to aim for fragments, they will likely find their way into your résumé. Again, be consistent in your writing style, and fragments will not stand out or seem inappropriate in the résumé as they do in other forms of writing.

You *do not* want to employ the use of fragments in your cover letter.

What Not to Include
Personal information

Do not include personal information such as your marital status, religion, race, etc. Employers are not allowed to ask questions about these things, and including them on your résumé might cause you to be discriminated against, but you would never know for sure. The only exception is if you are applying for international jobs, in which case some of this information is considered standard. Consult a professional or a manual on international résumés for more information.

Do not include a photograph with your résumé or a URL for your personal website that tells visitors all about your hobbies, summer vacation, and your dog. The only people likely to use a photograph with their résumés are those in the entertainment business such as actors.

Letters of recommendation

Do not send these with your résumé. Save them for later, such as following an interview.

Specific salary

Do not include your current or desired salary. Oftentimes a job posting will request that you include such information. Do not list concrete numbers on your résumé. Instead, if you must, address the issue in your cover letter. (See the section on cover letters for more information.)

A creation date

Do not list a creation date on your résumé, even if you are posting it online. Often, online résumé databanks have a system that denotes when your résumé was posted.

References

Do not list references on your résumé. At the most, you may include "references available on request" or something similar for visual appeal, but even this is debatable. It is a practice that is dying out. You can safely leave the line off the résumé because it is assumed that you will provide references at the appropriate time if requested by the employer.

Anything that can work against you

Have you been fired? Have you received unfavorable reviews? Is your GPA only a 2.0? Do not include anything in your résumé that can automatically disqualify you from the running. The résumé is not the place to explain why something went wrong in your past. It is the place to highlight your best selling features. If you do have something unfavorable in your past, be prepared to talk about it (in the best possible light) at the interview, but do not shoot yourself in the foot by putting it on your résumé.

All of the sample résumés and cover letters in this book are written by professional résumé writers who are members of one or more of the following organizations: Professional Association of Résumé Writers and Career Coaches; The National Résumé Writers' Association; and Career Masters Institute. Many of the writers hold one or more certifications in résumé writing; please refer to Appendix I for more information.

CHRONOLOGICAL RÉSUMÉS

XXXXXXX

1942 Pennsylvania Avenue • Boulder, Colorado 80302 • (xxx) xxx-xxxx

SUMMARY

Highly motivated team player with training and practical experience in marketing and advertising. Committed to achieving an employer's objectives. Strong work ethic. Skilled in identifying and meeting client's needs. Computer literate. Energetic, productive, and goal directed.

EDUCATION

Bachelor of Science in Journalism - Advertising, University of Colorado at Boulder. Graduation Date: May 2004.

Honors: Major GPA: 3.6 • Dean's List • Recipient of Kappa Kappa Gamma Outstanding Academic Award • Recipient of University Scholarship Award.

Courses include: Advertising Campaigns, Advertising Copy and Layout, Advertising Media, Advertising Research, Consumer Behavior.

Representative Course Project: Currently collaborating on the development of a comprehensive advertising campaign for White Wave Soy Foods, Inc.

Study Abroad in Italy. Selected to study art history in Florence, Venice, and Rome through the University of Colorado. Summer 1999.

EXPERIENCE

Marketing Intern, Palo Alto Theatre Works, Palo Alto, California. Summer 2003.
- Designated to manage promotion for the "Night Out on the Town" annual fundraiser. Responsible for media planning; sponsor solicitation; and writing copy for the brochure, invitation, program, and print media advertisements.

Sales Associate, Nordstrom, Palo Alto, California. Summer 2002.
- Ranked as the top-producing sales associate among a staff of six.

Undergraduate Teaching Assistant, School of Journalism, University of Colorado, Boulder, Colorado. Summer 2001.
- Assisted professor in "Madonna Undressed," an exploration of media exploitation.

Instructor, Bar 717 Ranch, Hayfork, California. Summer 2000.
- Taught horseback riding to disabled children. Supervised a group of 12 children.

Additional experience includes Salesperson, Eddie Bauer; Child Care Provider, The Stacy Family; and Peer Counselor, Financial Aid Office, University of Colorado.

AFFILIATIONS & ACTIVITIES

Computer Secretary, Kappa Kappa Gamma, Boulder, Colorado.
Conducted computer training sessions and secured funding for new computer equipment.

Volunteer, Adopt-a-School Program, University Hill Elementary School, Boulder, Colorado.

Volunteer, Project Read (adult literacy program), Redwood City Library, California.

XXXX
2400 30th Street #507
Boulder, Colorado 80310
(303) xxx-xxxx

OBJECTIVE: Seeking an entry-level position in the biotech industry, preferably in the research and development division.

SUMMARY

Corporate internship experience within the biotech industry. Technical skills include: Elisa, plasmid transformation, GC, NMR spectroscopy, IR spectroscopy, UV/light spectrophotometer, Delta Klett, centrifuge, gel scanner. Proficient on MS Word, Cricket Graph, MS Excel, Statworks, Filemaker Pro.

EDUCATION

Candidate for **B.A. in Molecular, Cellular, and Developmental Biology** from the University of Colorado at Boulder. Graduation Date: May 2004.

Recipient of a Hughes Initiative Grant for a research project.

EXPERIENCE

Genzyme Corporation, Framingham, Massachusetts. Intern, June-August 2003. Reviewed and proofread data from quality control tests which identified residual solvents and biotoxins in the drugs Ceredase, TSH, and Vianain. Uncovered and corrected previously undetected data errors. Developed a database for each drug. Conducted statistical analysis of data and produced graphs. Graphs charted test progress and assisted QC Managers in determining test revisions.

Cytochrome C Oxidase Subunits Study, University of Colorado, Boulder, Colorado. Lab Technician, January-August 2002. For an Independent Study/Hughes Initiative Grant, assisted in a segment of a research experiment.

SUMMER EMPLOYMENT

McDonald's Restaurant, 1999-2000; Perno Pontiac, 1998.

AFFILIATIONS & ACTIVITIES

Biology Tutor, University of Colorado.
Member, Phi Kappa Psi Fraternity: Pledge Class President; Academic Chairman.
Recording Secretary, Baker Residence Hall Board.
CU Ski Club

PERSONAL INFORMATION & INTERESTS

Age 22, single, healthy. As part of a military family, have lived throughout the United States and in England. Have traveled to Canada, Ireland, Germany, and Austria. Interests include chess, racquetball, astronomy, numismatics.

xxxxxxx

permanent address:
2284 Cody Way
Parker, Colorado 80134
(303) xxx-xxxx

university address:
1125 Grandview #1
Boulder, Colorado 80302
(303) xxx-xxxx

SUMMARY

Effective communicator skilled in developing rapport with people from all backgrounds. Experience living overseas. Fluent in Spanish. Maintains high standards of performance. Committed to achieving an organization's objectives. Adaptable, organized, and highly productive.

EDUCATION

Candidate **for B.S. in International Spanish for the Professions**, emphasis in **Business**, minor in **Mathematics**, University of Colorado at Boulder. Graduation: August 2003. Cumulative GPA: 3.5; Major GPA: 3.75.

Honors: Order of Omega Honor Society • Golden Key National Honor Society • Regent Scholar • Professional Women's Scholar • Spanish Honor Society • National Institute of Standards and Technology Fellowship.

Study Abroad, Universitas Nebressensis (through George Washington University), Madrid, Spain. Spring 2002.

EXPERIENCE

Superconducting Project Member, **National Institute of Standards and Technology**, Boulder, Colorado. September 2002-Present.
Serve as a team member researching economic/physical feasibility of high-temperature superconductors. Perform a wide range of technical duties.
- Contributor on published abstracts and papers.

Spanish Intern, **Isbell Metzner** (cultural management firm), Madrid, Spain.
January 2002-August 2002.
Provided assistance in coordinating international cultural conferences. Compiled demographic research on Hispanics in the United States. Researched United Nations' historical information for a 40th anniversary celebration.
- Performed Spanish-English translations of documents, correspondence, and magazine articles.

Volunteer, **Amigos de las Americas Volunteer Program**, Michoacan, Mexico. Summer 2000.
Assisted villagers in construction projects and taught health education.

AFFILIATIONS & ACTIVITIES

President, Spanish Club.
Membership Chairperson, Kappa Kappa Gamma.
Coordinator, Volunteer Clearing House.
Member, University of Colorado Club Water Polo.
Volunteer ESL Tutor, Baseline Middle School.

RONALD AMES

111 Bali Road   •   Harleysville, PA 19438   •   (215) 513-9131   •   ames@dotresume.com

PROFILE

Honors graduate in chemical engineering with hands-on experience in process development and optimization. Team player with excellent interpersonal and communication skills.

SKILLS

Experience with ASPEN PLUS, HYSYS, and Polymath. Proficient with MS Word, Excel, and PowerPoint.

EDUCATION

B.S., Chemical Engineering, Keystone College, Philadelphia, PA, **Magna Cum Laude / 3.8 GPA** (5/2004)

Awards
President's Scholarship   •   Silver Key National Honor Society   •   Pennsylvania Epsilon Honor Society

Course Highlights
Biochemical Engineering, Controls, Fluid Mechanics, Heat Transfer, Mass Transfer, Material Science, Polymer Processing, Reaction Engineering, Thermodynamics, Transport Phenomena, Unit Operations

Senior Group Project
Designed and priced a plant that produces methyl methacrylate from isobutylene.

EXPERIENCE

Engineering Intern / Operator (5/2003–3/2004)
Adkens Manufacturing, Inc., Cherry Hill, NJ
As intern, assisted in pilot tests to optimize process of creating platinum catalyst on carbon support. Designed experiments, assembled equipment, ran trials, and prepared samples for analysis. As operator, performed refinery processing procedures in accordance with engineering specifications.

Research Assistant, Science Foundation Engineering Grant (5/2002–8/2002)
Keystone College, Philadelphia, PA
Researched basic principles of reaction engineering and designed three labs for school's first planned course in biochemical engineering. Labs demonstrated enzymes hydrolyzing starch, action of yeast, and conversion of glucose to ethanol under various conditions.

Student Engineering Clinics in Cooperation with Industry

Miles Waste Treatment, Inc., Stillwater, NJ (1/2004–5/2004)
Worked on team that developed new process for producing ethyl acrylate from waste streams. Converted from HYSYS to ASPEN PLUS and optimized process with added conditions.

Foster Baking, Camden, NJ (9/2003–12/2003)
Served on three-member team that devised more precise method of measuring yeast activity. Created and tested apparatus that measures gas volume, tracked gas-producing activity of yeast over time, and verified measurements provided by supplier.

Keystone College, Philadelphia, PA (9/2002–5/2003)
Assisted senior-level students in developing micromixing lab for use in reaction engineering class. Researched micromixing, set up process, conducted trials, gathered data, and wrote lab procedure.

ACTIVITIES

Coordinated soccer meets for engineering students and recruited new players.

BEA K. BILLINGSLY
5555 55TH STREET
FLATLAND, TEXAS 79000
BKBILL5533@HOTMAIL.COM

(555) 555-5555

CERTIFICATION

Texas Teachers Certification, Elementary Education K-6   December 2004

EDUCATION

Bachelor of Science in Interdisciplinary Studies, FLATLAND UNIVERSITY, Flatland, Texas   **2004**

HONORS:
- *Overall GPA: 4.0: President's List, All Semesters*
- *Who's Who of College Students, Fall 2001 – Current*
- *All American Scholar, Fall 2001 – Current*

TEACHING EXPERIENCE

STUDENT TEACHING:

GREEN ELEMENTARY SCHOOL, Flatland, Texas   **2003**
Assisted classroom teacher with 18 first grade students (at least two with learning disabilities and four gifted and talented). Presented hands-on life experience lessons with abundant visual aids. Created enjoyable environment with creative bulletin boards featuring student works. Interface with parents, teachers, and administration. Recognized learning differences and expect all students to perform at their highest level.

CURRICULUMS AND PROGRAMS:
- Sharon Wells Math
- Core Knowledge Curriculum
- Phonics
- Universal Literacy Program -- Voyager
- Accelerated Reader
- Early Literacy Reading and Writing Program

INSIGHTS:
- Continuous self-evaluation strengthens effectiveness and enables strategic improvements.
- Lesson plans are a beneficial tool in measuring teaching goals.
- Classroom management is profoundly conducive to learning.
- Children need positive reinforcement as well as structure and management.

OBSERVATION/FIELD EXPERIENCE:

FLATLAND CHRISTIAN SCHOOL, Flatland, Texas   **Fall 2002**
Subject Matter Processes – Taught a two-week core knowledge unit on History / Social Studies to 15 fourth grade students. Developed curriculum guide. Received excellent evaluation.

BRIGHTNESS ELEMENTARY SCHOOL, Flatland, Texas   **Fall 2002**
Methods – Taught a one-week English unit to a gifted and talented class (30) and an average class (20), both departmentalized. Received excellent evaluation.

PROFESSIONAL AFFILIATIONS
- *Texas State Teachers Association, Current*
- *National Educational Association, Current*
- *Association of Texas Professional Educators, Current*

RHODA BLAIN

4 Hilltop Circle, Medford, NJ 03333
(home) 856.555.5555 · (cell) 609.777.7777 · rblain@aol.com

OBJECTIVE: A Graduate Assistantship

QUALIFICATIONS: Highly motivated graduate student with over 5 years work experience:

- Proven experience in secretarial and administrative settings
- Excellent typing skills (70 wpm) and computer skills
- Expertise in customer service, phone skills, and good ability to multi-task
- Background working with children who have behavioral and emotional difficulties
- Strong interpersonal skills, friendly, foster a positive work environment
- Work between 20–40 hours per week while maintaining full coarse load and good GPA

EDUCATION AND CERTIFICATIONS:

Masters Degree, Trenton University. Anticipated May 2004. EDS Program 2004–2005.
Major: School Psychology. GPA: 3.87
Bachelor's Degree. 2003. Southern College, Midstate University. Milltown, N.J.
Major: Psychology
Certified in CPR, First Aid, and Crisis Prevention

COMPUTER SKILLS:

Proficient at Microsoft Word, Excel, PowerPoint, E-mail, Internet Research. Type 70 wpm.

WORK EXPERIENCE:

SECRETARY, Licensed Psychologist Private Practice   **May 2002–Present**
Dr. Thomas Fletcher, PhD, Medford, NJ

Schedule appointments for 3 doctors. Track all billing, payments, and client accounts. Type reports, letters, and dictations. Handle phone and receptionist duties. Work 20–40 hours/week.
- Scored psychological tests and recorded results
- Initiated and implemented effort to have staff utilize computer for important paperwork
- Reorganized procedures to be more efficient and professional
- Trained office manager in using computer programs

SUBSTITUTE WEEKEND COUNSELOR   **October 2003–Present**
Family Service of Camden County, Mary Smith Center, Burlington, NJ

Assist case manager at partial care facility, helping children from adoptive or foster care families with behavioral and emotional problems.
- Demonstrated caring ability to provide attention and affection, and balance with appropriate discipline
- Conducted group activities and discussion groups, and supervised during free time
- Coached children in appropriate conduct and behaviors for different situations they face

VOLUNTEER GROUP ASSISTANT   **February 2004**
Robert Middle School, Cherry Hill, NJ
Assist school psychologist in after school discussion group on separation and divorce.

HOSTESS/CASHIER   1998–2003
Rose Diner & Restaurant, Mt. Laurel, NJ
Greeted and seated customers, handled register, trained other staff.

~~~~~

SAMANTHA BLAKE

13 Cobble Hill Road, Huntington, NY 11743
(555)555-5555 • sblake@yahoo.com

~ PROFESSIONAL INTEREST ~

Entry-level position in an organization providing social/human services.

~ EDUCATION ~

BACHELOR OF ARTS, PSYCHOLOGY, May 2004
State University of New York at Stony Brook, Stony Brook, NY

~ COMPETENCIES ~

Experience working with children and individuals needing emotional support
Trained in counseling techniques - Highly compassionate with excellent people skills
Effective working independently and as a team member
Computer skills including MS Word

~ WORK HISTORY ~

FAMILY SERVICE LEAGUE, Huntington, NY
Volunteer Counselor
September 2003 – Present

Respond to crisis hotline callers experiencing personal difficulties related to a variety of issues including anxiety, depression, suicidal thoughts, and interpersonal conflicts. Offer support and reassurance through calm and deliberate verbal exchanges. Summarize and compile information on each conversation including caller demographics, significant issues discussed, and follow-up or referral suggestions. Received several weeks of training on counseling techniques.

Child Care Provider
September 2001 – September 2003

Employed on long-term assignments by two Smithtown families, each with special needs children. Worked ten to thirty hours a week supervising homework and assisting with school projects. Provided transportation to activities, prepared meals, and assumed parental role. Fostered a secure and safe environment.

KINDERCARE CHILDREN'S CENTER, Hauppauge, NY
Day Care Counselor/Travel Camp Counselor
May 2000 – September 2001

As Day Care Counselor, provided basic child care and supervision to a group of one- to six-year-olds. Initiated games and activities to keep children engaged. As Travel Camp Counselor, helped coordinate and organize day excursions and outings. Offered well-received suggestions for program improvements for the following year. Developed an enhanced appreciation for cultural diversity. Chaperoned trips.

References available on request

TARA LAWRENCE COLE

90-34 Brownstown Circle • East Islip, New York 11796 • (631) 843-8385 • TLC@Healthmatters.net

CAREER GOAL

Health Care Management trainee position where a degree in Health Care Management, internship experience working within a progressive nursing home, and experience as a Teacher Assistant will be of value.

EDUCATION

Bachelor of Science in Health Care Management, January 2004
—with a minor in Business Administration
Long Island University *at* C.W. Post, Brentwood, NY

INTERNSHIP EXPERIENCE

Health Care Management Intern, Prince of Peace Nursing Home, Bay Shore, New York   8/03 – 12/03

- Reporting directly to Preceptor, acquired hands-on training through close observation and interaction with an interdisciplinary health care team throughout this 63-bed non-profit nursing home facility.
- Gained a comprehensive understanding of health care management, including insurance and billing processes with an emphasis on Medicaid and Medicare requirements.
- Provided general office support in areas of document preparation and data entry for cross-functional departments, including Business Office, Personnel, Medical, Social Work, Fundraising, Housekeeping, Laundry, Maintenance, Dietary, Kitchen, and Activities.
- Coordinated a fundraising project to secure monies for therapeutic equipment; visited the Foundation Center to research fifty philanthropic organizations; selected fifteen foundations based on review of published 990PF forms; composed and distributed letters of request for funding.
- Attended weekly Quality Assurance, Supervisory, and Safety meetings to learn about various issues impacting funding, budgets, special projects, quality resident care, employee relations, and regulatory compliance with New York State Health and Human Services and Conscience Policy guidelines.

WORK HISTORY

Teacher Assistant, East Islip Elementary School, Islip, New York   9/01 – 6/03

- Assisted in teaching general and special education students within an integrated classroom setting, implementing units that extend into all areas of the curriculum.
- Maintained full classroom management in primary teacher's absence with responsibility for teaching, testing and grading, record keeping, class conduct, and problem resolution.

CERTIFICATIONS

Certified Lifeguard; CPR and First Aid Certified – Infants, Children, and Adults, 1997 – Present

COMPUTER SKILLS

Windows 2000; Microsoft Word, Excel, Power Point, and Outlook Express; FC Search; Internet Navigation

Richard Costello

School Address:	Home Address:
513 Broadway, Apartment E45	378 John Street
Albany, New York 12204	Buffalo, New York 14901
(518) 231-8345 xxxxxxx@xx3.ithaca.edu	(617) 745-2568

A highly skilled, dedicated Personal Trainer with experience in sports conditioning and health clubs

SUMMARY OF QUALIFICATIONS
- Specialized skills and educational background in Personal Training with unique blend of professional experiences.
- Demonstrated ability to design, implement, and deliver fitness and training programs to individuals and groups.
- Experienced working with diverse populations: children, teens, adults, elderly, athletes, and special needs.
- Exceptional communication and motivational skills: interpersonal, written, coaching, and public speaking.
- Enthusiastic, outgoing, personable, motivated hard worker with high energy who enjoys a challenge.

EDUCATION
ITHACA COLLEGE, Ithaca, NY
B.S., Exercise Science   To be awarded May 2005

CERTIFICATIONS
Certified Personal Trainer, American Council on Exercise
CPR Certification, American Red Cross

EXPERIENCE
SIENA COLLEGE, Loudonville, NY   January 2003– Present
Assistant Strength and Conditioning Coach (Internship)
Serve as Assistant Strength and Conditioning Coach for 360 co-ed student athletes of 18 Division I athletic teams at Siena College. Sports include Football, Basketball, Baseball, Softball, Soccer, Lacrosse, Tennis, Field Hockey, Volleyball, and Golf.
- Devise and implement strength and conditioning programs for athletes during individual and group sessions. Educate athletes on corrective stretching and strengthening.
- Instruct athletes on corrective and high-performance exercising, using free weights, Swiss ball training, medicine ball training, and plyometrics training. Provide athletes with diet and nutrition consultation.
- Oversee athletes' strength and conditioning program: assess and monitor progress, set goals, and conduct tests on strength, power, and agility. Conduct team practices and training sessions for various sports.
- Developed Athletic Department's Web page for Strength and Conditioning program: www.Siena.edu (May 2005).

ITHACA FITNESS CENTER, Ithaca, NY   2000 – 2003
Personal Trainer
- Designed and implemented fitness programs and provided nutrition consultation for fitness center members.
- Conducted body-fat testing for weight-management program, using skin calipers and bioelectrical impedance.
- Coordinated programs for strength testing, flexibility testing, weight training, and sub-max Vo2 testing.
- Trained Ithaca High School Ice Hockey Team on strength and conditioning principles.

DIAMOND GYM, Elmira Heights, NY   1998 – 2000
Personal Trainer
- Created and facilitated fitness programs and provided nutrition consultation for gym members.
- Performed body-fat testing for weight-management program, using skin calipers and bioelectrical impedance.
- Supervised gym programs, including strength testing, flexibility testing, sub-max Vo2 testing, and weight training.

CITY HEALTH CLUB, Ithaca, NY   1998
Volunteer (Through Ithaca College)
- Assisted physically and mentally disabled health club members with therapeutic exercise and fitness training.

TECHNICAL SKILLS & PROFESSIONAL ACTIVITIES
Computer Skills: Microsoft Word (Windows, Excel, PowerPoint), WordPerfect, and Internet. Experienced in Web page design using Microsoft Front Page (Used during Siena Web page design).
Professional Affiliations: Mid-Atlantic Regional Chapter (MARC)-American College of Sports Medicine, Regional Member.
Awards: Named "Favorite Fitness Consultant," by the *Ithaca Journal,* 1999.
Student Activities: Member of the Fitness Club, Ithaca College.
Hobbies: First Degree Black Belt, Tae Kwon Do and First Degree Black Belt, Hap Ki Do.

Melody J. Courtney

87211 Jennywood Lane • Sherwood, Oregon 97140

555-555-5555 cell   *home 777-777-7777*

Elementary Education Teacher
Pre-Kindergarten–5th Grade

Motivating students to explore the world around them, carefully guiding them through necessary and diverse situations to formulate questions and develop strategies with which to answer those questions offering freedom in thought processes and learning.

Professional Profile

Success-driven, recent graduate, and ambitious ***Elementary Education Teacher*** with expertise in developing an intuitive connection with the student, tuning in to their specific learning needs, and providing clear, concise, and complete hands-on exercises. Experienced in developing and implementing an appropriate curriculum and planning highly effective lesson plans. Able to immediately grab students' attention, provide a strong presence, and command mutual respect. Possess outstanding communication skills with students, staff, and parents. Highly adaptable, multi-disciplined, organized, competent, and loyal. Strong team player with effectiveness in promoting school policies and practices. Additional expertise includes ***Health and Psychology*** with emphasis in ***Sports Coaching.***

Education

Bachelor of Science • Early Childhood / Elementary Education • *2003*
  Western Oregon University • Monmouth, Oregon
    • Honor Role student with emphasis in ***Health*** and ***Psychology***
Early Childhood Education • Oregon State University • *1998–2000*

History of Employment

Kindergarten Teacher • Columbus Elementary • McMinnville, Oregon • *2003*

Student Teacher • *Fourth Grade* • Columbus Elementary • McMinnville, Oregon • *2002–2003*

Caregiver • High Lookee Lodge Assisted Living Facility • *2002*
  Tenant care including administering medications. Provided cleaning, food service, and ground work for facility.

Membership Services Supervisor • Salem Boys and Girls Club, Swegle Branch • *2001–2002*
  Oversaw orientation of new members. Verified arrival and departure of 200 members daily. Supervised equipment check-outs and returns. Informed parents and members of upcoming events.

Concierge & Marketing / Sales • Eagle Crest Resorts • *2000–2001*
  Arranged hundreds of guest reservations daily. Advised businesses and traditional guests of local features to visit. Notified visitors of a variety of sales options being offered. Corresponded with guests, aiding in their vacation preparations.

Volunteer Activities

• Neighborhood Watch Co-Chairman • Preschool teacher's aide *(Fall 2001)* • Bible school teacher *(Summer 2000)*

JOHN DENNISON

E-mail: jden45@aol.com   56 Main Street • Boston, MA 67880   (659) 344–5566

PROFILE

Marine Business ... Investment/Financial Analysis ... Market Research

Talented professional with a solid academic foundation and cross-functional training in **business and marine management**. Demonstrated analytical, research, quantitative and problem-solving skills. Excellent communications, detail/follow-through and organizational skills; excel in fast-paced, demanding environments. Customer-service and team-oriented. Recognized for productivity and dependability. Advanced computer skills; adept in quickly learning new technology and applications. Fluent in Italian and conversant in Spanish.

Computer Capabilities – Operating Systems: Windows 00/98/NT. **Applications:** Microsoft Word, Excel, Access, PowerPoint, Front Page, Photoshop, Dreamweaver, Lotus Notes, C-PAS, financial applications. **Programming:** Knowledge of JavaScript, HTML, Visual Basic, website design/maintenance.

EDUCATION

BOSTON UNIVERSITY, Boston, MA, May 2004
Bachelor of Science in **Marine Business** with minor in **Resource Economics**
- Graduated magna cum laude, GPA: 3.9
- Financed college tuition and expenses through employment.

Relevant courses: Personal Finance Applications, Shipping & Port Management, Marine Resource Management, Human Use & Management, Economics of Resource Management, Economics & Politics, International Trade in Economics.

Activities: One of only 4 students chosen out of 230 applicants by the Alumni Relations Council to attend the Leadership Academy Training Program, a weeklong seminar held at Purdue University.

EXPERIENCE

Intern in Market Research – PETERSON TECHNOLOGIES, Providence, RI (1/04–5/04)

Acquired market research experience and contributed to business development efforts at one of the nation's top 15 Internet technology consulting firms. Researched and generated sales lead contacts, as well as company and industry data. Updated and maintained an extensive client database. *Accomplishments:*
- Established more than 2,000 new client leads, boosting sales during the summer months.
- Co-authored training manual for new interns using both print and multimedia applications.

Administrative Support – MONROVIA ENTERPRISES, Boston, MA (9/00–5/03)

Initially hired as part of work-study program and quickly offered salaried position based on diverse qualifications. Performed general office assignments in alumni research that included data entry and updating key donor files. Created several new databases that streamlined and enhanced information access.

Dock Manager – NEWPORT MARINA, Newport, RI (9/99–9/00)

Promoted within first month of employment to co-manage dock area, seafood market and lobster pound at one of the busiest marinas on the eastern seaboard serving recreational and commercial fishing fleets. Key role in managing major fishing tournaments with nationwide competitors. Liaison between commercial fisherman and area fish brokers. *Accomplishments:*
- Achieved record sales, resulting in one of the most financially successful years to date.
- Instilled teamwork; supervised and trained 8 employees in all aspects of marina operations.
- Initiated conversion to a computerized accounting system (QuickBooks), increasing efficiency.

Additional: Established seasonal landscaping service and grew business to 50 accounts with 50% repeat/referral clientele based on consistent service quality and excellent customer relations (6/97–9/99).

Jessica Devlin

64 Walnut Creek Drive, Yardley, PA 19089
(215) 919-5555 Home · (215) 919-8888 Mobile · jessdev@home.com

OBJECTIVE: Entry-level Mental Health Counseling position, such as Residential Counselor, Mental Health Counselor, Mental Health Associate, Clinical Case Manager, or Partial Care Counselor.

EDUCATION

Bachelor of Science, Liberal Studies, double minor: Psychology / Professional Education   May 2004
Rutgers University, New Brunswick, NJ

Relevant Courses:

Introductory Psychology	Mental Illness	Developmental Psychology	Transcultural Health
Introductory Sociology	Psychodrama I	Educational Psychology	Theory of Personality
Physiological Psychology	Loss and Grieving	Sociology of the Family	Abnormal Psychology
Essential Helping Relations	Social Psychology	Field Experience I & II	Intro. Criminal Justice

MENTAL HEALTH INTERNSHIP

Mental Health & Guardianship Advocacy, Public Defender's Office, Trenton, NJ   2002 – 2003
- Interned for 3 programs in mental health field within Public Defender's Office: Mental Health Unit (Mercer County Field Office), Guardianship Advocacy Unit, and Special Hearings Unit (Megan's Law).

- Interviewed individuals at in-patient public and private facilities, such as Hagadom State Hospital (specializing in geriatric psychiatric care), Trenton Psychiatric Hospital (adolescent and adults), as well as the Carrier Foundation (children and adolescents) for Mental Health and Guardianship Advocacy programs.

- Assisted attorneys In Megan's Law legal cases by interviewing defendants for upcoming hearings, documenting and evaluating statements, and preparing materials for the court.

- Performed follow-up case management, interviewing clients to complete cases assigned, and submitted timely documentation and reports. Ensured confidentiality of all records and communications.

EMPLOYMENT

Substitute Teacher, Hamilton Regional School District, Hamilton, NJ   2003 – present
- Teach all subjects as substitute teacher for elementary and secondary schools, following lesson plans detailed by classroom teachers, as well as maintaining positive class atmosphere and discipline.

Hostess / Cocktail Waitress, Rusty Scupper, Princeton, NJ   2002 – present
- Coordinate seating, efficiently and promptly, for popular downtown restaurant with seating for 550 indoors and outdoors. Seat 200 customers per 8-hour shift, while serving 1000 bar customers per 5-hour shift.

- Efficiently seat and serve group parties and banquets, such as four 2002 Holiday parties (75 customers each) in one day. Received recognition for top-notch customer service and positive attitude under stress.

- Entrusted with $450 bankroll at beginning of each shift. Maintain 99+% "count out" (cash reconciliation) accuracy for monies collected and disbursed daily.

- Chosen by management to promote upcoming shows and events via on-site and off-site marketing pieces and public relations appearances.

Administrative Assistant, Claims Administration, Public Defender's Office, Trenton, NJ   Summer 2001
- Maintained orderly and productive environment in busy office with 6 attorneys. Effectively answered and transferred incoming phone calls on 8 lines, and scheduled 50 – 60 appointments daily for all attorneys.

- Word-processed, edited, and revised large volume of homeowners' claims and legal settlement documents weekly (20 – 25 documents, each 75 – 80 pages in length). Consistently completed assignments with short turnaround time (within 24 hours). Received live dictation, composed and sent correspondence and memos.

COMPUTER SKILLS

Windows 98, MS Office 2000 – Word, Excel, Access, PowerPoint, MS Outlook, PhotoShop, Internet Explorer

Cara J. Fielding

266 Garfield Avenue
Lansdale, PA 19446

Phone: (215) 361-6133   caraf@dotresume.com

Objective

Junior Account Executive

Education

B.A., Public Relations Major   5/2004
BRYN MAWR UNIVERSITY, VILLANOVA, PA
Maintained 3.5 GPA while working full-time and attending school full-time;
earned 100% of college expenses.

Course Highlights

- **Public Relations Programs**—Worked as team member to prepare public
  relations programs for insurance company and convention center. Identified
  and met with clients, devised PR plans, and gave PowerPoint presentations.
- **Media Information & Gathering**—Participated in group project to develop
  campaign targeting new fitness magazine audience.

Experience

Public Relations Intern   6/2003–8/2003
DEWITT & JAMES, HORSHAM, PA
Award-winning marketing, advertising, and public relations agency.

Wrote press releases and research reports. Conducted Internet research on
resort industry competition, regional and national population changes, and
landfill locations. Used *Bacon's MediaSource* to find all city magazines,
newspapers, and radio/television/cable stations in major cities in six states.

Achievements

- Uncovered information that resulted in $13.3 million allotment to client
  (Keystone County, PA) from Governor Rendell's government proposal.
- Earned an A for internship and received excellent evaluations. Commended
  for research skills, professionalism, maturity, determination, and skill.

Nursing Monitor Technician   10/1998–present
MEMORIAL HOSPITAL, NORRISTOWN, PA

Work with nurses and other staff members in team effort to ensure best outcome
for patients on heart monitors. Train nurses and other employees in use of
monitoring equipment. Help save patients' lives through conscientious
monitoring and quick communication to nurses.

**Organizations/
Interests**

- Member of PRSSA (Public Relations Student Society of America).
- Photography buff (35 mm); called on by friends and relatives to photograph
  portraits and weddings.

Computer Skills

Proficient in Word, PowerPoint, and Internet research; familiar with Excel.

Lynn Franklin

Current Address:
100 Ridge Hall
Fulton, NY 55555

Home: (555) 555-5555
Email: lynnfranklin@aol.com

Permanent Address:
72 Hollow Hill Drive
Melville, NY 55555

Objective
Town Day Camp Director

Profile

Hard-working, academically successful university student with a passion for motivating and encouraging young children to excel. Experienced teaching and supervising children in large groups as well as on an individual basis. Flexible, easy-going, and compassionate with the ability to quickly develop a good rapport with children of all ages. A seasoned camp counselor that truly enjoys creating educational programs that satisfy the natural curiosity of young minds.

Summary of Abilities, Skills, and Attributes:
- Energetic, motivated, and dedicated • Excellent time-management abilities • Personable
- Proficient at coordinating group activities • Computer skills (MS Word, MS Excel, Internet)
- Exceptional sensitivity working with children from diverse backgrounds • Enjoys children

Education

Bachelor of Science, Childhood Education, Oswego State University, NY — anticipated 2004
Childhood Education (Grades 1-6) Major with a concentration in **Mathematics**
Classes include: Introduction to Education, Calculus I, Number Systems and Operations, General Psychology, Composition I & II, Macroeconomics, and Tools for Computing.

Relevant Experience

CLARKSTOWN DAY CAMP, Clarkstown, NY   Summer 2003
                                                          Summer 2002

Camp Counselor
- Supervised a group of 30 eight- and nine-year-old girls, five days a week during summers.
- Planned appropriate group activities and ensured full participation.
- Demonstrated excellent judgment while handling disputes between campers.
- Taught swimming to participating children in the group.

SAINT MARIA's ACADEMY, White Plains, NY   9/2001–6/2002

Teacher Assistant (Volunteer)
- Assisted teacher with class projects and activities.
- Supervised children on class trips:
  o Ensured that participating children had proper parental approval to attend activity.
  o Enforced school safety rules and procedures while on class trips.

ROCKLAND AQUATIC CLUB, Monsey, NY   4/1998–8/2001

Swim Instructor
- Taught swimming to children, age three to ten.
- Maintained water safety, at all times, while performing lessons.
- Alleviated the children's fear of water enabling them to swim by the end of the course.

Sarah T. Freeman

3030 Marigold Dr., Crystal, Texas 75000 (000) 999-9999
sfreeman59@yahoo.com

PROFILE

Intelligent achiever as demonstrated by outstanding academic standing + Mature and ambitious + Value continued education + Open-minded and tolerant of diversity + International traveler + Committed, diligent worker + Time manager + Honor loyalty and integrity + Decisive problem solver + Goals- and career-oriented leader + Bilingual: English/Spanish (learning Korean) + PC literate with proficiency in MS Office Applications

EDUCATION

SAINT GREGORY'S COLLEGE OF CALIFORNIA, Crest Ridge, CA   **2000 – 2004**
Bachelor of Arts in Politics
Cum Laude, GPA: 3.5/4.0

Relevant Projects:
- *Thesis:* The War on Drugs: A Battle that is Destroying America-Putting a Stop to Mandatory Minimums.
- *Group Project:* Comparison between U.S. and Canadian health care systems.
- *Group Project:* The death penalty in the U.S. – Do I agree.

EXPERIENCE

Intern   U.S. CAPITOL   Washington, DC   **Fall 2003**
Attended American University and assisted Senator Dianne Feinstein performing research for the Senate Minority Committee on technology, terrorism, and government information. Coordinated the Senator's schedule via computer data entry. Assisted pressroom employees and regularly interfaced with constituents in person and by phone.
- Gained insight into government processes at a federal level.
- Learned to use the congressional Research Center.
- Gained overview of how constituents directly affect the law-making process.
- One of only two chosen from US for prestigious internship.

English Teacher   ENGLISH FRIENDS ACADEMY   South Korea   **1998 – 1999**
Taught all levels of English to kindergarten through middle school classes ranging from five to ten children. Taught kindergarten computer basics.
- Motivated children to improve English skills.
- Successfully interfaced with parents and peers.

Other Employment:
Seasonal and temporary jobs as child care provider, secretary, and sales clerk.   **1993 – 2001**

COLLEGIATE ACTIVITIES

- Member, Portuguese Club   **2000 – 2001**
- Volunteer, Dorothy Day House (Feeding Homeless)   **2001**
- Volunteer, American Red Cross (Helping Flood Victims)   **2000**
- Volunteer, March of Dimes Walk America (Fighting Birth Defects)   **1998 – 1999**

Carla Goldstein

244 Strawbridge Court ♦ Scotia, NY 12334 ♦ (518) 782-4887

An experienced, highly skilled Teacher certified to teach elementary students, special education, and reading

SUMMARY OF QUALIFICATIONS
- Variety of successful teaching experiences: grades K-12, special education, reading classes, and private tutoring.
- Skilled in creating and presenting effective course work and related material that interests children to learn.
- Able to motivate children with various levels of skills and abilities to learn on individual and group basis.
- Proven interpersonal skills, having worked with and directed diversity of professionals, students, and staff.
- Proficient at evaluating individual students achievements and correcting problem areas in learning.
- Strong organizational skills; completed graduate studies in Education while teaching and tutoring.

EDUCATION & CERTIFICATION
College of Saint Rose, Albany, NY   2003
Master of Science, Education (Reading), 3.86 G.P.A.

Marist College, Poughkeepsie, NY   2001
Bachelor of Arts, Special Education / Psychology (dual major)

New York State Provisional Certification, Regular Education, K-6
New York State Provisional Certification, Special Education, K-12
New York State Certification, Reading

PROFESSIONAL EXPERIENCE
Voorheesville Central Schools, Voorheesville, NY / **Guilderland Central Schools,** Guilderland, NY   2003 – Present
Substitute Teacher (2004 – Present)
- Work in 2 school districts with full-time teachers in teaching elementary and special needs students.
- Assist with developing and presenting curriculum, including reading classes.

Kindergarten Teacher, long-term position (2003 – 2004)
- Collaborated with full-time teachers in developing daily curriculum and teaching lessons.
- Developed stimulating environment and activities to encourage learning and higher-level thinking.
- Evaluated students' progress and success by assisting teachers with filling out report cards.
- Conducted small group activities, including center activities.
- Participated in faculty meetings to discuss school policies and professional development.

RELATED EXPERIENCE
Ichabod Crane Primary School, Valatie, NY   Fall 2003
Special Education Teacher (November – December)
- Introduced multi-sensory learning activities related to themes. Led small group activities in math.

Reading Teacher (October – November)
- Reinforced students' skills in language arts, reading, and math by developing and implementing games.
- Oversaw small group activities, including writing centers.

Second Grade Teacher (September – October)
- Instituted unit on math concept at second grade level containing instructional centers for student participation.
- Coordinated reading groups, monitoring each student's progress and pinpointing problem areas.

Christopher Columbus Elementary School, Poughkeepsie, NY   Spring 2002
Third Grade Teacher
- Planned and presented science, language arts, and social studies lessons, according to classroom curriculum.

Winpfeimer Nursery School at Vassar College, Poughkeepsie, NY   Fall 2001
Kindergarten Teacher
- Supervised instructional centers, facilitating active participation in art and science.

VOLUNTEER EXPERIENCE
Treasurer, Temple Beth Emeth Youth Group, Albany, NY
Volunteer, Temple Beth Emeth Soup Kitchen, Albany, NY
Volunteer, Mt. Carmel Elementary School, Poughkeepsie, NY
Secretary, Marist College Chess Club, Poughkeepsie, NY

DIANA HANSON

12 Wesley Street, Brentwood, New York 11717   (631) 255-7711 • programmer@inet.net

Seeking an entry-level position in the capacity of:

SOFTWARE PROGRAMMER

- Bachelor's degree in Computer Science with over two years of accomplished help desk support experience.
- Analytical, detail oriented with strong programming skills; work diligently on long, tedious assignments.
- Maintain excellent interpersonal communication, time management, and problem resolution skills.

Languages: C++ Turbo, Basic, Cobol, Visual Basic, Pascal, Assembler
Software: Windows 98/2000, Microsoft Word, Excel, Access, and PowerPoint

RELEVANT EXPERIENCE

Sky-Force Technologies, Information Technology Department, Hauppauge, New York   9/03 – Present
Intern Computer Programmer / Help Desk Associate

Leading provider of advanced aerospace systems, components, and support to aircraft manufacturers and operators worldwide. Products include quality fluid measurement and management systems, avionic displays, and flight inspection systems for commercial, commuter, and military aircraft.

Programming
- Recognized department-wide as a "little genius" for early contributions in the beta programming of software modules for a complex scheduling program utilizing a Cobol-comparable programming language.
- Apply ghost procedures to delete all programs and data files on several lease-expired systems.
- Attend morning meetings to discuss projects and assignments, plan strategies, and suggest improvements.

Help Desk Support
- Work closely with a help desk team, providing hands-on support to end users with hardware and software problems including WAN connectivity, upgrades, configurations, data recovery, and extensive printing issues.
- Document requests for help desk support and outcome resolutions to monitor and track recurring problems.
- Interface between technicians and employees to identify problems and formulate solutions.

EDUCATION

State University of New York at Stony Brook, Stony Brook, New York
Bachelor of Science degree in Computer Science / Business Option, May 2004
Full athletic scholarship - Sophomore and Freshman; Big West Academic All-Star Team, 2000, 2001

*Software Applications on the PC | Structured Programming | Microcomputer Assembler Language |
Systems Analysis / Distributive Systems | Management | Accounting | Economics | Marketing*

Regents Diploma, 2000
Babylon High School, Babylon, New York
Business Student of the Year | National Service Honor Society | Class Historian

Elliot T. Hart

57 Arbutus Road ▪ Dix Hills, NY 11746 ▪ 631-555-5555 ▪ elliothart@hotmail.com

Seeking an Entry-Level Position in Human Resource Management

Experience includes:

Interviewing and Hiring / New Hire Orientations / Employee Scheduling
Training & Group Leadership

EXPERIENCE

Assistant Manager/Bartender, NICOLE'S PLACE—Syosset, NY   1/03 – Present

As the only assistant manager, reported directly to general manager in this high-volume restaurant establishment with ~60 employees and service on 3 floors. Primary functions similar to a human resources manager.

- Reviewed applications, interviewed, and hired approximately 25 bar staff.
- Conducted new-hire orientations to include job training and review of company policies. On occasion, fired workers in breach of duties or in violation of company guidelines.
- Scheduled the work hours of ten employees.
- Proactively took on additional responsibilities such as resolving paycheck discrepancies, work schedule issues, employee conflicts, and customer complaints.
- Managed inventory of bar items and verified accuracy of deliveries against purchase orders.

Bartender / Interim Bar Manager, HUNTINGTON COUNTRY CLUB—Huntington, NY   5/00 – 12/02

Established rapport, provided camaraderie, and served patrons in this private club catering to an upscale clientele.
Assumed bar manager's responsibilities for one month during boss's absence. Oversaw service operations including staff scheduling and bar readiness.

- Trained 6 other bartenders in basic and advanced bartending techniques including use of the computer touch screen.
- Maximized customer satisfaction by providing courteous service.

COLLEGE LEADERSHIP

President, Vice President, Philanthropy Chairman, Fund Raising Chairman & Recruitment Chairman
THETA CHI FRATERNITY (2001 – 2003)

- Raised membership 150% in two years.
- Led chapter meetings and events of 20-30 people according to Robert's Rules of Order.
- Headed a fundraising event for a homeless shelter that raised over $3,000.

COMPUTER SKILLS

Proficient in Windows, Word, PowerPoint, Internet, and e-mail. Some Excel and Access.

EDUCATION

Bachelor of Arts, Communications, January 2004. Adelphi University, Garden City, NY

DENNIS HAUSBURG

1116 Sellers Road
Hatfield, PA 19440
(215) 368-4076
hausburg@dotresume.com

GOAL

Environmental Scientist / Consultant in an organization that will benefit from my Phase I Assessment experience and strong communication, analytical, organizational, and computer skills.

EDUCATION

B.A., Environmental Studies, Temple University, Philadelphia, PA (4/2003); earned 50% of college expenses while maintaining 3.4 GPA in major.

Relevant Courses: Communication for Environmental Professionals, Environmental Science Ethics and Public Policy, Geochemistry, Law and Environment, Physical Oceanography, Remote Sensing of the Earth, Risk Assessment.

Course Highlights:

- Analyzed results of Phase I water testing.
- Created maps showing expansion of downtown Pittsburgh between 1930 and 1995 using aerial photographs, GPS (Global Positioning System), and remote sensing.
- Prepared environmental press releases, in-house memos, and technical reports.

EXPERIENCE

MILL CREEK CITIZENS FOR CLEAN WATER, Mill Creek, PA (5/2002–present)
Vice President
Serve as consultant to group established to resolve ground water contamination problem. Prior to formation of group, initiated investigation of pollutants in area following review of DEP (Department of Environmental Protection) press release. Researched effects of chemicals, interviewed homeowners, and found evidence of hazardous situation. Worked with affected residents to organize citizen's group; subsequently elected vice president. Recommended testing and proposed solutions at township meetings. Gained television and newspaper exposure of problem.

HATFIELD PRINT WORKS, Hatfield, PA (4/1997–present)
Customer Service and Print Manager
Assist owner and manage day-to-day operations in owner's absence; serve customers, perform routine and specialized printing work, and prepare invoices and bank deposits.

TAVERN WEST, Lansdale, PA (10/2002–8/2003)
SPRING VALLEY COUNTRY CLUB, Horsham, PA (5/1999–9/2002)
Server and Bartender
Helped managers open new restaurant and bar. Trained 10+ servers, provided front-line customer service, and suggested and implemented more efficient communication and organizational solutions. Translated for Spanish-speaking employees.

SPECIAL SKILLS

Computer: Microsoft Office (Word, Excel, PowerPoint), Web Design (HTML), C++ Programming, Hardware Maintenance and Repair.
Language: Intermediate Spanish.

VOLUNTEERISM

Federal Emergency Management Agency / Red Cross, New York, NY (9/2001).
Sorted supplies and provided meals to firefighters and other workers following 9/11 terrorist attacks.

JESSICA JEFFERSON

600 Broadway, Apartment #30D
Troy, New York 12211

(518) 273-4473
xxxxx@aol.com

OBJECTIVE

Seeking a challenging position as an Environmental Planner with an organization actively involved in regional planning where my skills and experience can be utilized toward protecting the environment.

EDUCATION

State University of New York, Albany, NY
Master's Degree in Regional Planning (MRP), 3.8 G.P.A.

To be awarded May 2005

State University of New York, Plattsburgh, NY
B.A., Environmental Planning & Resource Management, 3.5 G.P.A., *cum laude*

2003

HONORS

Dean's List
Crary Foundation Scholarship
Plattsburgh College Foundation Scholarship

RELATED COURSE WORK

Thesis: Growth Management in the Capital District (Urban Sprawl).

Key Courses: Environmental Planning, Planning Studio, Land Conservation, Statistical Methods, Small Town Rural Planning, Urban & Metropolitan Statistical Functions, Planning Law, Comprehensive Planning, Computer Mapping.

Independent Study: Generated planning maps of Jefferson county using GIS (ARC View) and Roots   Spring 2005

EXPERIENCE

CLOUGH HARBOUR & ASSOCIATES LLP, Albany, NY   May 2004 – Present
Consulting firm specializing in environmental planning and engineering, surveying, and landscape architecture.
Internship
- Assist with writing environmental impact statements and proofread environmental documents and reports for accuracy.
- Prepare SEQR environmental assessments and NEPA reports, which includes reviewing various federal and state maps.
- Conduct wetland delineation, which includes inspection of wetlands for soil characteristics and vegetation.
- Conduct site visits, which includes taking photos and organizing required paperwork, reports, and permits.

STATE UNIVERSITY OF NEW YORK, Albany, NY   September 2003 – Present
Graduate Assistant
Advise and help students with course work. Hold office hours for individual instruction and guidance. Facilitate classroom instruction and test administration for between 200-400 students.

UNITED STATES POSTAL SERVICE, Niskayuna, NY   Summer 2001
Letter Carrier
Handled and distributed mail. Worked in office and delivered mail on walking and driving routes.

TAMARACK FORESTRY, Canton, NY   Summer 2000
Traffic Controller
Directed traffic, cleared brush, secured roadways and residences after 2000 winter ice storm disaster.

ADDITIONAL SKILLS & QUALIFICATIONS

Computers: Microsoft Office, GIS (ARC View), and CADD.
Communications: Demonstrated interpersonal and counseling skills, public speaking, and written skills.
Foreign Languages: Conversational French.
Professional Affiliations: American Planning Association (APA), Member.

Angela Kelly

19 Nancy Street ♦ Utica, NY 12119 ♦ (518) 783-2263 ♦ xxxxx@xxx.edu

An enthusiastic, dedicated Teacher with certification to teach Pre-K through Grade 6

SUMMARY OF QUALIFICATIONS

- Experienced in teaching Preschool through Grade 6 in various positions and educational institutions.
- Skilled in creating and presenting effective lesson plans and related materials that interest children to learn.
- Able to motivate children with different levels of skills and abilities to learn on individual and group basis.
- Team player with strong interpersonal skills, having worked with diversity of students, professionals, and staff.
- Proficient in conducting standardized tests, writing profiles, and parent-teacher conferences.

EDUCATION & CERTIFICATION

Russell Sage College, Troy, NY   2002
Bachelor of Science, Elementary Education, *minor* **in Psychology, 3.105 G.P.A.**

Senior Thesis: Living with Asperger's Syndrome

Honors: Transfer Excellence Award Scholarship

New York State Provisional Certification, Pre-K-6 (Certificate # 065642676)

PROFESSIONAL EXPERIENCE

North Colonie Central School District, Southgate Elementary School, Latham, NY   2003 – Present
Support Teacher

- Provide teaching support in classroom, motivating students, and meeting educational goals in grades K–6.
- Reinforce lesson plans by working with small groups of students as well as special needs students.
- Teach lesson plans independently to classes with 20 to 25 students on variety of subjects.
- Fill in as substitute teacher throughout school district's 5 elementary schools as needed.
- Conduct testing and monitor students' progress, according to course curriculum and lesson outline.

SELECTED TEACHING PRACTICUM

Turnpike Elementary, Lansingburgh, NY   2002

- Designed and implemented daily curriculum for 4th Grade Class with 25 students.
- Led class independently in creating and delivering lesson plans and teaching materials.
- Evaluated individual student progress and conducted parent-teacher conferences.

School 16, Troy, NY   2002

- Developed and presented lesson plans and teaching materials for 1st Grade Class with 20 students.
- Served as substitute as needed and independently oversaw classroom full time for one week.
- Collaborated with full-time teacher in designing lesson plans and holding parent-teacher conferences.

Carroll Hill Elementary, Troy, NY   2001

- Presented one class per week for 1st Grade Class with 24 students.

School 12, Troy, NY

- Assisted teacher with daily curriculum and taught class as needed for 2nd and 4th Grade Class of 23 students.

Boys & Girls Club, Troy, NY   2000

- Coordinated intensive hands-on and one-on-one instruction to 15 special education preschool students.

RELATED EXPERIENCE

Self-Employed Home Day Care, LaGrange, GA   1984 – 1994
Childcare Provider

- Managed day care center, providing care and age-appropriate activities for Pre-K through Grade 6 Children.

VOLUNTEER WORK

YWCA, Troy, NY: worked with women and children, raised funds and food, and organized community dinner.
St. Peter's Church, Lagrange, GA: provided childcare services during Sunday services.

AWARDS

Certificate of Merit for Designing Discovery Box, The Retired and Senior Volunteer Program   2002

COMPUTER SKILLS

Microsoft Office, Microsoft Windows, FoxPro, Internet

David Martin Kohler

OBJECTIVE: HELP DESK / COMPUTER SUPPORT TECHNICIAN

PROFILE

- ☑ Recent computer center graduate with proven technical abilities.
- ☑ Demonstrated track record of achieving goals in a team environment.
- ☑ Highly motivated and dependable. Proven skills in problem solving, customer relationship management, and organization.

EDUCATION

The Computer Learning Center, Skillman, NJ   2004 – 2005
Computer Coursework completed in:

- ✓ Networking Essentials
- ✓ A+ Certification
- ✓ Intermediate Word 2003
- ✓ Beginning Word 2003
- ✓ Beginning Access 2003
- ✓ TCP/IP Protocol

- ✓ Beginning Windows NT
- ✓ Administering Windows NT
- ✓ Windows NT Core Technologies
- ✓ Windows NT Support by Enterprise
- ✓ Beginning Business on the Internet
- ✓ Beginning FrontPage 2003

Montclair University, Montclair, NJ   2000 – 2001
General first-year courses in Bachelor's Degree program (24 credits).

EMPLOYMENT

A Cut Above, Montclair, NJ   2001 – 2005
Receptionist / Cashier

- Successfully handled front desk and three incoming telephone lines for busy, upscale hair salon. Greeted and logged in steady stream of customers, coordinating appointments with hairdresser availability.

- Developed cooperative, team-oriented working relationships with owners and co-workers in this 12-station salon.

- Managed customer problems and complaints with tact and attention to prompt customer service. Received team and customer service awards.

- Experience gained in opening and closing procedures, cash register receipts, counter sales, light bookkeeping, and telephone follow-up.

Pro Soccer Camp, Princeton, NJ   Summers 1998 – 2001
Trainer / Coach

- Assisted Woman's Soccer Coach in 200-participant soccer camp. Asked to return as trainer for 3 seasons. Worked with individuals, as well as teams, to improve their attitude and resulting soccer performance.

ACTIVITIES

Jersey Waves Soccer Semi-Pro Team   1998 – 2002
- ✓ Team consistently ranked in top 10 semi-pro teams in the nation.

Washington Crossing High School Soccer Team   1997 – 2000
- ✓ Captain of team that won State Soccer Title in 1999
- ✓ Recognized as one of the top two mid-fielders In the state in 2000

175 Highland Road, Washington Crossing, PA 18977 • (215) 369-5555 • dmk21@bci.net

GREGORY MARTIN

67 Barkette Road
Tarrytown, New York 10098

(987) 662–7743
martin234@yahoo.com

PROFILE

Organizational Development/Change Management Professional with training and experience that provide a foundation for partnering human resources/OD initiatives with strategic business units to enhance productivity, performance, quality and service. Core skills include:

Project Management–Five years of project management experience that encompasses conceptualization, needs assessment and planning through execution, post intervention assessment, feedback and closure. Ability to integrate broader corporate values into functional project plans that yield deliverables aligned with enterprise objectives.

Training & Facilitation–Versed in OD interventions: training, process improvement, team dynamics, meeting facilitation, performance assessment and 360° Feedback instruments, coaching, as well as change management models and human factors issues.

Research & Technical Skills–Experienced in researching, formulating and conducting group training, including development of presentation materials. Competent researcher, utilizing electronic databases (InfoTrac) and survey methods; trained in performing data analysis using SPSS, ANOVA, T Tests and others.

EDUCATION

NEW YORK UNIVERSITY, New York, NY:
Master of Science in Industrial and Organizational Psychology, May 2004

Selected Projects & Research:

- Transformational leadership and change management study.
- Peer review and organizational citizenship behavior related to TQM and employee motivation.
- Study of lean manufacturing, participative management, cell concepts, flexible structures and related.
- Onsite studies of workplace safety, human factors and ergonomics issues.

Bachelor of Science in Psychology, *graduated magna cum laude,* May 2002

Awards/Honors: Provost's Awards (1998, 1999); Outstanding Social Science Award); Psi Chi Honor Society (1999). Self-financed 100% of college tuition and expenses.

EXPERIENCE

KENWORTH CORPORATION, New York, NY
Intern: Organizational Development Consultant (2002–2003)

Assisted the internal Senior Organizational Development Consultant in providing proactive OD consulting and interventions to enhance operational and human resources effectiveness, efficiency and quality in a Fortune 500 enterprise with 5,000 employees. Supported corporate training and development initiatives in coordination with the Human Resources Service centers, Learning and Development Unit, Corporate Library and Learning Centers, including diversity training, Corporate University offerings and customer service training.

Program Management, Training & Facilitation

- Planned, managed and facilitated Manager Information Network, a management peer group from 5 business units sharing best practices and fostering company's commitment to excellence. Initiated group's Intranet-based communication vehicle. Developed an organizational structure to allow group to become self-perpetuating.

- Designed modules on a range of business topics for management development programs. Designed and trained managers on effective use of quantifiable employee performance assessment tools. Recognized for exhibiting a group facilitation style that places participants at ease and encourages willingness to share information.

GREGORY MARTIN – Page 2

Program Management, Training & Facilitation continued...

♦ Served as co-facilitator for customer service training program for new hires. Demonstrated ability to energize training participants through enthusiasm and creativity.

♦ Participated in various phases of serving clients from responding to requests, to researching and observing several interventions.

♦ Collaborated on the remodel of the Learning Center to enhance usability, physical environment and selection of resource tools available for managers. Managed the Center's grand reopening project, including recommending and implementing ergonomic changes, project planning, budget administration and coordinating other activities.

UNICARE HEALTH, INC., New York, NY
Program Director - Intern (2000–2001)

Conceptualized, planned, executed, budgeted and directed a successful intergenerational pilot program at a health care organization. Demonstrated creativity in theme development and designing unique activities to maximize impact among multifunctional levels; program became an ongoing event.

PATRICIA MELANSON

63 Broadway, Brentwood, New York 11717 • (631) 577-9032 • production@media.net

OBJECTIVE

Position in the field of communications bringing directly related education, experience, and technical skills.

EDUCATION

Bachelor of Fine Arts, Communications
Hofstra University, Garden City, New York, 2003

Associates of Science, Broadcasting
LaGuardia Community College, Long Island City, New York, 1994

EXPERIENCE

Production Intern, The Mandy Wilson Show, New York, New York   2/03 – Present
- Work with producers, Viewer Service, and Audience departments in areas of topic research, guest selection and relations, ticket distribution, bookings, audience management, and general office support.
- Provided technical assistance to Control Room engineers during editing sessions.

Public Relations Assistant, Larry Spinner, *Jazz Musician*, East Hampton, New York   1/02 – 3/02
- Actively promoted artist's music and engagements throughout college towns and medical communities
- Distributed media kits and other marketing materials, conducted telephone campaigns, and performed Internet research to track local venues

Video Operator, Music Television Communications, Huntington, New York   1/01 – 3/01
- Reported directly to the Video Production Supervisor with responsibility for managing broadcast reception operations for nine network channels spanning the East and West Coasts
- Coordinated program back-up procedures, transmitted tones, monitored intervals, keyed program titles and graphics, and maintained log reports

Production Intern, The David Browne Show, New York, New York   9/00 – 12/00
- Researched, generated, and pre-approved show topic ideas reflecting viewer interests
- Conducted pre-show interviews by telephone as part of the studio's guest selection process
- Provided office support in areas of correspondence, filing, mail processing, and faxing

Production Intern, Media Communications, Hauppauge, New York   6/00 – 9/00
- Assisted in all phases of production processes demonstrating a proficiency in camera and lighting techniques, and an ability to work in accordance to floor plans and edit sheets

Faculty Assistant, Hofstra University, Garden City, New York   6/99 – 9/99
- Coordinated the computerized scheduling and technical set-up of audio and visual equipment
- Screened calls, processed equipment request forms, and maintained departmental logs and files

COMPUTER SKILLS

Hardware/Software: Windows 95/MacIntosh; MS Word/Excel; Quark Express; Louth Systems
Arts: Camera and lighting techniques; analogue film and video editing

PROFESSIONAL AFFILIATIONS

American Women in Television

RYAN R. MICHAELS
813–225–8745 ▪ Michaels@email.com

9876 Sand Crane Blvd. ▪ Tampa ▪ FL ▪ 33607

ELECTRICAL ENGINEER
Manufacturing Processes ▪ Operations Management ▪ Project Coordination ▪ Research & Development

Value To Employer	▪ Experience designing, developing, and testing electrical and electronic equipment; proficient in AutoCAD. ▪ Providing technical support and leadership to cross-functional teams working to improve product quality and refine workflow processes within manufacturing environments. ▪ Detailed and analytical competencies, with the ability to solve complex issues. ▪ Proven "take charge" leadership skills that result in solutions.
Education	**Bachelor of Science in Electrical Engineering** – expected May 2003 **Minor in Business Administration** Florida State University, Tallahassee, Florida ▪ Upper Division GPA 3.03/4.0 ▪ Relevant coursework: Microprocessors, C++, Electronic Circuits, Technical Writing, Intelligent Machines Design Laboratory, Management, Finance, Accounting, DSP, Communications Systems, Engineering Statistics, Digital Design
Internships	**Robotics Engineer** – August – December, 2001 FREIGHT MANUFACTURING, Atlanta, Georgia *(One of the world's largest manufacturers of advanced technology, components, and systems for all major automakers)* Collaborated with electrical and mechanical engineering teams in designing automated systems used for all product assemblies. Programmed PLCs by configuring process timing, setting tasks, testing, and performing quality checks. **Test Engineer** – Summers 2000 and 2001 JABIL CIRCUIT, INC., St. Petersburg, Florida *(A global leader in the electronic manufacturing services industry)* Liaised with representatives from two major client accounts (Intel and Cisco) in designing code modifications, writing software, testing new and existing products, and improving workflow processes. **Agricultural Engineering Research** – May - August 1998 FSU CITRUS RESEARCH EXPERIMENT CENTER, Tallahassee, Florida *(The world's largest citrus research, teaching, and extension center)* Partnered with agricultural engineers in modifying and testing citrus spray equipment.
Related Experience	**Telecommunications Specialist** – since March 1999 FLORIDA STATE UNIVERSITY – CIRCA, Tallahassee, Florida Selected from among 30 applicants to design and oversee installation of data/video network infrastructure, testing, and network maintenance. Train new hires on installation methodologies and network maintenance.
Memberships	Institute of Electrical & Electronics Engineers (IEEE) ▪ Campus Crusade for Christ
Leadership Positions	Reformed University Fellowship ▪ Eagle Scout

346 Windy Avenue
Brentwood, NY 11717

Geraldine Newman

(631) 808-0355
healthcare@united.com

Career Focus

Administrative-trainee position in:
Healthcare Management

Education

State University *of* New York *at* Stony Brook, Stony Brook, NY
Bachelor of Science, Healthcare Administration, 2003
Campus Leadership: Healthcare Management Club

Experience

Healthcare Facilities Intern, Long Island Day Care Center, Hauppauge, NY   6/03 – 12/03

- While learning, contributed to the general management of this 26-client adult day care facility.
- Worked collaboratively with the staff Registered Nurse, Certified Nurse Assistant, and Program Coordinator plan, develop, coordinate, and facilitate recreation therapy programs.
- Designed a customized form to define and measure Board members' knowledge of strategic planning for the center to ensure the provision of total quality care.
- Proposed budgets and plans impacting change management processes with a focus on mandatory training, practices, and procedures in alignment with regulatory guidelines.
- Observed and evaluated clinical charting procedures, admissions processes, and staff relations.
- Participated in Board meetings centered on facility operations and funding related issues.

Office Support Associate, Exhibit Presentations, Huntington, NY   *Part-time* 3/02 – Present

- Provide diversified office support in positions held over interim periods for various departments that include Sales, Billing, Purchasing, and Reception, in the following areas:
  - Preparing payroll for a combined sixty Union and non-Union employees.
  - Recruiting sub-contractors to fulfill job requirements on a per project basis.
  - Handling the invoicing, billing, reconciliation, and payables/receivables for 200 accounts.
  - Processing proposals and production work requests for various exhibit projects.
  - Sourcing vendors to ensure the cost-effective purchase and availability of products.
  - Training employees on computerized functions and effective Internet research strategies.
- Report to Account Executive to ensure open lines of communication and problem resolution.

Computer Skills

Windows 2000, Microsoft Word, Excel, Power Point, Word Perfect, Internet research

References

Exceptional References Provided Upon Request (Professors and Supervisors)

R.J. PEREZ

3 School Lane, Lloyd Harbor, NY 11743 • (631) 555-5555 • RJPerez@aol.com

CAREER INTEREST

Seeking a position in pharmaceutical sales.

EDUCATION

Bachelor of Arts, May 2004. Hofstra University, Hempstead, NY
Major: Communications; Minor: Business

SUMMARY OF QUALIFICATIONS

- Sales and marketing experience through college leadership endeavors and as an intern for Rolling Stone Magazine.
- Strong interest in the pharmaceutical industry. Knowledge of pharmaceutical sales acquired through personal research.
- Excellent oral and written communication skills. Professional demeanor.
- Highly energetic, motivated, and ambitious. Quick learner.

WORK EXPERIENCE

Sales/Marketing Intern, Rolling Stone Magazine, New York, NY   June 2003-July 2003

- Contacted new and existing clients to secure commitments for advertising space.
- Developed strong client relationships providing suggestions, service, and thorough execution of orders.
- Handled database management work including entry and retrieval functions.
- Prepared promotional material and media kits.

Intern, Media Advertising Associates, New York, NY   May 2002-July 2002

- Cold called prospective clients for sales department.
- Performed program prescreening at major television networks.
- Utilizing MS Excel, generated reports of network programs for sponsors.
- Verified program content compatibility with client guidelines.
- Assisted in preparing competitive advertising expenditure reports.

Travel Assistant, The Village Traveler, Huntington, NY   May 2001-August 2001

- Assisted with coordinating and booking travel arrangements for corporate accounts.
- Compiled information on clients and trips using industry-specific database system.

SKILLS

Computers: Windows 98/XP, Word, Excel, PowerPoint, Lotus Notes, Internet
Language: Bilingual, English/Spanish

ACTIVITIES

- Handled promotion and marketing efforts for the "X" Men Band.
- Academic Tutor Volunteer.
- Chairperson, Toys for Tots Holiday Campaign.

References available upon request

CARLA M. PFISTER

74 East Oldbrook Road   (000) 444-5555
Northbridge, NH 0000   pfister22@aol.com   Cell: (000) 666-7777

OBJECTIVE

A semester **internship** with a well-established accounting firm in Boston.

EDUCATION

Salve Regina University, Newport, RI
Bachelor of Science in **Accounting**   Expected May 2006

Academic Honors:
   Current GPA: 3.65/4.0
   Dean's List: two semesters

Relevant Courses:
   Accounting and Organizational Behavior
   Advanced Principles of Accounting
   Management of Human Resources
   Accounting Principles 1, 2
   Introduction to Computer Systems
   Intermediate Micro-computer Applications
   Problems in Urban Economics
   Principles of Economics 1, 2

EXPERIENCE

Northbridge Veterinary Clinic, Northbridge, NH
Nurse Assistant, Summers   2003 – 2005
   o   Assisted medical staff with boarding, washing, and appointments
   o   Worked with Bookkeeper on receivables and monthly billings

Brigham Gardens Living, Northbridge, NH
Food Service Employee, Summers   2001 – 2002
   o   Served food daily to 35 patients at an assisted living home
   o   Chosen to assist nurses with early-stage Alzheimer patients

SKILLS

Computer: MS Excel, Word, PowerPoint, Access, Internet search
Competent oral and written communications
Effective organizational and leadership capabilities
Highly competent sailor in regatta competitions

ACTIVITIES

Accounting and Finance Club, two years, SRU
Peer Leadership Team Leader
Relay for Life Feinstein volunteer for breast cancer
Sailing Team, two years, SRU
Peer Tutor in Business subjects, SRU

~ REFERENCES FURNISHED UPON REQUEST ~

Mark Quinn

Current Address:
123 Oak Street
Farmington, NY 99999

Cellular: (555) 555-5555
Email: mquinn22@yahoo.com

Permanent Address:
22 Main Street
Saratoga, NY 99999

Seeking an entry-level position in the capacity of:
Political Analyst

A highly motivated individual with a strong work ethic and a passion for international politics. Tactful, diplomatic, and experienced in dealing with people from diverse backgrounds. Hold dual citizenship with the United States and England. Multilingual: fluent in English and Italian, functional in Swedish and Norwegian, and studying Spanish and French.

Summary of Abilities, Skills, and Attributes:
- ♦ Research ♦ Analysis ♦ Organize and interpret data ♦ Oral and written communication
- ♦ Problem-solving ♦ Computer skills (MS Office, Internet, Front Page, C++, HTML, Adobe Photoshop)
- ♦ Works well individually and in teams ♦ Excellent time-management abilities

Education

B.A., Political Science and Philosophy, New York University, NY — anticipated 2004
- **Multidisciplinary Political Science Major**, concentration in International and Global Affairs; minor in International Studies with a **3.3 GPA; Dean's List,** 2003.
- Courses include: World Politics, Comparative Politics, Political Philosophy, Dynamics of International Conflict, Diplomacy in a Changing World, Democratization and Globalization, Global Democratic Revolution, Human Rights since 1945, International Economy – Global Issues.

College Papers: "The Balkans — Europe's Greatest Tragedy"; "How to Democratize Iraq —The Aftermath of Operation Iraqi Freedom".
Presentations: "What the Rest of the World Thinks of America"; "Europe and America".

Relevant Experience   (While attending College)

INSTITUTE FOR WORLWIDE RELATIONS, White Plains, NY   2000–2004
(A non-profit organization, with offices in London, New York, and Rome. Dedicated to increasing communication between cultures, promoting understanding, and facilitating dialogue on a political level.)

Conference Coordinator (Internship)
- Organized and coordinated two 50-person conferences on "European-American Relations in the 20th Century and Beyond" and "Young Leaders of Tomorrow":
    - o Worked closely with the directors on conference topics.
    - o Managed and planned all conference logistics.
    - o Corresponded accurately and clearly with participants and internal management.
    - o Solved problems and issues as they arose, ensuring a gratifying experience for all.

LITERACY, New York, NY   2001–2002
(A non-profit organization focused on literacy in the New York City Metropolitan area.)

Intern
- Drafted and edited the charter application for the LITERACY New York Charter School, resulting in its approval by the NY State Board of Regents in March 2001.
- Researched city and state laws.
- Communicated orally and in writing with city and state officials, highlighted concerns between various agencies and the school, and problem-solved issues.
- Simplified, reorganized, and maintained computer network.

Angel Ratswell

666265 SW Deviline Court • Beaverton, Oregon 77777

Email: angel200320@atbl.com

333-333-3333

Professional Profile

Highly motivated, versatile, and resourceful *professional* with a *Bachelor of Science* degree in *Psychology* and currently in a *Masters* program specializing in *Marriage & Family Counseling.* Over five years' experience with children ages 2-6 in a disciplined, learning atmosphere combined with performing human resource duties, training, and counseling for teachers, coworkers, and parents. Strong support experience in an office atmosphere with expertise in research and writing. Eager to excel, learn quickly, personable, and appreciated among peers.

Expertise Includes:
- Highly effective writing skills.
- Strong research and reporting abilities.
- Experienced in budgeting, financial planning, fund-raising, and donation solicitation.
- Naturally intuitive to children's needs with strong insight to unspoken needs.
- Strengths in listening, evaluation, and counseling.
- Effective database management and marketing.
- Development of programs/projects with effective implementation.
- Strong presentation skills, both written and verbal.
- Proven negotiation abilities.
- Proficient in assuring compliance with city, county, state, and federal governing agencies.
- Able to accept responsibility and delegate where needed.
- Well-developed organizational skills.
- Personable and work well with all types of personalities.
- Loyal, driven, honest, and committed to a job well done.

---------------------------------◆---------------------------------

Professional Experience

Associate Director · Educational Services • Portland, Oregon • *1998–2003*
Head Preschool Teacher *(promoted)*
Head Jr. Preschool Teacher *(promoted)*
Assistant Jr. Preschool Teacher *(promoted)*
Rapid upward progression in job responsibility from initial assistant, performing work as needed, to assuming Associate Director responsibilities involving the entire school, i.e., curriculum, teaching, training, counseling, supervising, providing assessments, budget planning, negotiations, parent involvement, marketing, and fund raising.

Receptionist/Office Assistant · In Basket Business Services, Portland, Oregon • *1993–1998*
Receptionist for 10 companies along with answering multi-phone lines. Data entry, including invoicing, posting payables and receivables, and verification of statements. Variety of office duties.

Marketing Coordinator · Automated Machine Tool, Portland, Oregon • *1996–1997*
Telemarketing for strong sales leads. Relief receptionist. Maintained database, literature files, and price books. Letter composition.

Certifications

Certified • Parenting Classes through the philosophies of Jane Nelsen, Ed.D., M.F.C.C.

Education

Ongoing studies to qualify for **Doctorate Degree in Child Psychology** - *emphasis in* **Play Therapy**
Master's Degree - Marriage & Family Counseling • George Fox University • Portland, Oregon Campus
Degree expected 2004
Bachelor of Science • **Psychology** • Portland State University, Portland, Oregon • 2001

FRED SMITZ

999 Jane Street
New Jersey, NY 07044

frsmitz@hotmail.com

Phone: (000) 222-2222
Cell: (000) 333-3333

QUALIFICATIONS PROFILE

Dynamic, forward-looking team player with a sound understanding in mechanical and aerospace engineering. Excellent working knowledge in CAD drafting, including ability to interpret and analyze data to develop and design models. Inspiring team leader with the ability to think laterally to provide solutions, exercising independent judgment and decision-making in the diagnosis and resolution of problems. Outstanding communication and interpersonal skills, with the ability to communicate effectively at all levels.

- ☑ CFD Analysis
- ☑ CAD Drafting
- ☑ Aerodynamics
- ☑ Space Systems

- ☑ Gas Dynamics
- ☑ Viscous Flow
- ☑ Stress Analysis
- ☑ Finite Element Analysis

- ☑ Engineering Graphics & Design
- ☑ Structural Design & Analysis
- ☑ Numerical Analysis
- ☑ Propulsion

Advanced skills in AutoCAD 2000/2002, Catia V5, Matlab R12, Ansys V5.5, and FLUENT

PROFESSIONAL EXPERIENCE

NEW YORK UNIVERSITY — New York, NY   2002

Research Assistant (Summer Position)

Reporting directly to Professor for New York's Propulsion Research Facility performing research and analysis for various projects; data extrapolation; aerodynamics; CFD analysis; and CAD drawings.

- Instrumental in managing complete set-up for solid motor rocket experiment; designed bed assembly and performed all CAD assignments utilizing AutoCAD.
- Collaborated with assistant professor regarding the usage and operation of the Waveview software for the new data extrapolation hardware to be used by thesis students; wrote a step-by-step technical manual for students on software use.
- Independently calculated aerodynamic coefficients for the RTD-1 at various altitudes in order to correlate CFD analysis results, enabling the matching of numbers in Missile Datcom program.
- Performed CFD analysis on RTD-1 and SPHADS vehicles to determine aerodynamic coefficients and visualize the flow over the rocket vehicles, resulting in possible design recommendations for both vehicles; testing and analysis was performed in FLUENT.
- Created and developed all CAD drawings for experiments, including Solid Rocket Motor (SRM) Safety duct GA/Detailed, SRM Bed Assembly GA, SRM Bed Assembly Detailed, Small Payload High Altitude Delivery System (SPHADS) GA/Detailed, SPHADS 3D, and Rocket Glider Vehicle 3D.

EDUCATIONAL RELATED EXPERIENCE

NEW YORK UNIVERSITY — New York, NY   2002 – 2003

Student

- Appointed as Project Leader for numerous group projects, supervising small groups of 4-6 and assisting team members in troubleshooting problems.
- Collaborated with project team in successfully designing an International Space Station (ISS) module designed for regular experimental purposes. In case of emergencies, module had an ability to separate from the ISS and serve as a safe-haven to crew.
- Analyzed and interpreted information from data to develop a CFD model of an external flow over a rocket vehicle for thesis project; rocket vehicles were modeled in AutoCAD and meshed in Gambit, while CFD analysis was carried out in FLUENT.

EDUCATION

NEW YORK UNIVERSITY   **Bachelor of Engineering** (2003)
Major: Aerospace Engineering

JULIE STEVENSON

1458 Jackson Avenue • San Diego, California 92109 • (858) 444-8149 • jstevenson20@aol.com

SUMMARY OF QUALIFICATIONS

Dedicated individual offering a Bachelor of Science in Nursing with more than two years of experience as a patient care associate. Experienced in providing end-of-life and palliative care. Successful in developing relationships with patients and families. Able to communicate effectively with Hispanic patients. Diligent worker, compassionate, and organized.

- Selected as one of two students out of 15 applicants for graduate-level class in palliative care.
- Completed student nursing rotations in a variety of clinical settings:
  - ✓ Harbor View Medical Center (Labor and Delivery, Nursery, Postpartum)
  - ✓ Grossmont Hospital (Orthopedics, Oncology)
  - ✓ Mesa Vista Hospital (Geriatric, Adult, and Adolescent Mental Health)
  - ✓ Mercy Hospital (Pediatrics, Children's After Hours Clinic)
  - ✓ Alvarado Medical Center (Medical Intensive Care, Medical Unit)
  - ✓ Mission Bay Hospital (Oncology)
- Researched and wrote brochure on childhood diabetes for community food shelter.
- Delivered effective presentation on the importance of health care in jails and prisons in America.
- Served as student government representative for two years.

Proficient in PC environment, computer charting, Meditech, Word, and PowerPoint.

EDUCATION / TRAINING

Bachelor of Science in Nursing, G.P.A. 3.8   Expected May 2004
University of California, San Diego, California

Certifications: Registered Nurse License (Expected June 2004), Basic Life Support (2003 - Present)

PROFESSIONAL EXPERIENCE

Patient Care Associate, Cabrillo Hospital, San Diego, California   2002 - Present
Provide care for three to five oncology and urology patients per day in cancer care center. Work under registered nurse supervision in 15-bed unit with low nurse-patient ratio. Monitor vital signs, assist with personal hygiene, insert Foley catheters, and draw blood.

- Designated charge patient care associate each shift; ensure all associates complete duties.
- Trained four patient care associates and certified nurse's aides.
- Educated in providing dressing changes and central line care for patients.
- Worked in telemetry unit for six months which increased working hours to full-time.
- Recognized in hospital newsletter, *Hospital Notes*, for providing excellent patient care.

Psychiatry Clinic Receptionist, University of California, San Diego, California   2000 - 2002
Worked closely with psychiatrists, psychologists, and social workers in student health center. Learned about mental health. Organized patient charts and emergency transport care. Scheduled appointments.

- Gained experience using health care software program Meditech.
- Trained and supervised three receptionists.

KEVIN STRONG

5555 Cattle Road, Ranchland, Texas 79000
222-222-2222 (Cell) Ψ   999-999-9999 (Home)
kstrong880@yahoo.com

PROFILE

- *Committed to personal success in fitness, health, and continued education*
- *Well-rounded, fun-loving, and personable individual who enjoys people*
- *Positive attitude and magnetic personality for motivating others*
- *Hands-on, instructive communication style; good listener/counselor*
- *Energetic, creative events planner with presentation experience*
- *Strategic planner and problem solver who uses initiative, follow up, and follow through*

EDUCATION

BS in Exercise Sports Science (Minor in Health), 2004, SUCCESS UNIVERSITY, Flatland, Texas
- Dean's List, Spring 2003

CERTIFICATIONS

American Fitness and Aerobics Association, 2004
CPR and First Aid, 2003

RELEVANT EXPERIENCE

Intern, AMERICAN FITNESS CENTER, Green River, Texas   **2003**
Served 400 hours as physical fitness intern, reporting to Fitness Specialist for large insurance corporation. Assisted members in measuring body composition, designed workout programs for at least 15 clients, conducted new member orientations, and instructed group strength training class of 30 members. Designed, coordinated, and promoted aerobithon for 75+ participants, to include kickboxing, spinning, and boot camp.

- *Received kudos from Fitness Specialist for being capable and dependable*
- *Received positive feedback from class participants*

Personal Trainer, SUCCESS RECREATION CENTER, Flatland, Texas   **2002 – 2003**
Performed assessments to include body composition, flexibility, and blood pressure for 50-100 members a week. Personal trainer to seven clients. Designed workout programs for 40+ members. Worked with physically challenged individual.

Events Coordinator: Orchestrated "Natural High Mountain Bike Race" involving 50 participants and including promotion, donation solidification, individual orientation, registration, and award presentations. Promoted and coordinated "Nutrigrain" sports challenge, which included monitoring member workout progress and awarding participants with sponsor prizes.

- *Employee of the Month, May 2003*
- *Helped choose new equipment for facility*
- *Collaborated monthly with other personal trainers for new ideas*
- *Presented health presentation to group of Boy Scouts*
- *Created enjoyable workout environment*

COMPUTER SKILLS

Computer literate with working experience in BSDI, Multi Media Fitness Program, Microsoft Word and Excel, Internet, and Windows ME/XP.

INTERESTS

Enjoy people, history and documentaries, outdoor activities, and physical fitness.

FUNCTIONAL RÉSUMÉS

JONATHAN BENTLEY, E.I.T.

100 Central Rd.
Middletown, MT 55555   JBentley@email.com   555-111-1212 (home)
                                                                              555-222-3434 (cell)

Dedicated civil engineer with experience in structural and transportation design and proven leadership abilities.

CORE COMPETENCIES

☑ Structural Investigation & Design   ☑ Construction Drawings   ☑ Impact Studies & Specifications
☑ Computer Aided Design (CAD)   ☑ Project Management   ☑ Groundwater Monitoring
☑ Conceptual Design & Development   ☑ Hydraulics & Hydrology   ☑ Floodplain Management
☑ Traffic Engineering   ☑ Soils & Earthwork   ☑ Construction Drawings
☑ Land Development   ☑ Budgeting and Scheduling   ☑ Standard Specifications

EDUCATION

Bachelor of Science: Civil Engineering, emphasis in Structures   May 2003
Northern State University, Uptown, NY

Relevant Projects

Urban Lake and Park Development for City of Centreville, NY
Scope of design included storm water runoff, earthwork, structural analysis of retaining wall, and parking/sidewalk design.
- Designated Project Manager of four-member team.
- Retained quality control over project scope to preserve manageable size and avoid State violations.
- Initiated communication with city engineers and Fish & Game personnel on project-related issues and guidance.
- Maintained project schedule and completed on time. Received an 'A' grade on project.

Highway Design for State of Massachusetts
The project scope included design of one-mile stretch of highway through private and public lands. Design challenges included steep terrain, storm water runoff, super-elevation for curves, and negotiating homes, businesses, and cemetery.
- Design included horizontal and vertical design based on minimal earthwork and minimal disturbance to local businesses and public land.
- Maintained project schedule and completed on time. Received an 'A' grade on project.

SELECTED ACHIEVEMENTS

- Earned status of Engine Boss and Incident Commander Type 4 and oversaw wildfire control, including methods of attack, personnel and equipment requirements, and strategic planning; maintained personnel and public safety.
- Supervised up to 150 personnel and all equipment needs including air tankers, engines, helicopters, and water tenders.
- Used sound judgment and decision-making skills to preserve safety of crew and implement strategic plans of attack against wildfires.
- Developed strong leadership and communication skills as demonstrated by high-level of performance by crewmembers.
- Implemented training regimens for crew; many members promoted as a result.

EMPLOYMENT HISTORY

Delivery/Yard Crew: Big Tree Lumber Co., City, MT   2003–Present
Forestry Technician: Tonto National Forest, City, CA   FT Seasonal, 2000–2003
Type 2, 3 and 6 Crewmember: Rural Metro Fire Dept., City, CA   FT Seasonal, 1998–1999

TECHNICAL & RELATED

MS Word, Excel, PowerPoint, and Project/AutoCAD/HEC-HMS/Haestad Methods - WaterCAD, SewerCAD, Flowmaster
Familiar Codes and Methods: NEPA, UBC, ASD, NDS, LRFD
Montana Commercial Driver's License

RAYFORD COLLINGSWORTH
8888 Pine Street, Plains, Texas 79400

(800) 999-5555
rcollingsworth87@nts-online.net

OBJECTIVE: Political Scientist position in the State of Texas

SUMMARY

BA in Political Science (Pre-Law) and Post-Baccalaureate in Education. One year's teaching experience at Crestview Middle School where motivation, classroom management, and creative presentation were essential. Three years' experience in retail sales where persuasiveness and supportive, timely customer service were a priority. Solely financed 100% of college education working near full-time schedule while concurrently managing demanding coursework and maintaining an excellent grade point average. Strengths include:

- *Rapport / Trust Building*
- *Assertive Communication*
- *Direct Problem Solving*

- *Teamwork*
- *Organization / Prioritization*
- *Proactive Decision Making*

- *Integrity / Work Ethic*
- *Participative Leadership*
- *Assessment / Discernment*

EDUCATION

Post-Baccalaureate, Education, 2004, BA in Political Science (Pre-Law), 2002 (GPA 3.9), MAJOR UNIVERSITY, Plains, Texas
24 hours toward Master's Degree in Education, *(GPA: 4.0)*

SKILLS SUMMARY

LEADERSHIP SKILLS

- Consistently trusted with greater responsibility than that for job level. Promoted to branch bank manager at early age.
- Willing to own responsibility and accept accountability as demonstrated in past employment.
- Accomplish tasks with minimal direction or supervision, yet work equally as well in team environment.
- Gravitated toward facilitating collegiate groups averaging 4+ members.
- Consider past experiences, customer/company needs, and ethical standards when problem solving / decision making.
- Accept new ideas, solicit consensus, and encourage active participation from team members.

INTERPERSONAL/COMMUNICATION SKILLS

- Very comfortable and confident presenting programs or information to small or large audiences.
- Use assertive communication to negotiate issues, mediate conflicts, and affect compromise and positive outcomes.
- Employ perceptiveness, sincerity, and respect for differences to build rapport and trust with diverse groups.
- Communicate effectively at multiple levels using appropriate language and interpersonal styles.
- Genuinely care for others and lend a hand to help those in need through volunteer activities.
- Able to write comprehensive and effective reports and business communications.

ORGANIZATION AND PLANNING SKILLS

- Identify and assess needs, draft plans, prioritize steps, implement action, and evaluate outcome.
- When coordinating projects, assign tasks, use resources, troubleshoot problems, and follow up to stay on track.
- Establish clear goals and objectives while inspiring team spirit and achievement.
- Set priorities and continuously monitor progress, adjusting when necessary to meet timely goals.
- Efficiently manage time as demonstrated by ability to coordinate college / work schedules.

WORK HISTORY

Teacher	PLAINS INDEPENDENT SCHOOL DISTRICT	Plains, Texas	2003 – 2004
Carpenter – Remodel	RAYFORD'S CARPENTRY	Plains, Texas	2001 – 2003
Sport Bike Specialist	GOOD TIMES POWERSPORTS	Plains, Texas	2000 – 2001
Package Expeditor	FEDERAL EXPRESS	Plains, Texas	1999 – 2000
Bank Associate, Manager	PLAINS NATIONAL BANK OF WEST TEXAS	Plains, Texas	1998 – 1999

MARY ANN GARRY
123 Randolph Street
Croton, New York 00000
(555) 555–5555

CERTIFIED MEDICAL ASSISTANT

A capable professional with solid qualifications in clinical medical assisting, including performing basic laboratory procedures, assisting with medical/emergency procedures, and taking medical histories. Thorough and accurate in completion of insurance forms and patient documentation. Demonstrate a sensitive, caring approach to patient care along with the ability to work cooperatively with all members of the health care team. Excellent interpersonal, organizational, problem solving, and communication skills. Computer proficient.

EDUCATIONAL BACKGROUND

Certificate - Medical Assistant Program, Clinical Specialty
Westchester Community College, Valhalla, New York (2003)

Certifications

Registered Medical Assistant, 1997 (#567834) - American Registry of Medical Assistants
Phlebotomy Technician • EKG Technician • CPR Certified
Level III Collection Services Technician • Psychemedics Sample Collection

CLINICAL and MEDICAL OFFICE SKILLS

Skin/Venipuncture … Specimen Collections (Urinalysis, Hematology & Psychemedics)
Medical Histories … Lab Procedures … Vital Signs … EKGs … Emergency Treatment
Assisting with Physical Examinations … Medical Terminology … Biohazardous Materials Disposal

HIGHLIGHTS of EXPERIENCE

♦ Conducted examinations involving complete patient medical histories, blood pressure readings, urine and blood sample collections, and drug screening for company serving the insurance industry. Frequently assigned to handle difficult clients and recaptured key accounts by ensuring timely service.

♦ Provided ongoing care to private, elderly patients. Took vital signs, administered medications and supplemental nourishment through IV therapy, and assisted patients with activities of daily living.

♦ Performed emergency services rotations at Memorial Hospital, assisting medical team in providing treatment at accidents and other emergency situations.

♦ Taught several courses in Medical Assistant Training Program at Health Education Centers, including anatomy, physiology, medical assisting, EKG, phlebotomy, and medical laboratory testing.

PROFESSIONAL EMPLOYMENT

Paramedical Insurance Examiner • <u>INSURANCE SERVICES, INC.</u>, White Plains, New York • 1996-2003
Instructor - Medical Assisting • <u>HEALTH EDUCATION CENTERS</u>, White Plains, New York • 1993-1996

PRIOR EXPERIENCE

Office Manager • <u>SCOPE COMMUNICATIONS</u>, White Plains, New York • 1993-1994
Customer Service Representative • <u>BOWEN CORPORATION</u>, White Plains, New York • 1991-1993

ANGELIQUE GATÉ
Unit 4/31 Mayfield Street, Arlington, VA 22201 • (703)555 5555 • agate@hotmail.com

FOCUS: OVERSEAS AID/COMMUNITY WORK • YOUTH & COMMUNITY CARE • PUBLIC RELATIONS

Globally focused graduate with strong awareness of complex socio-economic, cultural, ecological, and resource management issues. Successfully combine analytical and research expertise with flair for public speaking, presentation, writing, and communications. Keenly interested in developing a career in overseas aid, youth and community care, or marketing communications.

QUALIFICATIONS

POST GRADUATE DIPLOMA IN PSYCHOLOGY, *University of Queensland, Australia* (Anticipated 2004)
PSYCHOLOGY (BRIDGING COURSE), *Queensland University of Technology*, Australia 2000
BACHELOR OF ARTS (Social Science) Major: Community Work, *University of Melbourne,* Australia *2000*

KEY CREDENTIALS

COMMUNITY/OVERSEAS AID
- Data Collection & Analysis
- Reporting & Funding Proposal Development
- Regulatory & Government Affairs
- Childhood Development Phases
- Issues Management
- Budget/Funds Analysis

PUBLIC RELATIONS/MARKETING
- Public Speaking/Presentations
- Teaching & Training
- Special Event Coordination
- Program Development & Evaluation
- Media Communications
- Marketing & Promotions

Computer literate – Microsoft Office, Adobe Acrobat, Internet, e-mail.

EXPERIENCE SUMMARY

Communications, Research & Overseas Aid
- Conducted extensive interviews with people of drought affected villages in northwest India; aided by an interpreter, researched, documented, and compiled the effects of a 2 year drought.
- Composed a compelling case for food relief funding; produced and presented proposal to the National Dairy Development Board for distributing the nutritional dietary product *Khichidi*.

Public Relations, Promotions & Media
- Propelled promotional ideas into definitive action plans, leading to highly profitable and successful special events. Driving force behind complete project coordination including media communications, advertising design, venues, entertainment, outside broadcasts, and promotions.
- Generated impressive profits and record crowds to the *Miss Indy Competition*. Coordinated complete event from lighting and sound professionals, to judges, contestants, patrons, and sponsors.
- Promoted radio events and competitions, conducted live-air crosses from outside broadcast vans, secured prizes from sponsors, and managed prize distribution at 'live' locations.

Teaching & Organization
- Coproduced developmentally appropriate programs for children of varying ages, in conjunction with Child Care Director. Commended by parents, and enjoyed by children, programs incorporated stimulating educational activities that were both safe and fun.

EMPLOYMENT SYNOPSIS

Promotions Coordinator, *Kawana Waters Hotel*, Queensland, Australia	4/2000–Present
Promotions Officer, *Sea FM Radio,* Queensland, Australia	1998–Present
Field Worker/Researcher, *Self Employed Women's Association*, India	11/2000–12/2000
Dental Nurse/Assistant, *Lostock Hall Dental Surgery,* England	6/1997–9/1997

REFERENCES UPON REQUEST

Mary J. Hamilton

234 W 3rd Avenue ▪ Marysville, California 95999
Home: 535-344-0555 ▪ Cell: 535-511-9988 ▪ E-mail: mjh@isp.com

Objective: Currently interested in an internship that involves learning about orchard production and management. Would like to work for a company that specializes in agriculture production.

PROFILE

- Enthusiastic and committed, willing to do what it takes to reach company goals.
- Dynamic leader and team-builder, consistently motivating others to succeed.
- Exceptional organizational skills, punctual with excellent ability to multi-task.
- Successful in promoting an organization and generating funding.
- Pleasant personality, work well with all types of people.
- Excellent communication and interpersonal skills.

EDUCATION

CALIFORNIA STATE UNIVERSITY, Chico – Expected completion Spring 2004
Bachelor of Science in Agricultural Business, emphasis in Management

Course Work Completed: Introduction to Plant and Soil Science, West Coast Crop Production, Farm Accounting, Agriculture Management Information Systems, Introduction to Agriculture Business Economics, Introduction to Soils, Introduction to Managerial Accounting, Agriculture Systems Quantitative Methods, Agricultural Ecology, Agriculture Systems and Issues, World Food and Fiber Systems.

Currently Enrolled In: Agriculture Production Economic Analysis, Agricultural Markets and Pricing, Agribusiness Management, World Food and Hunger Issues, Agricultural Machine Systems.

Research Projects: Fall 2002 Agriculture Systems and Issues class, completed a presentation and research paper on Farm Labor. In the same class, completed individual presentation on estate taxes and how they affect family farm operations. Currently involved in projects of stock market analysis, futures market analysis, and net worth forecasting analysis.

Computer skills: Proficiency in Microsoft Word, Excel, Access, and PowerPoint; knowledge of website design; proficient in Internet and e-mail.

ACTIVITIES AND ORGANIZATIONS

Member of local sorority **Kappa Sigma Delta** – Fall 2000 to Present

- Elected Vice President, this position oversees all chairs in the sorority and oversees the completion of all tasks, Spring 2003.
- Played intramural softball and flag football with my sorority, currently softball champions for two consecutive years, Spring 2003.
- Elected Rookie educator, this position is very important because it develops organizational and communication skills, Fall 2002.
- Elected secretary, which involved making executive decisions and overseeing the participation of all events, Spring 2002.
- Held position as fundraiser chair, which involved organizing and planning fundraisers for community and sorority, Fall 2001.

Mary J. Hamilton – Page 2

ACTIVITIES AND ORGANIZATIONS (Continued)

- Summer 1998 USAC study aboard program in Turin, Italy, six-week program studying Italian. Traveled to Greece, France, and Mexico for vacations. Completed 2 years of college-level Spanish.

COMMUNITY ACTIVITIES

- Participated in clothing drives and Adopt-a-Family during holiday season for American Red Cross.
- Volunteer for Community Challenge, which raises money for the Boys and Girls Club.
- Volunteer for Derby Days, which raises money for Children's Miracle Network.
- Participated in a mentoring program for young girls in the community.
- Volunteered at humane society.

WORK EXPERIENCE

Ski Instructor, Alpine Meadows, Tahoe, Nevada – 1998 to 1999
Skills were to monitor the safety and instruction of children's ski programs.

Internships: West Coast Realty, Reno, Nevada – 1999
Experience included on-site inspections and study of real estate.

ANDREW HATTON

18 Parring Road, Toms River, NJ 08754 • (732) 929 5555 • andrewhatton@hotmail.com

FOCUS: GRADUATE OPPORTUNITIES ~ MARKET LEADERS & MULTINATIONALS

Fresh to the workforce and highly motivated to take the first steps on the path towards a fulfilling career. Strongly enthusiastic for securing entry-level marketing, advertising, human resources, or graduate opportunity, but eager to demonstrate the necessary attitude to achieve an employer's goals. Cited by past employers for good-natured, cooperative outlook, willingness to work hard, and strengths in contributing to the enthusiasm and leadership of teams. Sound academic results emphasize personal commitment towards growth.

KEY CREDENTIALS

DIRECT EXPERIENCE IN:
- High-Impact Service Delivery
- Customer Relationship Management
- Team Building & Motivation
- Complex Problem Solving & Decision Making
- Cash Control & Auditing
- Team Supervision & Training
- Staff Rosters/Skills Analysis
- Client Instruction/Education
- Retail Sales & Solution Selling
- Inventory Control
- Risk Management/Store Security

EXPERTLY TRAINED IN:
- Change Management
- Organizational Development
- Employee & Labor Relations
- Human Resources Generalist Affairs
- Product Lifecycle Management
- Training & Development
- Brand Management
- Business Development
- Competitive Analysis
- Market Research & Strategy
- Tactical Marketing Plans

Computer literate: Word, Excel, PowerPoint, Publisher, Internet, and e-mail.

QUALIFICATIONS

BACHELOR OF BUSINESS, *Swinburne University of Technology* Melbourne, Australia 2001
Majors: Marketing & Human Resource Management

VICTORIAN CERTIFICATE OF EDUCATION, *Canterbury Grammar School* Melbourne, Australia 1996

- 1996 House Prefect
- 1st XVIII Football
- Athletics Team

- 1995 House Colors
- 1st XVIII Football Colors
- Athletics Colors

CERTIFICATIONS & TRAINING

Certified & Registered Ski Technician, *Salomon, Look, Marker, Rossignol*
Bronze Medallion, *Surf Life Saving Australia*
Certificate in First Aid, *St. John's Ambulance*
Food & Beverage Hygiene Certificate
Responsible Serving of Alcohol, *Liquor Licensing Commission*

STRENGTHS & ACCOMPLISHMENTS

ORGANIZATION/WORK FLOW MANAGEMENT
- Commended by customers and management alike for ability to meet the challenges of high pressure, fast-paced environments
- Juggled multi-faceted tasks energetically and capably; responded to customer enquiries, processed transactions, raised orders, and controlled cash to meet the "impossible" deadline

RETAIL SALES/MERCHANDISING/PROMOTIONS
- Maximized average dollar sales in retail environments; listened for unspoken clues to influence customer's buying decisions; gained reputation for ability to mobilize slow moving stock
- Developed outstanding relationships by individualizing each client; nurtured loyal/regular clients, remembering pertinent facts from previous communications

PROFESSIONAL EXPERIENCE

Developed and consolidated outstanding customer service skills through a diversity of workplace experiences during high school and university studies. Tirelessly committed to part-time casual employment to supplement full-time university studies, without sacrificing academic results.

CHARTER SPORTS, Colorado USA, *Ski Technician*..Nov 00-Apr 01
National company specializing in high-ticket ski equipment, accessories, and clothing - rentals and retail sales.
Achieved exceptional sales by applying influential selling techniques. Sourced unavailable or out-of-stock items to "make the sale" and optimized service delivery via personalized communications. Maintained merchandising displays for maximum customer impact. Frequently entrusted with leadership responsibilities including staff rosters, stock ordering, and risk management.

- Identified problematic human resource issue triggering potential staff shortages in peak season; seasonal employees were unwilling to accept positions citing management's reluctance in guaranteeing continued employment over the entire season. Constructed detailed business plan forecasting an improved recruitment strategy for the following season that would save costs and boost productivity/revenues.

GOVERNOR HOTHAM HOTEL, Melbourne, Australia, *Barman/Waiter/Retail Assistant* 1998-2000
Multifaceted role rotating throughout core revenue generating areas while simultaneously studying at University. Earned "stripes" as a responsible leader, entrusted to open and close the bar, manage cash control for main bar, restaurant and bottle-shop, initiate purchasing orders, conduct stock takes and audits, and preside over the smooth and profitable running of the hotel in the manager's absence. Commended by management for personable style in all customer communications.

BUILDING CONTRACTOR, Melbourne, Australia, *Builder's Laborer*..1996-1998
Supported qualified tradesman with hands-on assistance on a variety of construction projects.

CASH CONVERTERS, Toronto, Canada, *Sales Representative* 1997-1998
Front-line customer service and sales.

OAKDALE MEATS, Toronto, Canada, *Assistant*..1997
Casual work in wholesale boning room, working to stringent quality control, health, and hygiene standards in a deadline dependent environment.

FIORELLI'S RESTAURANT, Melbourne, Australia *Food & Beverage Attendant* 1997
Upmarket Melbourne restaurant reputed for high-quality service delivery.
Delivered high-caliber food and beverage service to patrons. Ensured comfort with surroundings, accurately recorded orders, resolved complaints, and offered timely, efficient responses to enquiries. Set tables, scheduled bookings, and managed bar.

HARRY HEATH'S SUPERMARKET, Melbourne, Australia, *Sales Assistant*..............................1994-1996

J. WALTER THOMPSON, Melbourne, Australia, *Work Experience Student*......................................1994

PERSONAL

Leisure interests include snowboarding, surfing, fly-fishing, music, concerts, photography, golf, and cricket. Traveled extensively throughout Japan, Canada, US, Greece, Turkey, Italy, Austria, Czech Republic, Germany, Belgium, England, and Mexico.

Lord Somers Camp: Developed strong alliances and worked under extreme conditions to hone team and leadership skills in this camp designed to explore inner strength and self-worth.

MEMBERSHIPS

- Member, Old Camberwell Grammar Football Association; member social committee, U19 Victorian Squad; past Member, 1st XVIII
- Past member, Australian Scouting Association (7 years); Member – Melbourne Cricket Club.

REFERENCES AVAILABLE UPON REQUEST

Thomas Hiller

55 Glendale Road, Apartment 3 ♦ Schenectady, NY 12207 ♦ (518) 433-7854 ♦ xxxxx@aol.com

An enthusiastic, highly knowledgeable professional with a Bachelor's degree in Environmental Science and expert skills in environmental planning conservation laws, consulting, health, and safety

PROFESSIONAL SUMMARY
- Experienced in planning projects and managing resources that have positive impact on environment.
- Skilled in providing environmental consulting and training to contractors and businesses of all sizes.
- Demonstrated leadership skills with ability to coordinate large-scale projects and groups of people.
- Able to control invasive species, manage forests, assemble field data equipment, and collect samples.
- Proven ability to write environmental documents and reports collected from field data and lab tests.
- Outstanding organizational, interpersonal, public speaking, presentation, and teaching skills.

SKILLS & ACCOMPLISHMENTS
Environmental Planning & Project Management
- Designed and implemented field study to study trout habitat selection in Lake Champlain Watershed (SUNY).
- Evaluated and measured air samples using lab techniques to determine legal limits of air quality (Alpine).
- Consulted clients on industrial hygiene from collections of airborne pollutants data (Alpine).
- Played key role in industrial health and safety on industrial demolition and construction projects (Alpine).
- Coordinated projects, reports, budgets, staff, and clients (Alpine / EZ / YWCA / USMC).

Land Conservation & Resource Development
- Provided assistance and made recommendations in creating and preserving wetlands drainage basin to prevent flooding of lands surrounding commercial storage facility (EZ).
- Enhanced landscape by removing nuisance vegetation and introducing beneficial trees, grass, and soil (EZ).
- Introduced environmental plans according to local zoning laws and guidelines (EZ).

Environmental Law & Regulations
- Informed clients on legal standards, mitigation techniques, and abatement projects (Alpine).
- Applied in environmental planning projects and land conservation efforts, federal and state conservation laws, NEPA, SEQRA, OSHA regulations, permits, and public policy (Alpine / EZ).
- Gained knowledge of nonprofit land acquisition techniques, including easements, donations, tax incentives, rights of first refusal, revolving funds, and undivided interests on land (EZ / SUNY).

Specialized Training & Abilities
- Completed upper-division coursework in Environmental Planning, Wetlands, Environmental Law, Environmental Impact Assessment, Soils, and Advanced Environmental Science Writing (SUNY).
- Conducted training classes and educational programs for department staff and students (USMC / YWCA).

PROFESSIONAL EXPERIENCE
Air Technician, Alpine Environmental Services, Albany, NY	2004 – Present
Grounds Planner, Call EZ Storage, Tampa, FL	summers 2000 – 2003
Program Coordinator, YWCA, Gloversville, NY	2000
Sergeant / Communications Specialist, United States Marine Corps	1995 – 1999

EDUCATION
Plattsburgh State University, Plattsburgh, NY	2004

B.S., Environmental Science, 3.23 G.P.A.

LICENSES
New York State Asbestos Handler & Sampling Technician, NYS Department of Labor, Division of Safety & Health

AWARDS
Good Conduct Medal, USMC
National Defense Medal, USMC
Overseas Deployment Ribbon, USMC

COMPUTER SKILLS
Microsoft Office

CHRISTIE H. HUGHES

813-248–9562
hughes@email.com
9876 Burnt Ash Lane, Tampa, FL 33602

Career Focus

Medical Sales

Education

Bachelor of Science in Speech Language Pathology/Audiology, Minor in Sign Language – Expected May 2003
University of Florida, Gainesville, Florida

- Coursework included Anatomy & Physiology, Anatomy & Physiology of Speech and Hearing Mechanisms, Introduction to Hearing Disorders, Hearing Science Physics, Vocal Disorders, Fluency Disorders, Introduction to Speech Science, Language Development and Disorders, Phonological Development and Disorders

Central High School, Tampa, Florida – 1999

Special Skills

- Proficient in using and understanding sign language
- Understand hearing mechanisms and throat anatomy & disorders
- Adept in Microsoft Word and WordPerfect

Selected Leadership Highlights

As the first point of contact for companies, presented a friendly, warm, and caring attitude; went the extra mile to make each client feel important; listened carefully to client requests; correctly routed calls; and scheduled appointments.

As the primary greeter at the tanning company, tasked with *selling and upselling products and services to first time and returning customers.*

As Chairperson of Anchor Splash, led the university-wide, Panhellenic fundraiser for the Service for Sight philanthropy. Coordinated the activities, liaised with the media, collected and tracked donations. *Raised the most money of all Delta Gamma chapters in the State of Florida.*

As Director of New Membership, served as role model and leader to the new members for two consecutive semesters. Created a nurturing environment to make everyone feel welcome, solved problems, and educated the new members on Delta Gamma principles.

As Head of the House Corporation, tasked with enforcing rules in the Chapter apartment. Served as liaison between the new members, officials, and alumni; mediated and resolved problems. *Developed a reputation for creating win/win solutions.*

Part-time Employment During College

Administrative Assistant, Law Offices of Michael J. Krakar - Current

Receptionist, Tan USA – 2001 to 2002

Receptionist, Terry Sellers & Associates, P.A. – 2001 to 2002

Receptionist, Tampa Bay Property Management Co. – 2000 to 2001

Katherina Ivanova

12456 Connecticut Avenue, NE • Washington, DC 20036 • Katdance@aol.com • Home: 202.456.7890

Enhancing learning with passion and leadership

Extensive training in dance including classical ballet (since the age of 3), modern dance, and jazz
Five years of working with children and peers in a work / camp environment
Flexible and adaptable, adjust to new situations easily and quickly
Very outgoing person who can get along with everyone; high energy level
Experience in various leadership and teaching roles
Knowledgeable with information on personal safety and injuries; certified in CPR / First Aid
Performed with the Salado Rangerettes in the 2000 Cotton Bowl
Runner up in Miss Texas Scholarship Program, 2001

EDUCATION

Bachelor of Fine Arts in Dance, University of Texas at Austin, Austin, Texas, August 2003, GPA: 3.85
Diploma, St Mary's High School, Arlington, Virginia, 1999 GPA: 3.95

PROFESSIONAL TRAINING

Ballet Training

- Nineteen years of training in Ballet to include Russian, RAD, and Checetti methods of ballet.
- Trained in several states and internationally including Virginia, Kansas, New Jersey, and Mons, Belgium.
- Apprenticed with the Shore Ballet Company with the Academy of Dance Arts. Performed in such pieces as the Nutcracker, La Sylphide, Snow White, and Aladdin.
- Attended the Burklyn Ballet Theatre in Stowe, VT in 1992, performing in Les Sylphide, and several modern pieces choreographed by the artistic Director Angela Whitehill.
- Participated in several master classes and workshops with the following people; Angela Whitehill, David Howard, Cheryl Noble.
- Studied under Yacov Sharir, Lyn Wiltshire, Andee Scott, Holly Williams, Libby Lovejoy, Kent DeSpain, and Andrea Beckham while at the University of Texas.
- Passed Grade 4, Grade 5, Grade 6, in the RAD Syllabus. Received marks of Highly Commended in the Pre-Elementary RAD exam and Commended in the Elementary RAD exam. 1992 - 1995

Modern Training

- Seven years training in modern dance. Trained mainly in Graham technique. Four years of modern dance at Academy of Dance Arts in Red Bank, NJ, and three years as part of degree program at the University of Texas.
- Master Classes: Cloud Gate Dance Company.

Jazz Training

- Six years of jazz training at the Academy of Dance Arts. Participated in high school Dance team; also member of the Rhythm and Cheer All-Stars which trained solely in jazz.
- Master Classes: dancers from the Broadway show Fosse.

Choreographic experience

- A piece called "Crash" in 1997 in a program called SEPA (Student Enrichment Program for the Arts).
- Solo piece for a Star Makers Dance Competition from the Broadway show Evita: "He Must Love Me."
- Lyrical piece for Star Makers Dance Competition for high school dance team.

OTHER EXPERIENCE

Assistant Director of Drama
CONGRESSIONAL SCHOOL CAMP
Falls Church, VA
Summer, 2001 and 2002

Created games that pertained to drama for all age levels from 6-14 years old. Taught children the basics of acting and directing plays. Hosted a two-week intensive drama specialty camp culminating in a special production put on by the children. Assisted the director by demonstrating exercise and activities to the children or escorting them to other areas of the camp. Occasionally led classes.

Supervised children in before/after camp program. Played games with the children, read stories and watched movies with them. Developed good relationships with children and their parents.

- Helped the children who were homesick or afraid of new places by relating personal events and experiences of being a military child and having to move often while growing up.
- Provided children with a glimpse of my background in dance and drama. Answered questions about how to further their education in the fine arts.
- Improvised and expanded the wide variety of games for the children.
- Developed team atmosphere with staff of 100+. Bonded with fellow staffers making overall climate comfortable and pleasant.
- Truly enjoyed children and sharing my passion of the arts.

Lead Counselor
RAVEN ROCK OUTDOOR MINISTRIES
Sabillasville, MD
Summer, 1998 and 1999

Supervised children at an active overnight camp. Charged with care of the children 24/7 for six days a week or until the child's camp term was finished. Created, demonstrated, and led activities. Provided children with a wide variety of games and activities to include archery, mountain biking, hiking, and many invented/adapted camp games like executive marbles and real-life Clue. Led the daily Bible studies and evening worship ceremonies which were similar to campfire sing-a-longs.
- Able to relate well with the children and help them with shyness and/or home-sickness.
- Learned very good life lessons—realized that teachers learn just as much from the children.
- Worked well with the staff at the camp. At the end of the first summer, director requested that I return the next year.
- Emotional partings at the end of each session made me smile to know that I touched a child's life and they had touched mine.

Katherina Ivanova

BRADLEY LI-NYGUEN

14 Westlake Drive
Framingham, MA 01702

E-mail: chinli@bigpool.com

Cell: 508 875 1699
Residence: 508 789 098

GRADUATE CANDIDATE: SOLICITOR ~ PARALEGAL

Accredited Para-Professional Interpreter in Mandarin & English Languages (NAATI)

Double-degree in law and business, advanced training in immigration law, accreditation as a para-professional interpreter, and "real world" employment experiences combine to distinguish this graduate from student peers in preparation for the rigors of law practice. Multilingual talents and an ease for understanding the nuances of cultural communications will best serve organizations servicing international markets, or clients with diverse ethnicity. A self-sufficient and independent worker, equally comfortable in collective "brainstorming" and team collaborations. Patience, a quiet demeanor, and a willingness to listen and analyze have served to resolve conflict and find solutions.

Expertly trained in:
| Sale of Goods | International Marketing | International Economics Law

Direct Experience with:
| Cross-Cultural Communications | Customer Service | Legal Research
| Operations Management | Contract Negotiations/Mediation | Expenditure Control
| Documents/Speech Translations | Events Management

EDUCATION

Bachelor of Business (Accounting)
Bachelor of Law
University of Massachusetts (2003)

Additional Training:
Immigration Law & Practice—A Training Course for Migration Agents
Faculty of Law, University of Massachusetts (2002)

ACADEMIC SHOWCASE
Selected projects highlighting academic talents in law

- **Project: Sale of Goods**
  Key contributor in three-member team, challenged to analyze a real-life consumer issue using the state's Sale of Goods Act as the benchmark for resolution. Assumed role of group leader to mediate and refocus team efforts from heated debate that threatened the project's momentum, to a mission with a common goal. Presented joint efforts to the class, receiving a Credit for research and analysis.

- **Project: International Economics Law**
  Solo project, conducting six-months of intensive research to produce a ten-thousand-word essay on the implications of Taiwan joining the World Trade Organization and the impact on the country's trade relations with Taiwan and China. Processed and analyzed volumes of information, and devised personal research strategy—selecting only credible sources from academic journal articles and official media releases. Successfully delivered the project on deadline.

- **Project: International Marketing (Bachelor of Business)**
  Group project of seven participants tasked to conduct a comprehensive analysis of an existing company—*Bono Enterprises*, and create a strategic marketing plan complete with recommendations for expansion into the Japanese export market. "Impossible" timeframes for delivering the project, vast amounts of information, and a group with disparate views on strategy challenged the deadline and endangered project quality and momentum. Personally resolved critical issues by mediating between groups, and steered research by offering online and in-person support. Conducted research into the Japanese business environments and legal obligations governing exports, and produced SWOT analysis. Submitted research to the company's Managing Director. Awarded a High Distinction.

COMMUNITY INVOLVEMENT

President, UMA Taiwanese Students Association, 1999

Elected President of the UMA Taiwanese Students Association in 1999.

- Immediately identified multiple benefits of consolidating four independently operating associations for Taiwanese university students to one cohesive association offering significant cost benefits, a stronger membership base, one leadership team, and opportunities for larger scale special events.

  Despite robust resistance from universities, lobbied extensively to form groundbreaking association. Conducted measured step-by-step strategy for collaborating on special events in 1999, and introduced committees that formed the basis for friendship. In mid-2000 the amalgamated Taiwanese Students Association was formed with one base of centralized funding and one leadership committee that showed immediate inroads in the quality of upscale events at quality venues, and attracted students from Taiwan seeking cultural or academic assistance.

- Represented the association—negotiating with fund sponsors, community services, and local businesses to provide students with discounted services, products, and information.

Treasurer, UMA Taiwanese Students Association, 1998

Appointed to position of Treasurer in 1998, overseeing and authorizing the membership budget including all expenditure allocations and membership dues. Created budget, forecasted spending targets and purchasing power, and personally investigated and compared product costs.

- Raised revenues from discos, cruises, and an annual dinner that netted a profit of $500.
- Spearheaded monthly newsletters and an annual booklet in Taiwanese that provided educational and cultural information to international students.
- Twice awarded second-level funding from the University of Massachusetts Students Association for participation in the International Food Festival, and efforts in presenting University orientation information to Taiwanese high school students.

Business Interpreter

Translated business letters, accounting issues, marketing, and contracts with customers and service providers for a small business owner lacking English fluency.

- Frequently identified incorrect charging and/or calculations from suppliers, raising matters of conflicts in invoices and documents.
- Advocated for business owner providing explanations of business practices and aligning them to local government by-laws and regulations.

EMPLOYMENT EXPERIENCES

AMAANDO PTY LTD   1993–Present
Importer and wholesaler for vehicle spare parts nationally and internationally
Sales Executive
Simultaneously juggled work commitments with double-degree studies meeting all deadlines. Received and processed orders, supervised deliveries, and assigned product pricing. Resolved quality, warranty, sales, and distributorship issues with customers, and managed inventory control and logistics.

PERSONAL

Multilingual: English, Mandarin, Japanese, Hakka, Taiwanese, and Cantonese

Leisure interests include exercise/gym work, computer networking, open source software and operating systems, and researching intellectual property rights. Enjoy technologies, as an intermediate user of Microsoft Office Professional, Internet, e-mail, Windows XP/2000/ME/98/95, and OpenOffice.

EDEN MILLER, PA-C

67 Walden Road
Somers, TX 89776
(973) 580-9978
e-mail: emiller34@aol.com

OBJECTIVE	To apply well-rounded clinical training and skills as a **Physician Assistant** in an acute care environment.
CLINICAL SKILLS & PROCEDURES	Excellent experience in urgent care, primary care and hospital environments, providing high-quality professional care to a wide range of patients. Recognized by physicians/supervisors for maturity, dependability and clinical capabilities. Successful in quickly building rapport and gaining patients' trust/confidence.

- Completing patient histories; providing patient education and intervention.
- Performing and dictating complete & focused physical examinations, which include pelvic exams, presurgical exams and newborn physical exams.
- Development of diagnoses (including differential), assessments and treatment plans; comfortable in discussing diagnoses with patients.
- Skilled in performing various procedures: venipuncture, IV therapy, Foley catheter and NG tube insertions, ABGs, suturing/stapling and removal.
- Assisting in surgical procedures such as inguinal and umbilical hernia repairs with mesh, laproscopic and open cholecystectomies, laparoscopic appendectomies, valve repairs, coronary artery bypass grafts, complete and simple mastectomies, surgical incision of lipomas and exploratory laparotomies. Preparation of SOAP notes.
- Pre- and post-operative management, fluid and electrolyte management and direct wound care experience.
- Interpretation of x-rays, CAT scans and MRIs.
- Certified in Advanced Cardiac Life Support (ACLS).

EDUCATION & TRAINING	B.S., Physician Assistant Program, May 2004 SOUTHLAND COLLEGE, Austin, TX

- Passed PANCE exam, April 2004

Clinical Rotations:

Typical comments from evaluators:

"Excellent in obtaining histories and putting patients at ease."

"History and physical exam presentations are top rate."

"Exceptional general medical knowledge."

Medical training and experience in the Physician Assistant program acquired through 12 clinical rotations in various medical settings (2001-2004):

PETERSON MEMORIAL HOSPITAL, Austin, TX

- Pediatrics Department, including Neonatal Intensive Care Unit
- General, OB/GYN & Cardiac Surgery
- Internal Medicine

CULVER HOSPITAL, Austin, TX

- Emergency Medicine

MALVERN PSYCHIATRIC ASSOCIATES, Austin, TX

- Psychiatry

PARKER & ASSOCIATES OB/GYN, Austin, TX

- OB/GYN – Private Practice
- Elective – OB/GYN

EDEN MILLER, PA-C   PAGE 2

Clinical Rotations   WEST ASSOCIATES, Austin, TX
continued…
                                   ◆ Ambulatory Medicine (urgent and primary care experience)
                                   ◆ Preceptorship – Ambulatory Medicine

                                  MONROE HOSPITAL, Austin, TX

                                   ◆ Elective – Medical/Psychiatric
                                   ◆ Preceptorship – Medical

                                  AUSTIN MEDICAL CENTER, Austin, TX

                                   ◆ Elective – Ambulatory Medicine

RESEARCH   PETERSON MEMORIAL HOSPITAL, Austin, TX (1999-2000)
PROJECT   **Research Assistant** – Emergency Research Education Department

                                   ◆ Recruit patients, draw blood samples, start IVs and maintain daily documentation
                                      as assistant to Dr. Smythe in the Nuclear Medicine Lab.

MEMBERSHIPS   Student Association of the American Academy of Physician Assistants
                                  American Academy of Physician Assistants
                                  Texas Academy of Physician Assistants

Yoga and Healing Massage

Sara Moon
Certified and Licensed Massage Therapist
Yoga Instructor

800.555.1212 • moonyoga@aol.com

ABOUT SARA: *"Sara's training and experience combine the natural relationship between yoga practice and massage to promote deep holistic healing."*

PROFESSIONAL PROFILE

Sara is a certified licensed massage therapist through the Shiatsu School of California where she learned and practiced many healing massage techniques. She also studied under Dr. Vincent Saporito who pioneered structural medicine by bringing structural deep tissue, primal scream, psychotherapy, and yoga together.

Sara trained with well-known healer, Anna Forrest, and during her studies she did an internship for two non-profit foundations, "Home Place" and "Yoga Star". Through these foundations, Sara provides a safe environment for people, who are in shelters, treatment centers, prisons, and inner city communities, to practice yoga.

Sara currently volunteers at the *Land of Yoga* in Pasadena, California and periodically at the *L.A. Yoga House*. Some of her massage therapy clients have included comedian, Chris White and head writer, Linda Smith, of the CBS show *Landslide.*

YOGA ~ HEALING MASSAGE:

- **Yoga Instructor** - Sara works close ly with her students on alignment and adjustments. She is also skilled in helping with injuries both physical and spiritual.

- **Traditional Thai Yoga Massage** - Originating from the time of the Buddha, Thai Massage focuses on stretches involving important acupressure points helping to remove blockages and restore the natural energy flow which can lead to disease.

- **Shiatsu Massage** - This massage helps to alleviate pain by balancing the underlying causes. Pressure is applied to the meridians (energy lines) promoting good health by stimulating the energy flow (Ki).

- **Deep Tissue Massage -** With this massage, slow deep strokes are used for releasing stress from the deeper layers of muscle tissue which cause inflammation and the blockage of oxygen. This deep tissue massage stimulates recuperative powers within the body helping to remove toxic build-up.

- **Swedish Massage** - Relaxing and rejuvenating this massage uses a variety of techniques promoting the flow of blood back to the heart, increased oxygen in the blood, and the release of toxins from the muscles.

EDUCATION & TRAINING

Shiatsu School of California (2003) ~ Sri Pattabhi Jois (2002) ~ Anna Forrest, Teacher Training (2002)
Yoga Training, Mark Blanchard and Brenda Strong (2001)

EMMA WILLIAMS

18/101 Johnson Avenue, Chermside Qld 4032 ♦ 0402 333 444 ♦ (07) 8888 9999 ♦ ewilliams@beonline.com

PROFILE

Innovative and inspiring English and Drama Teacher dedicated to imparting a passion for reading, creative writing, acting, live theatre, and critical analysis.

STRENGTHS

▶ Assist students to build confidence, and find ways to express themselves, through English and Drama.
▶ Relate well to students while maintaining the organization and authority necessary to bring out their best.
▶ Identify individual learning needs and develop strategies to enhance learning for each student.
▶ Develop and utilize numerous creative strategies to help students understand complex concepts.

EDUCATION

Bachelor of Education (Secondary English and Drama) – University of North Queensland, Cairns, 2003
♦ Awarded Golden Key National Honour Society membership for consistent academic excellence

Speech and Drama, Grade 5 (Honors) – Australian College of Music, Sydney, 2001

ACHIEVEMENTS

♦ Selected from field of applicants to co-write pilot TV program with noted screenwriter, J. Moore.
♦ Co-researched and created workshop entitled "Impact of Technology on Children's Literacy", while still a 1st-year university student.
♦ Independently conducted above workshop for 100+ attendees at the Early Childhood Conference, Brisbane, when my co-presenter suddenly became ill.
♦ Selected as Queensland state finalist in the Jaycees public speaking competition.
♦ Stage-managed Year 12 school musical production, "Just in Time", for Stafford Private School.
♦ Prepared Year 8 Choral Speaking Choir for regional performance for Macgregor Girls' School.
♦ Awarded Dux of entire senior year for secondary education.
♦ Elected to serve as School Captain during senior year.
♦ Awarded the Rosalyn Carlyle Memorial Award for consistent effort and application during senior year.

ACTIVITIES

▶ Performed roles in numerous productions, including Myrtle May in "Harvey" (University of North Queensland Theatre Department); Moitle in "Ma Baker's Tonic" (James Cook University Theatre Department); and Ophelia in "Hamlet" (Stafford Theatre Group).
▶ Independently undertook physically and mentally challenging 9-day Outward Bound course to further strengthen communication, leadership, teamwork, and problem-solving skills.
▶ Served as committee member of "World Week 6 – Multicultural Festival" for 3 consecutive years.
▶ Served as St John's Ambulance volunteer to provide first aid at numerous public events.
▶ Assisted in designing poster campaign to raise awareness of refugees for Austcare.

EXPERIENCE

Student Teacher – Years 8, 9, 10, and 11, Stafford Private School, Stafford, Queensland, 2003
Student Teacher – Years 8, 9, and 12, Macgregor Girls' School, Macgregor, Queensland, 2002
Student Teacher – Years 8, 9, and 11, Stafford Private School, Stafford, Queensland, 2001
Student Teacher – Years 8 and 9, Buderim Girls' School, Buderim, Queensland, 2000

COMBINATION RÉSUMÉS

XXXXX

322 Pine Acre Lane • Coraopolis, PA 15358
(xxx) xxx-xxxx • xxx@comcast.net

SUMMARY

Well-rounded and motivated with ability to read people and communicate effectively. Strong work ethic. Rapidly acquires new skills. Focused, judicious, and inquisitive.

EDUCATION

Moon Township High School, Coraopolis, PA. Graduation Date: June 2004.
    Four years of Drama/Theatre • Three years of Building Trades
    Honor Thespian, 2003 • Academic Letterman, 2002 • Theatre Letterman, 2002.
    Who's Who Among American High School Students • Outstanding Production Work
    Award, 2002 • National Society of High School Scholars, 2002/2003.

Jakarta International School, Jakarta, Indonesia. 2001.
Singapore American School, Republic of Singapore. 1998-2001.
Kingsway Christian Academy, Perth, Western Australia. 1997-1998.

ACTIVITIES & AFFILIATIONS

- Theatre Performances in high school productions in Texas, Singapore, and Indonesia.
- State Level UIL Theatre Participant, 2001 • Regional Level UIL Theatre Participant, 2002 • Main Stage Performer, Texas Thespian Festival, 2003. Chosen to advance to National Competition.
- Certified S.C.U.B.A. Diver and Deep Water Diver, 1989-Present.
- Singapore American Community Action Council – Singapore American School Football (traveled to and played in Korea); Singapore American School Baseball; Umpire for Minor League. 2000-2001.
- Youth Council, International Baptist Church. 1999-2001.
- Singapore American School Interim Trip – Traveled in, studied history of, and performed community service in Hong Kong.
- Trained for Mixed Martial Arts Tournament, Wrestling/Boxing, 2002-2003.

EXPERIENCE

Owner (part time), Woodworking Business, Coraopolis, PA. October 2001-Present.
    Build and sell speaker boxes and podiums. Work requires precision and patience.

Apprentice, DoAll Construction, Coraopolis, PA. Summer 2003.
    Acquired skills in maintaining high quality while meeting tight deadlines.

Checker, Food Basket, Coraopolis, PA. June 2002-August 2003.
    Promoted from Sacker to Checker. Provided personable customer service while working efficiently.

Host, Marco's Mexican Restaurant, Coraopolis, PA. Summer 2001.
    Promoted from Busperson to Host.

LANGUAGES

Well versed in French; familiarity with Mandarin.

ADAM DANIEL BERTOLLI

<u>Current</u>:
100 Harris Point Avenue
Warwick, RI 00000
(401) 222 – 6666, x0000

E-Mail: abertolli@aol.com

<u>Permanent</u>:
22 Jonathan Drive
Midtown, RI 00000
(401) 000 – 0000

PERSONAL PROFILE

➤ Highly motivated to begin and achieve employment objectives in the criminal justice field.
➤ Proven experiences of working well under stressful conditions.
➤ Rule-oriented, fair, and disciplined in giving or carrying out orders.
➤ Dedicated, focused, and diligent in executing and maintaining the highest level of abilities to reach all planned objectives and goals.

EDUCATION

Stetson University, Warwick, RI
Bachelor of Arts degree in **Administration of Justice**   Expected May 2005
Horton Davis College, Lafayette, CT
Major in **Criminal Justice** (Transferred to Stetson University)   2002 – 2003
LaBelle Catholic Prep Academy, Providence, RI
College Preparatory Diploma   June 2001

College Scholarships:

► Stetson University, Dean's Scholarship, $6,000 per year
► Horton Davis Scholarship, one year, $8,000
► Horton Davis Grant, $1,000
► LaBelle Catholic Prep Academy College Scholarship, $1,500

College Honors:

► Grade Point Average: 3.6/4.0 (*cum laude)*
► Dean's List, Horton Davis College and Stetson University, three semesters
► Rhode Island State Police Entrance Exam score: 91%,   October 2004

High School Achievements:

► National Honor Society
► Rhode Island Honor Society
► National Italian-American Honor Society
► High School Book Club founder and President
► Three years on Division One Football team, Captain, senior year
► Division One Super Bowl Championship Award

Adam's integrity, sincerity, and personal achievements mark him for high success in life.
      – Brent Keenan, Guidance Counselor, LaBelle Catholic Prep Academy

ADAM DANIEL BERTOLLI   PAGE TWO

_____ RELATED WORK EXPERIENCE _____

Department of Safety and Security, Stetson University, Warwick, RI
Dispatcher   9/12/03 – Present
- Dispatch vehicles to officers' campus beats and patrols
- Relay emergency information to on-duty guards
- Maintain day logs and incident reports
- Keep professional radio contact, serve as operator on emergency calls, and assist Newport Police with information on law violations

R. I. Department of Environmental Management (D.E.M.), Lincoln, RI
Park Ranger, Lincoln Woods State Park– Level Three Supervisor   Summer 2004
- Supervised and trained 12 new rangers, assigning patrols within 150 acre park
- Kept day logs, incident reports, and vehicle inspection sheets
- Charged with first to respond, handle, and assist in medical emergencies violations of law occurring in Park while on duty
- Served as eyewitness for R.I. State Police and R.I. D.E.M. Enforcement

Park Ranger, Lincoln Woods State Park, – Level Two   Summer 2003
- Enforced and maintained Park rules and regulations, reporting violations to a supervisor
- Provided park rules of conduct and general information to 5000 summer visitors
- Kept professional radio contact
- Maintained and updated bicycle inspection sheets

Svensen–Gustafson Investigative Services, Inc., Providence, RI
Security Guard   1/22/02 – 4/19/02
- Assisted Brown University Police with traffic control at campus events
- Ensured the safety of students and families during winter events and graduation
- Patrolled designated University buildings for the well being of students and staff

_____ SKILLS _____

- Computer: MS Word, PowerPoint, Access, Excel, Internet search capability
- Experience with finance duties as ADJ club treasurer
- Excellent organizational and project planning skills

_____ ACTIVITIES _____

► Administration of Justice Club, Stetson University, Treasurer
► Student Ambassador, Stetson University
► Treasurer, Class of 2005, Horton Davis College
► Student Ambassador, Horton Davis College
► S.E.E.D. (Student Events Excluding Drinking) committee member
► S.A.R. (Student Admissions Representative)

~ References readily furnished upon request ~

Cheryl Bloom, R.N.
89 Pine Road • Monrovia, NY 09927 • (555) 555-5555
cbloom@comcast.com

Registered Nurse

- Strongly motivated graduate with experience in hospital, sub-acute, and other health care settings.
- Clinical skills combine with dedication to excellent patient care, compassion, and professionalism to integrate patients' medical and emotional care.
- Able to relate to patients quickly and work effectively with physicians, peers, and other health care professionals. Conscientious, team-oriented, and eager to learn.

Education, Licensure & Certification

B.A. in Nursing, 2002
Chenneworth College, Croton, NY

Registered Nurse, New York State License, 2003

Basic Life Support with Automatic External Defibrillator, American Heart Association
CPR, American Heart Association
Certified Nursing Assistant, New York Nursing Assistant Registry, 2000

Additional: Math and Sciences courses, Flynn Community College, Monrovia, NY

Areas of Knowledge & Skills

- Physical Assessments
- Vital Signs / Blood Glucose
- Catheter Insertion
- Finger Sticks
- Patient & Family Education

- Dispensing Medications / Intravenous Therapy
- Documentation / Care Maps
- Nasopharengeal & Oral Suctioning
- Application of Dressings / Wound Care
- Cast Care / Pin Care / Traction Care / Tracheostomy Care

Clinical Training

Acquired hands-on clinical experience and knowledge in nursing procedures while completing several rotations at the following facilities. Experience with patients ranging from pediatric to geriatric.

Medical-Surgical	Rockport General Hospital
OB/GYN	Melville Memorial Hospital
Pediatric	Montessori School
Gerontology	Evergreen Health Care Center, Mediplex, Kimberly Hall, Meadowbrook

Healthcare Experience

Jackson Memorial Hospital, Croton, NY   **2000-present**
Patient Care Technician

- Provide post-operative care to patients on an 80-bed Medical-Surgical Unit.
- Diverse responsibilities include: monitoring vital signs, blood glucose and tube intake/output, collecting specimens, assisting with personal hygiene and feeding, and recording patient status.
- Transport patients to medical procedures and operate portable electrocardiogram.
- Educate patients and family members on home care.

SARAH E. BOURNE

1463 North Mesquite Trail • Austin, Texas 78721
Residence: 812.555.1234 • Cell: 917.123.4589 • sebourne@yahoo.com

Legal Assistant / Paralegal dedicated to providing superior support to legal staff

Well qualified and highly motivated **paralegal professional** with exceptional attention to detail. Creative and enthusiastic with proven record of success in prioritizing and processing workflow. Knowledgeable of Texas and New Mexico document filing practices. Strong initiative, ability to make decisions effectively and independently. Advanced computer skills including complete proficiency in use of Microsoft Office and SoftPro software. Values offered:

Reliability and commitment	Exceptional interpersonal skills
Articulate, strong communication skills	Outstanding research capabilities
Keen ability to learn new situations quickly	Time management skills
Flexible in changing environments	Thorough, confidential, and ethical

EDUCATION

Paralegal Certificate, Baylor University Legal Assistant Program
Summer Intensive Program, Waco, Texas, 2003
Internship with residential real estate practice

Bachelor of Arts, History with Political Science Minor, Texas Christian University
Fort Worth, Texas, 2000
Phi Alpha Theta: History Honor Society
Pi Sigma Alpha: Political Science Honor Society

LEGAL EXPERIENCE

Paralegal Intern
Johnson & Tyler, LLP
Waco, Texas
January, 2003—Present

Process loan documentation in a residential real estate practice. Explain loan process to clients. Open and prepare new client files. Order title searches and surveys. Manage client files during closing process. Assemble loan documentation for recording and filing. Retrieve documents from lending institutions, contact lenders for essential information, and make daily deposits into trust accounts.

- Processed 10-15 files per day during peak volume in summer.
- Excellent time management and planning skills.
- Complemented by clients for customer service skills.
- Committed to resolving issues before they become a problem.

Legal Secretary
Cohen, Tucker & Smith, LLP
Albuquerque, New Mexico
Summer, 1998

Answered phones and greeted clients. Performed administrative duties to include making copies, sending letters to clients and other attorneys, and billing clients. Excellent phone and interpersonal skills. Commended for attention to detail.

Abygael Brown

98 Ben Franklin Drive • Cherry Hill, New Jersey 07896 • abrown@aol.com • Work: (555) 333–3333

Qualifications Profile

Highly motivated and dedicated Year 12 Graduate with a strong record of academic achievement. Proven performer with effective combination of sales ability and customer service expertise. Experienced in dealing effectively on all levels in business. Customer service and team oriented.

Expertise

♦ Congenial and enthusiastic contributor to and supporter of team goals.

♦ Manages client expectations and develops effective working relationships with clients.

♦ Honest, confident, and hardworking with keen judgement and record of integrity and dependability.

♦ Strong communication, interaction, and relationship-building skills acquired through work experience and volunteer activities.

♦ Award winning performer with the ability to complete projects and deliver results in both individual and team assignments.

♦ Outstanding record of performance, reliability, confidentiality, and ethical business standards

♦ Conveys information in an effective and well-organized way; listens actively and gains cooperation from others.

Professional Experience

JD Coldridge & Associates – New Jersey, NJ   Dec 2003 to Jan 2004
Office Administration (Summer Position)

Supported and assisted managers in the efficient management of administrative services for the company through competent word processing skills, excellent public relations and effective time management. Scope of responsibilities included phone enquiries; invoicing; mail processing; filing; stock control; and spreadsheets.

Main Accomplishments:

➤ Established and maintained effective business relationships with external and internal customers, improving communication between customers and company.

➤ Resolved numerous business functions on a day-to-day basis; including customer enquiries, information requests, invoicing, and stock control.

➤ Independently researched, responded to, and followed up on requests from management personnel.

➤ Utilized skills in MS Excel, creating spreadsheets to effectively track job site costs.

Village News Newsagency – Cherry Hill, NJ   Oct 2000 to Nov 2003
Customer Service/Sales (Casual)

Under general supervision performed customer service; enquiries; sales; cash sales; stocktaking; and merchandising displays.

Main Accomplishments:

➤ Advised customers on the location, selection, price, and use of goods available from the store, with the aim of encouraging them to buy and to return to buy in the future.

➤ Processed and received customer payments for goods by cash providing correct change as required.

➤ Priced items and rotated stock by bringing old stock forward on shelves during quieter times.

Continued

Abygael Brown

Page 2

➢ Provided a high level of customer service and client relations based on outstanding communication and interpersonal skills.

➢ Assisted in working out totals for cash and other takings at the end of each working day and preparing money for bank deposits.

➢ Developed a thorough understanding of operating cash registers, automatic ticket issue machines, and other computerized equipment within the store.

Education

Higher School Certificate

All Saints Anglican School

Co-Curricular Achievements

Senior Debating Team – participating in various debating competitions	2001 to 2003
Athletics & Cross-Country School Representative	2001 to 2003
Duke of Edinburgh Award – completion of Bronze, Silver & Gold Level	2001 to 2003
Senior Choir	2001 to 2003
American Schools English Competition – Credit	2003
Cast Member for School Production "The Proposal"	2003

- Awarded Best Actress – Northern Rivers Drama Festival
- Highly Commended – Gold Coast Drama Festival

Highly Commended in MLTAQ French Speaking Competition	2001 & 2002
Bronze Community Service Award – 1.5 hours	2002
American Science Competition – Credit	2002
Vocal Ensemble	2002
Wind Ensemble	2001

Community Activities

Volunteer, Southport Special School (assisting children with reading, sport & craft)	2001 & 2002
Volunteer, World Vision 40-Hour Famine	2001

Certificates

First Aid Certificate	2001 & 2002

References Available Upon Request

TONY DEMARCO
12 Butterfield Court • West Hampton, New York 11933 • (631) 446-3201
tdemarco@optonline.net

OBJECTIVE	To secure a Cytotechnologist position within a hospital environment.
EDUCATION **1/00 to 8/03**	State University of New York at Stony Brook, Stony Brook, NY **Bachelor of Science in Cytotechnology, Minor: Biology - *(current) G.P.A., 3.85*** - Golden Key National Honor Society
9/96 to 5/98	Suffolk County Community College, Selden, NY **Associate of Arts in Liberal Arts** – *With Distinction* - Pi Alpha Sigma
SEMINARS **2002 to 2003**	LABORATORY CORPORATION OF AMERICA • Uniondale, NY AMERICAN SOCIETY FOR CYTOTECHNOLOGY • Scottsdale, AZ QUEST DIAGNOSTICS • Melville, NY • Wrote review of Quest Diagnostics seminar for *The Spindle* (Publication of Greater New York Association of Cytotechnologists).
CYTOLOGY EXPERIENCE **2001 to 2003**	GOOD SAMARITAN HOSPITAL • West Islip, NY **Cytology Specimen Preparation Assistant** • Prepared gynecological and non-gynecological specimens slides for Cytotechnologists using ThinPrep machine, stained and coverslipped slides. • Calculated monthly statistics, logged abnormal reports, and prepared five-year look-backs for review. • Organized and correlated Quality Assurance data. • Gathered data for Q-Tracks and Q-Probes. • Implemented Excel program for calculating monthly statistics. • Acquired experience in the use of Cerner Computer System.
SENIOR PROJECT	LABORATORY CORPORATION OF AMERICA • Uniondale, NY • Wrote and presented comprehensive report on "Ergonomics at the Microscope."
STUDENT VOLUNTEER **2002 to 2003**	STONY BROOK UNIVERSITY • Stony Brook, NY • Distributed information and fielded Cytology Q&A for admitted students. • Presented an introduction to Cytotechnology to high school students. • Teaching Assistant for BIO 202 (Introduction to Cell and Molecular Biology).
EMPLOYMENT **Summers** **1998 to 2001**	INAYAT MAMOOR, D.D.S. • West Islip, NY **Receptionist** • Provided office support functions, sterilized instruments, and poured models.
COMMITTEE/ MEMBER	• Dean's Advisory Committee, 2001 to Present • Commuter Student Association Member, 2000 • Cytotechnology Program Admissions Committee, 2003
PROFESSIONAL MEMBERSHIPS	• American Society for Cytotechnology • American Society of Cytopathology • Greater New York Association of Cytotechnologists • New Jersey Association of Cytology
SKILLS	• Microsoft Word/PowerPoint/Excel, Adobe Photoshop, Cerner, Lytec Dental

GREGORY JOHN GARSON

9000 59th Street, Flatland, Texas 79000

P. O. Box 986, Green River, Texas 76000

gg95@hotmail.com

(800) 555-0000

(543) 866-9900

SUMMARY

- General knowledge of daily investment firm operations
- Experience researching stock and updating broker/dealer transactions
- Self-motivated; use initiative and high energy to meet goals
- Organized and decisive; set effective priorities and implement decisions to meet operational needs
- Leader; own responsibility and accountability
- Flexible; easily adapt to change, new concepts, and work environments

EDUCATION

SUPERIOR UNIVERSITY, Lubbock, Texas   9/01 – Present
Bachelor of Business Administration in Finance expected   *5/04*
Master of Science in Family Financial Planning expected   *12/04*
GPA 3.0   Dean's List Spring 2002   The American Scholars National Honor Society

INTERNSHIP EXPERIENCE

Intern, THE PROVIDER/MONEYCO, Broxton, Pennsylvania   5/03 – 8/03
Gained insight to the financial industry as sit-in phone team observer. Attended in-service training classes for wholesale and investment representatives. Prepared documents needed to implement plans selected by clients. Expanded product knowledge, especially on variable annuities.
- Increased confidence as presenter delivering two speeches.
- Gained functional overview of daily operations of insurance / investment firm.
- Sold company on idea of an intern in spite of poor global market.

Intern, HUDD, SACCO & CO., Bradford City, New Jersey   5/02 – 8/02
Gained exposure to the mutual fund industry as a whole. Sat in on mutual fund managers' training program and observed sales / marketing calls. Prepared forms and agreements to complete sales. Increased product knowledge. Reduced office burdens by managing front desk.
- Earned internship from outstanding interview.
- Delivered perfect attendance.

WORK EXPERIENCE

Office Assistant, DAVID WELLS, INC., Green River, Texas   5/01 – 8/01
Prepared proposals to sell services that addressed client needs. Gained overall perspective of the day-to-day operations of a financial office. Greeted customers, routed telephone calls, and performed clerical duties.

Landscape Assistant, GREEN RIVER PARKS & RECREATION, Green River, Texas   5/00 – 8/00

HONORS/ACTIVITIES

- Member, The Marketing Association   2004
- Member, The Finance Association   2004
- Member, Student Government Association   2001 – 2004
  - ~ Elected as College of Business Senator 2001 – 2002 and 2002 – 2003 (Re-elected)
  - ~ Served on Budget and Finance Committee, 2001 - 2002 and 2000 – 2001 (Re-elected)
  - ~ Elected to Student Government Communication Committee, 2001 – 2002
  - ~ Elected to Student Government Medical Service Fee Advisory Board, 2001 – 2002
- Elected Member, Student SU College of Business Leadership Council (Re-elected)   2003 – 2004
- Elected Member, Greek Council for Christ   2002 – 2003
- Member, Kappa Sigma Fraternity   2001 – Present
  - ~ Chaplain 2001 – Present
- Eagle Scout   1998 – Life

MARTINIQUE HILL

14 Westlake Drive
Framingham, MA 01702

E-mail: martiniquehill@hotmail.com

Cell: 508 875 1699
Residence: 508 789 098

PSYCHOLOGY • COMMUNITY OUTREACH • RESEARCH

Self-governing psychology graduate—practical, focused, and analytical. Acknowledged for capacity to identify core issues, devise solutions, empathize, and communicate across all levels. Academic and employment experiences demonstrate an individual setting high expectations and pursuing defined outcomes—despite the challenges of changing priorities, diverse viewpoints, and pressure-cooker environments. An energetic debater, passionate communicator, voracious learner, and effective mediator; cited by peers and lecturers as a good listener and supportive problem-solver. Well-organized researcher and statistical scrutineer; a proficient and accurate report writer.

CORE COMPETENCIES

Expertly trained in →

- Psychological Assessments
- Welfare
- Report Writing
- SPSS Statistical Analysis
- Ethical & Professional Issues
- Counseling Psychology
- Quantitative Analysis, Design & Measurement

← Direct experience in

- Research Studies; participant interviews, research collection, and statistical analysis
- Office Administration; workflow management, inbound/outbound communications
- Recruitment and Interviews
- Customer Service/Retail Sales

Technology skill set includes:
SPSS (Versions 8.0 to 11.5), Microsoft Word, Excel, PowerPoint, Internet, E-mail, and Windows 2000/ME/98/95

EDUCATION

Postgraduate Diploma of Psychology
University of Massachusetts, 2003

Bachelor of Social Science (Psychology & Business Law)
Australia University of Technology, 2002

Dedicated to ongoing professional development through formal course work, workshops, seminars, and on-the-job training. Recent highlights include Family Law and its Relationship to Psychology seminars; Effective Interviewing Techniques, and Basic/Intermediate Word

THESIS

"The Social Ties of International Students at Universities"

Conducted 9-month research project for 12,000-word thesis. Devised research questions, presented proposal at conference of peers and academics, interviewed participants, analyzed data, and produced conclusions.

- Overcame international participants' apprehension over meeting new people and the demands of the study on their time through persistence, rapid response, and a professional attention to their concerns.

- Sourced information in an area where research is scarce and largely outdated. Followed-up leads, e-mailed authors and conference presenters, and gained access to materials; utilized the resources of large city libraries and the Internet.

RESEARCH PROJECTS ~ HIGHLIGHTS

Psychological Assessment: Awarded High Distinction for producing a comprehensive psychological report based on personal observations, interviews, and psychological test results from a volunteer participant.

- Overcame geographical distance issues and time scheduling conflicts; assumed a lead role in coordinating team handovers and juggling the collection and distribution of the one WAIS-111 test allocated to the study.
- Sustained impeccable standards of psychological practice by satisfying strict confidentiality protocols—despite pressure from the subject to reveal findings.
- Quickly adapted to psychological testing methodologies, conquering inexperience in area.

Abnormal Psychology: Key member of 4-person team conducting literature review on postnatal depression; review evaluated non-medication-based interventions and treatments, including counseling, group therapy, hospitalization, education, and training. Demonstrated breadth of topic knowledge via a 30-minute PowerPoint tutorial and received Distinction result.

- Personally defined and allocated group tasks that circumvented an impasse in decision-making.
- Spearheaded e-mail communication "ring" with each team member progressively adding sections allocated.

Counseling Psychology: Videotaped a 30-minute counseling session with a student peer, questioning and providing guidance and support on a real-life issue. Post-session, conducted personal performance evaluation and produced critique report complete with improvement recommendations.

- Successfully applied philosophies of "do no harm" and "treat with respect."
- Developed strong rapport with the client, nurturing a supportive, empathic, and respectful atmosphere for the individual to divulge confidential issues comfortably. Applied micro-counseling skills including attending, listening, summarizing, and feedback.

RELEVANT EXPERIENCE

FRAMINGHAM PSYCHOLOGY CLINIC   7/2003–Present
Administration Assistant (Volunteer)

Multifaceted role conducting statistical analyses, juggling routine daily office operations, and observing the inside workings of a specialist practice via case discussions and access to confidential reports. Study psychologists' methodologies and decision-making processes, and during monthly seminars with legal professionals and other specialist psychologists, monitor and seek to clarify information for own professional development.

- Analyze case data including dates, numbers of sessions estimated, and case types; raise reports for business principals to periodically review and use in strategic planning sessions.
- Won reputation for discretion and confidentiality in all client interactions, particularly when initiating contact for appointment reminders or rescheduling.

AUSTRALIA UNIVERSITY OF TECHNOLOGY   8/2002–7/2003
Research Assistant

Handpicked by principal researcher to join small research team investigating the social ties of international students. The research aims to elevate community awareness of the challenges faced by international students at Australian Universities.

Piqued the curiosity of potential case study candidates at international student orientation sessions, requesting assistance to participate in the study. Despite the challenges of overlapping schedules and a gradual loss of interest by participants, successfully applied powers of persuasion to resurrect student interest in the study, citing the importance of "trailblazing" for international students in the future.

- Successfully secured 50% of the study participants, with more indicating intentions to come "on board."
- Co-developed questionnaire in collaboration with supervising lecturer.

JODY KELIN

Home Address:	*Cellular:* 609.123.4567	*School Address:*
12 Meadowbrook Drive	*Home:* 732.987.6543	*15 Medford Court*
Lakewood, NJ 01234	*E-mail: jkelin@rutgers.edu*	*Newtown, NJ 66666*

GOAL:

A challenging technical position for an entrepreneurial computer professional

PROFILE:

Entrepreneurial computer professional with proven track record saving clients time and money. Started technical consulting business in high school, successfully providing support services to small businesses and individuals. Consistently demonstrate innovative suggestions for maximizing efficiency and service in the workplace. Excellent customer relations skills, well organized. Dedicated. Strong work ethic.

EDUCATION:

College of Science and Mathematics, Rutgers University.
BS – CIS Anticipated graduation: December 2003
Relevant Coursework:

- Object Oriented Programming
- Computer Architecture
- Data Organization & Database
- IT Security
- HCI & Usability Testing
- System Analysis and Web Design
- Project Management
- Data Communications and Networking

TECHNICAL SKILLS:

PC Networks: Configuration and installation of routers, switches, and hubs; as well as wireless technologies including configuration of access points, routers, network storage, and printing devices

Operating Systems and Software: Windows 2000, XP, 9x, Me, AS/400, MS Office, MS Access, Excel

Hardware: Mastery of PC hardware components and peripherals, troubleshooting, and installation including RAM, hard drives, various adapter cards, NIC installation, and configuration

Languages: Working knowledge of C++, Basic, JavaScript, COBOL, and HTML programming languages

PROFESSIONAL EXPERIENCE:

PRIVATE CONSULTING, Owner / Founder. 1996 – Present.
Started own business providing technical consulting to small businesses as well as residential help.

- Provide extensive variety of technical help including: troubleshooting, technical support, networking, and building PCs
- Offer training in hardware and software usage
- Establish and/or increase security for wireless networks. Configured firewalls
- Consistently demonstrate technical abilities to retrieve critical data (when back up does not exist or files have been corrupted), restore information (by accessing old images from hard drive), execute temporary access to "lost data", resolve security breaches (to laptops on wireless networks)
- Exhibit strong interpersonal skills and consulting abilities with clients

PROFESSIONAL EXPERIENCE (continued):

SENIOR SALES ASSOCIATE, The Gadget Place. 2001—Present.
(Senior Sales Associate 2003 — Present; Sales Associate 2001 — 2003.)

Run daily register reports, weekly payroll reports, and make daily bank deposits. Utilize AS/400 system in order to achieve high level of customer service. Handle maintenance and upgrading of POS systems throughout store. Supervise a staff of 10—15 employees.

- **AWARDS:** Achieved Sales Associate of the Month 10 times; Recognized for highest % Replacement Service Guarantee (RSG) 4 times; Highest % increase in sales from last year in volume group
- Work 30 hours per week while carrying full-time college course load
- Demonstrate strong customer relations skills. Proven ability to match customer needs with appropriate products
- Initiated effort, subsequently implemented in all stores, to provide managers with on-site access to corporate website. This allowed better and more efficient customer service
- Instrumental in effort to make register sites more efficient and ergonomically correct, through the suggestion and subsequent installation of flat panel monitors, and use of mice

CASHIER, Acme Foods Market. 1997—2000

- **AWARDS:** Cashier of the Month, Most Accurate Cashier, Quickest Cashier

PROFESSIONAL AFFILIATIONS:

Computer and Technology Club at Rutgers University

~~~

MARJORY C. KRAMER

5000 Germania Ave. ■ Flatland, Texas 79000
(800) 932-4488 ■ (800) 489-3330 Cell
mck44@hotmail.com

PROFILE

- BBA in Finance
- Organized time manager; astute; detail-oriented
- Reliable leader; assume ownership of responsibility
- Excellent written and oral communicator; good listener
- Pleasant demeanor; perceptive; easily establish trust and rapport
- Superior work ethic includes diligence, availability, loyalty, and punctuality
- Broadminded and open to change; tolerant and flexible

EDUCATION

SUPERIOR UNIVERSITY, Lubbock, Texas   2001 – 2004
Bachelor of Business Administration (BBA) in Finance expected 5/04
Overall GPA: 3.6

Relevant Coursework:

Economics	Financial Statement Analysis	Portfolio Management
Investments	Intermediate Accounting	Real Estate Finance
Corporate Fin. I & II	Principals of Money, Banking & Credit	Managerial Communications

Projects:
Investments – Tracked a virtual portfolio on Internet. Received A on project.
Financial Statement Analysis – Chose and analyzed NASDC company performance. Received A.

HONORS

- **Presidents List: Summer II 2001, Fall 2002; Dean's List: All other semesters.**
- **Golden Key International Honor Society and National Society of Collegiate Scholars, 2002**
- **Alpha Lambda Delta Honor Society and Phi Eta Sigma Honor Society, 2003 – Present**
- **McFadden Leaders Scholarship and Metro Alumni Scholarship**

WORK HISTORY

SEA BASS RESTAURANTS, Flatland & Rock Cove, Texas   2001– Present
Cashier (2004), Bartender (2004), Server (2001 – 2003), Hostess (2001)
Ensure superior customer service. Handle payment transactions, cash out each server, and balance drawer daily. Also trained new servers and hostesses as well as coordinating hostess schedule.
- Praised for add-on sales, teamwork, congeniality, and accommodating attitude.

MISS PETITE STORES, Rock Cove, Texas   1999 – 2000
Sales Associate
Assisted customers in retail clothing store, handling cash and credit transactions. Developed excellent sales techniques and repeat clientele. Gained experience marketing and promoting sales.

ORGANIZATIONS AND VOLUNTEER ACTIVITIES

The Finance Association	2002
The Marketing Association (Can Food Drive)	2002
Beta Alpha Psi (Habitat for Humanity and Race for the Cure)	2001 – Present

COMPUTER SKILLS

PC literate with working knowledge of Microsoft Word, Excel, PowerPoint, Access, Outlook, Windows 98/2000/ME/XP, and the Internet.

Timothy Marland

804 Boulevard ◆ St. Louis, MO 00000 ◆ tmarland@cybermail.com ◆ (555) 555-5555 ◆ Cell: (555) 000-0000

EDUCATION

May 2004

B.S. Accounting, with honors
Dean's List; President of Accounting Club
Missouri Baptist College, St. Louis, MO

Educational Highlights and Projects:

Contemporary Issues in Intermediate Accounting — Co-led team of 4, focusing on 10K detail of company selected for study, Private Brands Corporation, to analyze their solvency. Took on major role of figuring debt to equity ratios, earnings per share, common stock outstanding, executives' compensation, and pension plan expense of their various business units. Prepared a 10-page report of findings to support company's value to potential investors and presented it orally to class. Commended by professor for thoroughness and received grade of A.

Internal Auditing — Participated in a group performing an operational and financial audit of a hypothetical company. Discussed different opinions of business practices with regard to strengths, weaknesses, and recommendations. Gained insight into alternative ways of looking at situations.

Individual and Business Taxes — Became thoroughly familiar with the details of all tax forms and worked from memory to perform tax computations.

Introduction to Finance — Applied APR to such calculations as installment loans, payments, and annuities.

Other Coursework Included:

Managerial Accounting, Advanced Financial Accounting, Cost Management, Capital Budgeting, and Working Capital Management.

PROFESSIONAL QUALIFICATIONS

Computer skills in MS Word, Excel, Access, and Turbo Tax ... strong work ethic ... multitasking ability ... conscientious ... reliable ... very organized ... good time manager ... work equally well independently or with a team ... eager to learn and grow.

EMPLOYMENT

2000–Present

MAIL CARRIER, U.S. POSTAL SERVICE, ST. LOUIS, MO

- ◆ Sort and deliver a moderate to heavy volume of mail by vehicle or on foot.
- ◆ As a float person, cover any of five different routes.
- ◆ Perform a full range of postal product sales and customer service responsibilities.
- ◆ Financed 70% of tuition costs with earnings.

VOLUNTEER WORK

1997–Present

- ◆ Youth advisory member through church affiliation. Plan, implement, and oversee entertaining weekend and after school activities with a spiritual focus for ages children 4-15.
- ◆ Since 2001, have taken on responsibility of bookkeeper for Summer Bible Camp attended by 180 children.

DAVID J. MORROCO

66 Sheridan Lane
West Seneca, New York 14224

(716) 555-2897
dmorroco@hotmail.com

DATABASE ADMINISTRATOR
EDI System Analyst / Information Manager / Application Specialist

Professional Profile:

Skilled MIS graduate with successful track record of enhancing efficiency, integrating data, implementing new technologies, and ensuring the smooth operation of IT systems. Hands-on experience in technical support, database management, staff training, and web development. Ability to interpret and convey technical ideas to user community, resulting in greater compliance and cooperation. Demonstrated commitment to upholding the highest standards of quality and accuracy.

Core Skills: Database Design / Integration ... Technical Troubleshooting ... User Education ... System and Multi-User Interface ... Customer Support ... Web Design ... Needs Analysis ... MOUS

Computer Skills:

MOUS Certification: Microsoft Word
Web Tools: FrontPage, Dreamweaver, Flash, Fireworks, Netscape Composer, HomeSite, and PhotoShop
Applications: Lotus Notes, Emacs, and Microsoft Excel, Access, and PowerPoint
Operating Systems: UNIX and Windows
Languages: Java, JavaScript, HTML, Visual Basic, and SQL

Education:

State University of New York at Buffalo
Bachelor of Science – Business Administration   2003
Concentration: **Management Information Systems**
GPA: 3.4/4.0   Member, Management Information Systems Association

Experience:

<u>West Seneca Public Schools</u>, West Seneca, New York   9/02-Present
Adult Education Teacher
Instruct adult Medical Office students in the use of Microsoft Office Suite applications. Help students enhance their PC skills to improve employment opportunities. Maintain students' attendance and performance records. Plan weekly lessons and grade completed projects.
➤ *Customize lesson plans to address each student's level of knowledge and comfort with materials.*
➤ *Teach students with little or no prior computer experience and promote enthusiasm for the benefits of technology.*

<u>ATS Systems</u>, Buffalo, New York   8/02-11/02
Technical Support Intern
Provided technical support for Sony VAIO desktop and notebook computers through the 1-800 customer support line. Resolved callers' issues by troubleshooting problems and providing technical solutions. Documented calls and maintained daily activity and outcomes log.
➤ *Consistently met productivity goals, handling 6-8 calls per hour to successful resolution.*
➤ *Increased customers' confidence in Sony's line of PCs and peripherals by meeting callers' needs in a professional and timely manner.*

David J. Morroco   **Page Two**

<u>M&T Bank, IT Department</u>, Buffalo, New York   1/02-05/02
Access Database Intern
Built new Access databases to import and compare monthly Excel personnel records for 1,000 employees.
Designed automated methodology to identify new hires, attrition, and changes in static data. Implemented
improvements and documented development steps and technical specifications. Generated queries, forms,
and reports.
➢ *Developed two Access databases to import and compare Excel spreadsheets in order to track changes.*
➢ *Increased department efficiency dramatically and reduced the time needed to generate reports by over
  500%.*

<u>State University of New York at Buffalo</u>, Buffalo, New York   8/01-1/02
Student Web Developer
Designed and created web pages for the Professional Staff Senate's and Faculty Staff Senate's meetings.
Posted meeting minutes and agendas. Tabulated and constructed staff lists. Created specialty web pages for
upcoming Senate events.

References:

Furnished upon request.

Olivia M. Owens

34 Beacon Hill Lane ▪ Centerport, NY 11721 ▪ 631-555-5555 ▪ omo234@optonline.net

Seeking an Entry-Level Position in Marketing
Recognized as one of NYU's Best Students in the Marketing Department

EDUCATION, AWARDS & DISTINCTIONS

Bachelor of Business Administration, Marketing, 2004. NEW YORK UNIVERSITY, New York, NY
Major GPA 3.8, Overall GPA 3.6, Recipient of two academic scholarships.
One of two graduating students to receive departmental honors from the Marketing Department's faculty.
American Marketing Association Honor Society, American Advertising Federation Honor Society.

Associate of Science, Business Administration, 2002. Nassau Community College, Garden City, NY
Overall GPA 3.8, National Dean's List, Glenn A. Sparrow Award for Community Service.

COLLEGE LEADERSHIP, ACTIVITIES & PROJECTS

Vice President, New York University's Advertising Club, 2003-2004
Contributed to doubling the club's membership by enhancing outreach efforts to all students. Created and disseminated flyers, updated database of prior members for e-mail campaign, and announced meetings whenever possible to encourage participation. Coordinated and assisted with the organization of high quality speaker programs.

Participant & Presenter, National Student Advertising Competition, 2003
Working on both the creative and media sub-teams, planned media buys and wrote advertising copy including the slogan and tag line for a soft drink campaign that formed the basis of this college competition. Honored with a leading role in the project, made presentation to a panel of five judges as well as a large regional audience from 20 colleges.

Participant, Chancellor Awards Committee, 2001-2002
Served as a student representative helping run a survey to determine the recipients for Excellence in Teaching and Distinguished Professor Awards at Nassau Community College. Compiled survey responses from students and created six summary reports. Presented findings at a board meeting of ten college deans.

Marketing Projects: Consumer Behavior, Retail Management & Business Policy Courses, 2002-2004
Analyzed marketing strategies for real and fictional companies. Conducted PowerPoint presentations and wrote several 20-30 page reports on business strategies for marketing, customer service, public relations, and advertising. Authored company mission statements, press releases, and ad copy.

GENERAL BUSINESS EXPERIENCE

Marketing Assistant, 1-800-FLOWERS, Westbury, NY   Summer 2003
  ➢ Utilizing Excel spreadsheets, tracked sales statistics from Internet and retail purchasing.
  ➢ Coordinated the production and shipping of seasonal merchandise displays.
  ➢ Wrote captions and handled other copywriting for company's Web site.

Administrative Assistant, SBR CORPORATION, Northport, NY   Summer 2002
  ➢ Compiled, reviewed, and disseminated information relating to inventory management.
  ➢ Answered incoming calls from clients and vendors and handled inquiries as appropriate.
  ➢ Drafted and typed correspondence for company president and other senior staff.

COMPUTER SKILLS

Windows, Word, Excel, PowerPoint, Internet, and e-mail.

KANCHANA PERERA

124 Melville Road
Rocklin, CA 95677

E-mail: kanchi@rockman.com

Telephone: (916) 600 0323
Mobile: (916) 622 8071

GRADUATE ACCOUNTANT • ASSISTANT FINANCIAL/COST ACCOUNTANT • ACCOUNTS OFFICER
Proactive graduate, distinguished from peers by impressive academic results through degree studies, and "real world" experience both locally and overseas. Determined, analytical, and big picture focused; praised for ability to consider all options, strike appropriate solutions using available resources, and strive to accomplish desired goals. Work equally well independently or in results-focused teams. Acknowledged throughout academic and work life for strong attention to detail, and unswerving commitment to service that builds enduring client loyalty. Astute outlook and inherent business savvy supports intense personal interest for helping business to flourish. Strong knowledge of tax, with long-term interest in environmental and social accounting.

Professional strengths include:

- Management Accounting
- Taxation Compliance
- Financial Reporting
- General Ledger Maintenance
- Cash Flow Statement Preparation
- Payroll
- Accounts Receivable/Payable

- GST BAS Reporting
- Small Business Management
- Balance Sheet Preparation
- Cash Flow Statements
- Lease
- Trustees & Trusts
- Superannuation Investments

- Financial Advice & Counseling
- Stock Market Movements & Assessments
- Environmental Accounting
- Social Accounting
- e-Business

Technology: Solution Six, Microsoft Word, Access, & Excel; MYOB

EDUCATION

Bachelor of Business (Accounting)
Distinctions in Management Accounting, Taxation & Strategic Decision-making
RMIT University (2002)

Diploma in Business
Distinctions in Business Statistics and Business Information Systems
Perth Institute of Business & Technology (1998)

ACADEMIC PROJECT HIGHLIGHTS

- **Strategic Decision Making:** Team of 4 assigned project to calculate product volumes, safety margins and pricing, and consider expansion and investment options as a team "company" with CEO, Accountant, Marketing Manager, and Sales Manager. Challenged by tight deadlines, achieved team consensus by formalizing a joint collaboration by all parties to meet project objectives. Assumed role of company accountant to evaluate company performance, produce financial reports, and position the "business" for future prosperity. Project concluded with a well-received classroom presentation of research and findings. **Result: High Distinction.**

- **Environmental & Social Accounting.** Studied the environmental impact of storm water pollution, and researched the dollar cost to society and the health impacts over the short- and long-term. Composed and produced report that compared Australia with Singapore and the U.S.A., and presented assignment to class. **Result: Distinction.**

- **Cost Accounting.** Key contributor to team of 3, assigned to develop a cost driver report based on an authentic confectionary manufacturer. Circumvented reluctance of industry to participate by researching former student records and identifying an individual working in industry who permitted access to observe Ernest Hillier chocolate manufacturing plant. Personally researched processes from product order through receipt and production needs. **Result: Distinction.**

- **Relational Database Design & Development.** Two-person project to design an organizational database using Access. Complicated by a lack of desire by businesses to meet deadlines or participate, embarked upon internal University search, securing the interest of the RMIT gymnasium. Created the ERD and designed database, devising fields for student number, surname/first name, expiry date, and student history. Completed project received **Credit** result, and was later adopted by the RMIT gym staff as the foundation for their new database system.

EMPLOYMENT CHRONOLOGY

AUSTRA SELECTIONS   9/2001–Present

Bookkeeper

  Accounting System: MYOB. Report to: Company Director.

  Manage financial bookwork including all bank reconciliations, cash flow statements, and projected budgets. Produce BAS statements quarterly complying with all taxation legislation. Provided financial counsel to business owner, citing the financial and market advantages of expanding product distribution into general retail outlets. Owner embraced idea and is currently in negotiations with major department chain and German-based product manufacturer.

NEIL W. CURWOOD PTY LTD, Melbourne   7/2000–7/2002

Junior Accountant

  Software: Solution Six, MAS, AMS, LAS, Solution Six Tax. Report to: Company Director.
  Areas of Specialization: Companies, trusts, partnerships, superannuation funds, individuals and high-wealth returns.

  Assumed increasingly complex duties in line with willingness to expand professional expertise. Worked in close collaboration with clients, providing accounting and taxation advice, preparing annual income tax returns, and coaching in goods and service tax compliance.

  Progressively entrusted to prepare complex financial statements; interim and annual reports for manufacturing, retail, service, and investment businesses; prepare audits for superannuation funds, wages, debtors, and stock. Researched changes in accounting standards and tax issues, reported to business principal, and worked in close collaboration with decision makers from banking, tax office, and statutory bodies on behalf of clients. **Highlights:**

- Saved client from potentially costly tax office audit, by uncovering and resolving previously unidentified erroneous data when preparing year-end financial statement.

- Located incorrect data on client's previous taxation return mistakenly claiming a non-claimable loan repayment. Prepared amended tax return, overcoming any future issues with the tax office.

- Won client praise for research on the new Goods and Service Tax (GST) legislation; identified opportunities for clients to claim immediate 100% tax deduction for GST-related expenditures on new plant and software.

- Received letters of appreciation by two clients citing professionalism, timeliness, and accuracy in completing tax returns.

- Immediately identified problem with software installation that had eluded officer manager and staff, and caused system to become inoperable. Quickly reversed problem, and updated the system winning appreciation from the office manager for time and money saved.

DON PEIRIS WEERASINGHE LTD, Sri Lanka   8/1997–12/1998

Accounts Trainee

  Prepared bank reconciliations, cash flow statements, tax returns, and salary sheets; conducted end of year stocktake, and handled daily banking.

PROFESSIONAL MEMBERSHIPS

Member, Chartered Accountants Students' Society • CPA Passport Member
• Student Member, The Chartered Institute of Marketing, UK

COMMUNITY • SPORTING • ACADEMIC LIFE

- Assistant Treasurer, RMIT Student Association
- College Rugby Team Representative (1995–96)
- Past Member, Commerce Society (1993–96)
- Member, College Computer Club (1993–96)
- College Representative, Badminton (1992–94)

Recipient, *Best Attendance Award* over 3 consecutive years

KELLIE PRENTICE

Apartment 4, 204 George St
Columbia, MD 21045

E-mail: kp@hotmail.com

Mobile: 410 666 555
Residence: 410 444 211

STRATEGY CONSULTANT TRAINEE • BUSINESS UNDERGRADUATE
Member, Golden Key International Honor Society

Graduating business management student, distinguished by peers through top 5 course status, and appointment to the Dean's Honor Roll. Focused, intuitive, and analytical. Acknowledged for capacity to formulate workable strategies by assessing short- and long-term goals, applying a big picture vision, and addressing current business realities through observation and innovation. Skilled in meeting deadlines, working in environments of changing priorities and pressure, and quickly grasping new concepts. Natural curiosity has prompted a passion for travel and communicating with people worldwide.

Professionally trained in:

- Basic Financial Accounting & Management
- Marketing & Sales Fundamentals
- Team Management & Communications
- Events Management

- Business Legalities
- Research & Statistical Analysis
- Strategic Planning
- Business Policies
- Sports Management
- Organizational Behaviors
- Business Development

- "Red Carpet" Customer Service
- Customer Retention Strategies
- Employee Incentives
- Cost Containment & Optimization

Technology skill set: Word, Excel, PowerPoint, Internet, e-mail, Windows, HTML

EDUCATION

Bachelor of Business Management
Current Exchange Student: California State University
Dean's Honor Roll
Member, Golden Key International Honor Society
University of Queensland (2003)

ACADEMIC EXCELLENCE
SELECTED PROJECT HIGHLIGHTS

Project: Recreation Facilities & Events Management

AWARDED HIGH DISTINCTION AS A PROJECT LEADER, coordinating 30 team members staging an aquatic and field sports fun day. Overcame nonproductive adversarial atmosphere that threatened the project's momentum, by assigning specific work tasks and encouraging "ownership" from initial task delegation to completion. Managed core functions of sponsorships, marketing, and risk management; set guidelines, chaired meetings, and became the primary point of follow-up for critical issue resolution.

Project: Business Policy & Strategy

DISTINGUISHED AS ONE OF ONLY 4 STUDENTS to win a High Distinction (Grade 7) for solo efforts in assuming the role of a consultant in preparing a business report on an Australian-based enterprise. Analyzed the organization's strategies and business environment and assessed the efficacy of operations that formed the basis of a detailed series of recommendations. Inhibited by lack of access to confidential corporate information, scoured publicly disclosed company reports, financial statements, media releases, interviews, and print media to build a solid understanding of the company's strategic position. Devised several successful scenarios and formulated a strategy cited by the lecturer as "excellent."

Project: Business Research Methods

Solo research project. Identified complex business problem to solve and submitted a proposal outlining survey designs and analysis methods. "*Analysis section was exceptionally good*" cited course lecturer. Award a 6+ Grade high distinction.

EMPLOYMENT EXPERIENCES

MARYLAND CAMPERLAND   1/1997–1/2003
Camping retail outlet and repair workshop services

Sales Assistant

Rapidly acknowledged as a leading sales performer in the team demonstrating a strong customer service focus, and tireless commitment towards continuous improvement. Augmented university business studies by applying theory to a practical retail sales environment, presenting improvement and growth strategies to management—many of which were successfully, and profitably, executed.

In personal time, created a business improvement plan, citing the benefits of an integrated strategy spanning advertising restructures, customer retention plans, employee motivation and productivity ideas, and cost-containment blueprints.

Contributions & Results:

- Identified shortcomings in targeted audience advertising that failed to win new customers, or meet the price advantages of large chain store competitors. Surveyed the buying habits and demographics of existing customers, and concluded advertising exposure in local newspapers was ineffective in reaching the desired audience. Recommended successful multitiered strategy incorporating both print media advertising in tandem with a direct mail campaign.

- Capitalized on the "personal service" qualities of the store building brand equity to compete against price-based competitors and increase customer retention. **Devised newsletter concept designed to:**

  - ✓ Transform customers' perceptions of the business from "just a camping shop" to a valuable information resource. Newsletter would incorporate a rich mix of information for the hobbyist and dedicated camper such as favorable camping locations, "real life" customer stories, general camping information, new product information, featured items, and frequently asked questions.

  - ✓ Elicit customer involvement through "ego-boosting" activities—asking for product or camping advice and personal stories.

  - ✓ Promote a sense of "family" by highlighting "Employees of the Month," or a featured staff member in profile, to win customer recognition and loyalty.

- Devised staff motivation/recognition programs intended to increase sales activities, instill pride, and acknowledge superior performances. Built upon existing business credibility by displaying photographs of staff involved in camping, hiking, or fishing activities to suggest hands-on experience with product and applications. Lobbied management to launch a staff rewards program to recognize consistent achievement, and spearheaded the highly successful "Staff Member of the Month" board.

- Reversed shrinking profit margins impacted by traditional product discounting to make the sale. Created series of recommendations citing the advantages of producing goods more cheaply in-house, and promoted methods to offer value-added accessories in place of price reductions.

- Cut 25% from production costs by designing a new swag to be manufactured in-house. The new swag attracted higher sales, featuring more attractive design and better value for money.

- Accomplished 2% cost reduction in manufacturing process by slicing 10cm from product fabric design without compromising product quality.

REFERENCES

Available upon request

Rachel Smith

98 Ben Franklin Drive		Home: (609) 666–1111
Cherry Hill, New Jersey 07896	rachelsmith@aol.com	Home Fax: (609) 666–7777

Career Focus – Wildlife Attendant

Compassionate and dedicated high school student with a long time interest in animal care and study. Genuine love and concern for the well-being of all animals. Committed to continued learning and improvement of skills within the animal and wildlife fields. Confident and able to learn new skills quickly.

Expertise

- ◆ Long standing interest and desire to succeed in wildlife and animal studies.

- ◆ Demonstrated track record for achieving goals in a team environment.

- ◆ Proven experience within animal care environments, successfully gaining valuable knowledge and insight into the proper care and welfare of animals.

- ◆ Proficient leadership, planning and business writing skills gained as Treasurer/Secretary for Venturers Scout Association. Includes managing reports, paperwork, and organizing unit activities.

- ◆ Outstanding record of performance, reliability, confidentiality, and ethical business standards.

- ◆ Self-motivated, energetic, resourceful individual with a strong ability to find most efficient ways to organize and perform work.

- ◆ Excellent communication and interpersonal skills; readily establish rapport with individuals of various ages and cultures.

Education

Cherry Hill State High School – Cherry Hill, New Jersey	2000 to Present

Level 1 Nutritional Adviser Program (Animal Nutrition)

Course Includes: Small Animal Nutrition in Health
The Food
Small Animal Nutrition for Clinical Situations
Marketing

Professional & Work Experience

IGA – Cherry Hill, NJ	Oct 2003 to Present

Cashier/Customer Service (Casual)

Highly regarded team member for leading supermarket chain performing a variety of functions, including point of sale operation, customer service, cash handling, and EFTPOS transactions.

Main Accomplishments:

- ➢ Provided exceptional customer service, maintaining a positive attitude when interacting with all customers, coworkers, and professional staff.
- ➢ Processed and received customer payments for goods by cash, check, and credit/debit cards, providing change or cash out as required.
- ➢ Calculated and kept records of amounts received and paid, regularly checking the cash balance against this record.
- ➢ Maintained a high level of customer service and client relations by assisting customers in finding products within the store.

Continued
Rachel Smith

Cherry Hill Veterinary Clinic – Cherry Hill, NJ   Mar 2003 to Apr 2003

Veterinary Assistant/Animal Attendant (work experience)

Team member of local veterinary clinic responsible for assisting veterinary staff in surgery preparation, cleaning of kennels and surgery, feeding of animals, hydrobaths, dog walking, and general clerical duties.

Main Accomplishments:

➢ Assisted veterinary staff and surgeons on an "as needs basis" during consultations, surgical procedures, and treatments.

➢ Provided therapeutic massage to stimulate blood circulation, relieve tired muscles, and stimulate the skin by bathing and grooming animals with the hydrobath.

➢ Assisted veterinary staff in monitoring surgical and anaesthetic recovery of animals.

➢ Ensured the care and well-being of kennelled dogs by taking them on walks to stimulate muscle and blood circulation, while at the same time providing an effective and enjoyable environment.

➢ Cleaned and prepared comfortable sleeping quarters for animals.

Island Destiny Cruises – New Jersey, NJ   Oct 2002 to Dec 2002

Waitress (Casual)

Valued team member for showboat cruise restaurant performing a variety of functions, including customer service, taking of orders, serving of food and drinks, answering of questions, and cashiering.

Main Accomplishments:

➢ Maintained a calm and reassuring demeanor under high-pressure situations.

➢ Provided a high level of customer service and client relations based on outstanding communication and interpersonal skills.

➢ Calculated bill orders and took payments by cash and credit/debit cards, providing change where necessary.

City & Country Vets – New Jersey, NJ   May 2002 to Aug 2002

Veterinary Assistant (work experience)

Team member of local veterinary clinic responsible for assisting veterinary staff in surgery preparation, cleaning of kennels and surgery, feeding of animals, hydrobaths, dog walking, and general clerical duties.

Main Accomplishments:

➢ Assisted veterinary staff and surgeons in the preparation of physical exams and surgical procedures.

➢ Performed a variety of duties to assist in the proper care of animals, including preparing food (including special diets), ear cleaning, cleaning of enclosures, dog walking, and hydrobaths.

➢ Treated minor injuries and reported serious health problems to veterinarians.

Community Activities

Treasurer/Secretary – Adventurers Scout Association

School Activities

Big Band

Senior Concert Band

Involvement in all school productions

REFERENCES AVAILABLE UPON REQUEST

PATRICIA L. THORN

813-444–9632 ▪ thorn@email.com

2483 Beach Lane, Tampa, FL 33601

Career Goal	**Reporter ... Producer** qualified by superior communication, writing, and storytelling skills. Creative and personable, with the ability to remain calm and collected under pressure. Fluent in French and Creole.
Education	**Bachelor of Science** – expected May 2003 *Telecommunications (Specialization News) with an outside concentration in French* University of South Florida, Tampa, Florida
Telecommunications Highlights	→ *Selected from among 20 applicants for the role of News Producer* on WUFT-TV 5, a Public Broadcasting Service (PBS) affiliate serving 20 counties.
	→ *Recognized for writing and producing pieces on relevant issues* including housing funding for the homeless and the effects of holiday depression.
	→ *Interviewed high-profile personalities* including Lt. Governor Frank Brogan and gubernatorial candidate Bill McBride.
	→ *Volunteered with the Radio Reading Service* reading newspapers on the air for the visually impaired.
	→ *Instrumental in positioning the local Eye on Entertainment series to feature national entertainers.* Personally interviewed David Copperfield and Comedy Central comedians Dave Attell and Daniel Tosh.
Related Experience	WUFT-TV 6 (PBS Affiliate), Tampa, Florida – since 2002 *News Producer* for the noon news show; assign stories, write teases, design boxes and graphics, and ensure a smooth flowing program. *Reporter* for the evening news show and tasked with writing, shooting, and editing packages.
	Cable News Network, Atlanta, Georgia – 2002 *Intern* tasked with *field producing special projects.* Aided in producing segments, coordinated with PR agencies in scheduling guests, and wrote scripts.
	WRUF-AM 850, Tampa, Florida – since 2001 *Host and Producer* for the weekly radio show "Eye on Entertainment." *Anchor and Producer* for the midday news show.
	WUFT-Classic 94, Tampa, Florida – 2000 to 2001 *Reporter* for the evening news.
Selected Leadership Highlights	*Official Ambassador, Florida Cicerones* One of 70 selected from an applicant pool of over 650 to promote the University of South Florida to visitors, conduct campus tours, and foster alumni relations.
	Recruitment Counselor / Junior Panhellenic Vice President, Panhellenic Council One of 72 counselors selected from over 200 applicants to serve on the 2002 recruitment team. As Vice President, oversaw the organizational selection process of directors and assistant directors.
	Vice President of Administration / Executive Secretary, Kappa Alpha Theta Held executive leadership roles for two consecutive years.
Volunteer Activities	University of South Florida Dance Marathon ▪ Very Special Arts Festival District 1 Commission Campaign

SIMON WANG

7 Moore Street
Signal Hill, CA 90806

E-mail: swang@bigpool.com

Mobile: (360) 544-3344
Business: (360) 511 221

MARKETING GRADUATE

Hotels • Product Expansion • Leisure Markets • Government

Resourceful marketing and business graduate, distinguished from peers for capacity to organize, collect information, and deliver to strict deadlines. A receptive and action-focused team leader and principal organizer; competent in planning project activities, assigning workloads, and following-through. Good-natured humor, incisive edge, and nonjudgmental approach responds well to team "brainstorming" and provides the impetus for working independently. Keen to pursue entry-level roles in marketing, sales, market research/analysis, promotions, and product development/expansion that will benefit from "no compromise" philosophy that rejects "second best" and missed deadlines.

Degree level studies in:

- Consumer Behaviors
- Business Marketing
- Marketing Models

- International Marketing
- Advertising and Promotions Management

- Market Research
- Strategic Market Planning
- Service Marketing

Technology: MYOB, Microsoft Office, Internet, e-mail, HTML, Windows NT/XP/2000/ME/98/95, SPSS

EDUCATION

Bachelor of Arts (Asian Language–Japanese)
University of California (Anticipated 2004)

Bachelor of Business (Marketing)
Sub major: Accounting for Business
University of Technology, Fairfield (2003)

Advanced Diploma in Asia-Pacific Marketing
University of Sydney (Australia) 2001

ACADEMIC HIGHLIGHTS ~ MARKETING

Marketing Research
Partnered with team of three students to gather and interpret information from target market audiences that would allow the special event organizer to plan future mental health service conferences. Volunteered competencies in data analysis and performed all calculations that provided the fundamentals of report recommendations. Actively participated in formal presentation to THEMHS (The Mental Health Services Conference Inc. of Australia and New Zealand) with the company adopting the timetabling guidance. Awarded "Distinction" for depth of analysis and presentation.

Market Analysis & Forecasting
Project tested competencies in gathering information, interpreting raw data, and setting forecasts for future sales activities and market trends based upon outside influences, competitor activities, and the economic climate. As one of a team of four, reviewed the most effective methods for analysis, settling on Excel spreadsheets for the software's capacity to deliver the necessary results. Presented data analysis findings to the course lecturer and was awarded a "Credit" result.

Marketing Plan
Team of six assigned to prepare a full marketing plan for an aquatic and fitness center—Cook & Phillip Park. After full briefing of the client's market, product demographics, and future aspirations, conquered the challenge of gathering comprehensive data from both the company and external sources. Personally conducted all data analysis, presenting to the client's Managing Directors who praised the research and later embraced several of the recommendations. Awarded "High Distinction." (Plan & CD-ROM available).

EXPERIENCE NARRATIVE

TOYS ESSENTIAL!   3/2001–Present
Marketing Director

Transformed a hobby into a business launching a start-up import trading company to supply radio controlled cars and accessories into the North American market from Europe and Asia.

In partnership with two friends, established business plan, secured supplier network, and produced action strategy for penetrating the retail market locally.

Initially retailers were unreceptive citing little need to expand existing stock levels with an unknown and unproven product range. Networking with retailers at race events across California progressively elevated product interest, with potential buyers viewing cars in action and noting robust construction. Personal relationships flourished with requests for product catalogues, and eventual agreement to stock the products in hobby stores.

Entered into trade and payment agreements, and established a protocol for dealing with customer complaints or unavailable stock that would sustain business relationships over the long-term.

Investment in advertising is planned for late 2004 to expand the business by capitalizing on opportunities during the peak Christmas retail period.

GOLF PARADISE   2000–2001
Range Assistant
Reported to: Range Supervisor

Casual engagement up to 4-days weekly retrieving lost golf balls from the range. Cleaned and maintained the golf ball collection and washing equipment.

MEMBERSHIPS | ASSOCIATIONS

Member, UTS Scuba Diving Club
Member, New South Wales Radio Controlled Racing Car Club

PERSONAL

Enjoy scuba diving, golf, movies, traveling, snowboarding, fishing, and gym-work.
Multi-lingual: Mandarin Chinese, English, and Japanese.

NEWSLETTER RÉSUMÉS

SUE L. CHENG
telephone: 3399-7744

6E Tower, Hillsdale Bay
Taipo, NT, Hong Kong
e-mail: slcheng@hongkong.net

OBJECTIVE

Seeking to apply skills and knowledge of e-business, e-government and telecommunications markets in the Asian-Pacific Region. Project management and cross-cultural communications (Western and Asian) acquired through experience in diverse business environments.

EDUCATION

M.B.A. with concentration in Management of Global Information Technology and e-Commerce Marketing, 2003
KOGOD SCHOOL OF BUSINESS, AMERICAN UNIVERSITY, Washington, D.C.

Selected Management Consulting Projects:

- **Redman, Brotter & Williams Communications, Washington, D.C.:** Conducted comprehensive assessment of the business practices of the Washington D.C.-based public relations firm. Designed a detailed e-business plan for a focusing on process improvement and communication strategies, integrating order fulfillment, service delivery and customer relationship management, resulting in significant reduction in daily operating costs.

- **ADI Management Institute, Alexandria, VA:** Conducted an on-site analysis of the organization's management information systems requirements and designed procurement system that integrated contracting, accounting and receiving processes, resulting in more responsive, user-friendly system with real-time trackable data.

- **PacSystems Inc., Arlington, VA:** Analyzed existing business model and global expansion opportunities for a B2B e-marketplace serving the U.S. packaging industry. Conducted extensive research of major international packaging markets in Asia and Europe. Designed and presented to senior executives the region-specific data for effective market positioning. Commended on research depth and dynamic presentation style.

Awards:

- Case competition winner out of 10 teams in the Managers in International Economy class on Steinway's entry strategy to the China market. Professor's comment: *"You made the best presentation on that case ever; no one else was even close."*

B.S. in Communications, graduated summa cum laude, 1996
VIRGINIA COMMONWEALTH UNIVERSITY, Richmond, VA

INTERNSHIPS

FORSTERI INTERNATIONAL, Washington, D.C.	2000-2001
CAPITAL CORPORATION, Washington, D.C.	2000-2001

Intern—During the MBA program, completed internships related to business outreach, e-commerce marketing and e-business/e-government analysis. Engagement projects included:

Capital Corporation—Conducted market risk analysis on telecom, Internet and e-commerce development throughout the Greater China Region (China, Hong Kong and Taiwan) and identified global market trends, growth areas and investment opportunities for Aster Technologies, a client of the international investment and consulting firm. Results were published for senior decision makers on Aster's Intranet.

Forsteri International—Assessed e-business policy/leadership and e-government readiness in the China market for the global technology and policy consulting firm and clients, including Dunston-Patterson, Jones Smythe, and Hamden. Contributed research and analysis to company publication, *"Risk E-Business: Seizing the Opportunity of Global E-Readiness."* Utilized contacts in China and acted as liaison between firm and Chinese Ministry of Industry Information that regulates Internet and telecommunications development.

SUE L. CHENG
telephone: 3399-7744   Page 2

EMPLOYMENT

AMERICAN UNIVERSITY, Washington, D.C.   1996-1999
Project Manager, Multicultural Affairs

Initiated, created and marketed cultural training initiatives, special events and educational programs; conducted workshops on cross-cultural issues. Designed department's website and served as webmaster. Coordinated, authored and produced all office publications. Accomplishments:

- Revamped, secured funding and successfully promoted the academic training program. Results: increased participation rate 30% and achieved the highest retention rate organization-wide (34% above national average). Served as consultant to other organizations to establish similar programs.

- Appointed by President to direct the cross-functional strategic planning efforts that resulted in the development of the effective Leadership Training Institute.

- Chosen as internal consultant for the human resources practice in staff recruitment and retention to improve the university's diversity progress.

TECHNICAL SKILLS

Microsoft Office Suite, Lotus Notes, SQL, HTML, SPSS, Datatel, Netscape Communicator, NJStar (Chinese Language Software), Compass Marketing Software and PageMaker.

LANGUAGES

Fluent in Chinese (Mandarin and Shanghai Dialect) and English

REFERENCES

Available on request

MARIA TERESITA GOMEZ

OBJECTIVE: FBI Honors Internship Program

HIGHLIGHTS OF QUALIFICATIONS

☑ Self-motivated, disciplined individual with an intense desire to succeed
☑ Able to achieve results independently and as a cooperative team member
☑ Successfully developed and implemented aerobic programs for all athletic levels
☑ Resourceful, creative and diligent. Noted for consistent professional manner.

LEADERSHIP

- As Freshmen Orientation Leader, addressed groups of incoming freshmen on academic requirements and college life, and assisted them in registration process for 3 orientations.

- In the Marathon Township Police Department Intern Program, entrusted with collecting evidence, such as fingerprints, and accurately cataloguing in police database. Assisted in speed surveys in the ride-along program.

FITNESS PROGRAM COACH

- Personally instructed and motivated groups in aerobic exercises (3 classes weekly @ 30 students) for 2 private fitness centers.

- As Exercise Coach at Dennison College, oriented new members to gym, tailoring the basic program to meet their varying levels and goals. Supervised and evaluated 10 work study students in gym. Monitored gym members' fitness level progress and made recommendations for improvement.

PERSONAL ACHIEVEMENTS

- Achieved Dean's List status for 4 years.

- Won titles as Dennison College Bench Press / Dead Lift Champion (2001 – 2003) and Body Building Champion for 2003.

- Elected President of Police Explorers (Boy Scouts of America) during high school.

EDUCATION

May 2004 Bachelor of Arts (B.A.) anticipated
Criminal Justice and Administration and Planning,
Dennison College of Criminal Justice, New York City

Certifications: Water & Boat Safety, Brown Belt (Karate)

EMPLOYMENT HISTORY

Freshman Orientation Leader   2000 – 2004
and Exercise Coach
Dennison College, New York City

Intern, Marathon Township Police Dept.   2000
Marathon Township, NJ

Aerobics Instructor   1998 – 2000
Pump Iron Gym, Hillsborough, NJ
Synergy Spa, Princeton, NJ

COMPUTER SKILLS

Windows 2000, MS Office 2000 – Word, Excel,
PowerPoint, MS Outlook, WordPerfect, Internet, e-mail.

LANGUAGES

Proficient in Spanish – conversation, reading and writing.
Knowledge of French and Portuguese.
Currently studying Chinese.

PROFESSIONAL MEMBERSHIPS

Aerobic Association International, member since 1998
International Sports Medicine Assoc., member since 1998

Present Address: 355 W. 101st Street, New York, NY 10025 ▪ (212) 765-5555 ▪ mariagomez@juno.com
Permanent Address: 65 Michael Lane, Hillsborough, NJ 08844 ▪ (908) 281-5555

MARIA D. HASSON

813–246–8855
hasson@email.com
2384 Pineview Drive, Brandon, FL 33511

CAREER FOCUS

Project Analyst
Program Manager

QUALIFICATIONS

Articulate and engaging
professional distinguished by …

- Proven ability to see the big
  picture and design practical
  solutions to achieve
  objectives.

- Effective communication,
  listening, and interpersonal
  skills.

- A unique combination of
  analytical and creative
  competencies in approaching
  and resolving challenges.

- The ability to work
  independently or as part of a
  team.

- Superior visionary,
  implementation, and time
  management skills with
  attention to detail and
  excellent follow through.

ACADEMIC HONORS

- National Society of Collegiate
  Scholars
- Golden Key National Honor
  Society

HIGHLIGHTS OF VALUE OFFERED

*As a Graduate Assistant, made recommendations, embraced by the Head of
Audiology, to …*

- Create a practical win–win solution to the court's inadequate
  amplification issues: Capitalize on the court's budgeted dollars to loan
  out ADA/IDEA compliant hearing aids resulting in additional
  business, revenue, and alliances for the University's clinic.

- Resolve inventory shortages in the clinic by conducting a supply audit
  and implementing monthly tracking and restocking systems.

- Eliminate pricing discrepancies and loss of revenue by developing and
  enforcing a standard product pricing list for retail items.

As Resident Assistant, implemented …

- Developed programs in diversity and education for residents of Sledd
  Hall.

EDUCATION

UNIVERSITY OF MIAMI, Miami, Florida
Completed 45 credit hours of **Graduate Education** in Audiology

- Logged approximately 300 hours of clinical experience

Bachelor of Arts, CSD – 2001
**Business courses included Macroeconomics, Microeconomics,
Financial Accounting, Managerial Accounting, Statistics, and
Computer Software (MS Office)**

- Named to the **President's Honor Roll 6 out of 7 semesters**
- **CLAS Anderson Scholar of High Distinction**
- Recipient of a **4-year Florida Academic Scholars** Award

PROFESSIONAL EXPERIENCE

Graduate Assistant, Doctor of Audiology Program
Department of Communication Sciences and Disorders
University of Miami, Miami, Florida
August 2002 to December 2003

Office Assistant
Smith & Williams, Miami, Florida – 2002 and Summer 2003
Wallace E. Jones, Esq., Miami, Florida – 2001 to 2002
Phillip Chambers, M.D., Miami, Florida – Summer 2000
Harry Longfellow., C.P.A., Miami, Florida – Summer 1999

Resident Assistant, Division of Housing
University of Miami, Miami, Florida - January 2000 to May 2001

Shelly Shane

555 Rt. 23, Summit, NJ 07901
908-918-5555
shelshane@world.net

EDUCATION

May 2004 Bachelor of Arts
Elementary Education
Stockton State College
Stockton, New Jersey

Dean's List, GPA 3.4

OBJECTIVE

A position as a **Kindergarten School Teacher** utilizing my proven abilities to create a positive learning environment.

CERTIFICATIONS

Education Certification K-6 and Special Education Certification K-6 **(New Jersey, New York)**

Substitute Teacher K-12 **(New Jersey, New York)**
First Aid and CPR

MY PRIMER OF SKILLS

- **Attentive and adaptable** to individual learning styles; **active listener** who engages each child's sense of curiosity and creativity.
- **Balance** new educational ideas with traditional ideas and techniques; **bolster** each child's self-confidence by positive reinforcement.
- **Create** team **cooperative** learning environments and innovative activities; **care** deeply about quality education for all.

MEMBERSHIPS

NJ Teachers' Association
Natl. Child Care Association
NJ Child Care Association
Stockton Teachers Club – Pres.
Stockton Girl Scouts Volunteer

EXPERIENCE

January 2004 – present
Student Teacher K - 2
Summit Elementary School
Summit, NJ

- Teach or team teach six classes in math, reading, language arts and special education. Use thematic approach to all classes.

2003 – present
Co-Lead/Lead Teacher
Extended Day Care Program
Stockton School District, NJ

- Manage before and after school care program for 160 students in K – 6th grades, with tutoring and enrichment programs.
- Teach summer enrichment classes to K – 8th graders in science, drama and arts.

2002 Summer
Program Coordinator
Stockton School District, NJ

- Oversaw and coordinated summer programs for five sites serving 600 students.
- Supervised five program site coordinators and 40+ enrichment class teachers.
- Troubleshot and served as liaison with the Director of Community Education and the Extended Day Program Coordinator.

CURRICULUM VITAE

DAVID JOHN SAMUELS

22 McDonald Street, New York NY 10014
Home: (000) 333–3333 ▪ djsamuels@hotmail.com

QUALIFICATION SUMMARY

Dynamic, forward-looking team player with 5 years' experience, both tertiary and work experience related, in biotechnology. Combines extensive technical, analytical, and interpretive skills with practical field experience. Possess strong interpersonal skills: experience working with multi-discipline research/scientific teams and professionals. Proficient in English, Hebrew, and French. Areas of expertise include:

- GC-MS & LC-MS Analysis
- Solvent Extraction Methods
- Analysis of Biological Molecules
- Traditional & Advance Techniques in Microbiology & Molecular Biology
- Water Quality Guidelines
- Multivariate & Univariate Statistics
- Ecological Risk Assessment Principals & Methods
- Chemistry Microbiology Of Pollution Associated With Mining

EDUCATION

Ph.D., Environmental Biotechnology   1999 to 2003
UNIVERSITY OF NEW YORK, *New York*

- **The use of microbial phospholipid fatty acid profiling to measure the impact of acid rock drainage on microbial communities in sediments.**

  - Performed analysis, identification, and quantification of microbial biochemical markers such as phospholipids, PHAs, and ubiquinones using GC-MS and LC-MS.
  - Conducted physio-chemical and microbiological analysis of polluted sediments and water samples (ie. Heavy metals analysis, BIOLOG analysis, viable count, microbial morphology, 16s rRNA analysis, etc.).
  - Carried out multivariate statistical analysis to correlate physio-chemical parameters with biological ones.

Bachelors, Biotechnology   1996 to 1999
UNIVERSITY OF NEW YORK, *New York*

- **Course included:** Biochemistry, microbiology, immunology, and molecular biology.

  Course provided professional qualifications in biological sciences with an emphasis on DNA technology and its applications, combined with a firm basis in the industrial aspects of biotechnology.

  - Appointed as Project Leader for the establishment of a quality control plan for a pharmaceutical plant project, supervising up to 10 students and assisting team members.
  - Acknowledged for strong skills in statistics, biochemistry and molecular biology, assisting fellow students in problem diagnosis and troubleshooting.

PROFESSIONAL EXPERIENCE & TRAINING

Scientific Officer – Microbiology Department, Environmental Division   1999 to 2003
ANSTO (AMERICAN NUCLEAR SCIENCE & TECHNOLOGY ORGANIZATION), *New Jersey*
Team member of waste management project responsible for the evaluation of microbial molecular indicators for the measurement of ecological impact at a national research institute for environmental risk assessment.
Key Contributions:

- Research results on comparisons between polluted and unpolluted sites accepted for publication in the prestigious international scientific magazine "The Journal of Microbial Ecology," with two other collaborative publications anticipated.

PROFESSIONAL EXPERIENCE & TRAINING CONTINUED...

➤ Implemented quality control parameters in order to standardize and streamline the administration and analysis of experiments.

➤ Key player in the integration of team members' research through statistical analysis, contributing significantly to the scientific knowledge of the organization.

➤ Collaborated with team members in determining the relationships between environmental stressors (heavy metals, pH, flow, etc.) and microbial communities biomass and diversity.

➤ Trained team members on the various procedures for using statistical programs; enlisted as technical specialist due to high level of technical skills.

➤ Conducted an in-depth analysis on the various sediments to determine the ecological impact of acid mine drainage pollution on microbial communities through organic chemistry, analytical chemistry, biochemistry, microbiology, and analysis of vast amounts of data using multivariate statistics.

➤ Collaborated with project staff on the application of microbial bioindicators to determine ecological impact and recovery.

➤ Performed a number of projects and tasks unsupervised due to consistently solid performance. Projects included:

- Analysis of microbial phospholipid biomarkers using GC-MS and statistically analyzing the data.
- Analysis of microbial respiratory ubiquinone biomarkers using LC-MS.
- Analysis of microbial communities using carbon utilization assay (BIOLOG).
- Analysis of microbes using traditional microbiological methods.

➤ Assisted senior scientists in the evaluation and comparison of methods for assessment of environmental microbial communities.

Research Assistant (Work Experience)   1999

DNA LABS – NEW YORK IVF, *New York*

Worked in a developing capacity as a research assistant with increased responsibility for paternity tests, DNA fingerprinting, Southern Blotting, PCR analysis, and individual projects using gel electrophoresis.

Key Contributions:

➤ Wrote and submitted report for special in-house project to establish the relation between microdeletions in the AZF regions of chromosome Y and male infertility.

➤ Collaborated with chief scientists in the preparation and execution of paternity tests, including preparation of the gel for electrophoresis, preparation of samples, and amplification with PCR.

Research Assistant (Scholarship Program)   1999

CSIRO – FOOD SCIENCE NEW JERSEY, *New Jersey*

Performed a variety of research and analysis assignments in the field of food microbiology using independent judgement and diagnosis, including testing different batches of media with different inocula, assessing results, media making, resuscitation of lyophilized cultures, serial dilutions, and spread plating.

Key Contributions:

➤ Independently conducted several international collaborative studies in methods and media for enumeration of yeasts and moulds in foods.

➤ Played a key role in the optimization of international standard quality control techniques in the field of food microbiology.

➤ Wrote and submitted report for international collaborative study aimed at setting international quality control standards for specialized media.

SCIENTIFIC SKILLS

ANALYTICAL CHEMISTRY TECHNIQUES

- ☑ Solvent Extractions
- ☑ UV Absorption Spec.
- ☑ Particle Measurement Analysis
- ☑ Solid Phase & Column Chromatography, TLC
- ☑ Biosynthesis & Chemical Structures of Fatty Acids
- ☑ Liquid Chromatography - Mass Spectrometer Analysis, HPLC
- ☑ HP4500 Inductively Coupled Plasma - Mass Spectrometer (ICP-MS)
- ☑ Microwave Assisted Acid Digestion (MLS1200 Mega laboratory microwave digester)
- ☑ Vista Simultaneous Inductively Coupled Plasma Atomic Emission Spectrometer (ICP-AES)
- ☑ CNS2000 – for rapid determination of Carbon, Nitrogen, and Sulphur of mineral and environmental samples
- ☑ Identification & Quantification of Compounds using Gas Chromatography - Mass Spectrometer Analysis (extensive knowledge, 4 years experience using various instruments, i.e., HP 5890 series II coupled to VG TRIO, Varian Saturn GC-MS, etc.)

STATISTICAL ANALYSIS – MULTIVARIATE & UNIVARIATE TECHNIQUES

- ☑ ANOVA
- ☑ Student T-tests
- ☑ Covariant Analysis
- ☑ Regression Analysis
- ☑ Redundancy Analysis (RDA)
- ☑ Hierarchical Cluster Analysis
- ☑ Principle Component Analysis (PCA)
- ☑ Canonical Correspondence Analysis (CCA)
- ☑ Non-Parametric Multidimensional Scaling (nMDS) Ordination

MOLECULAR BIOLOGY & microbiology TECHNIQUES

- ☑ Paternity Tests
- ☑ Southern Blotting
- ☑ Bioreactor Operation
- ☑ Media Preparation
- ☑ Serial Dilutions
- ☑ 16s rRNA Analysis
- ☑ Gel Electrophoresis
- ☑ DNA Fingerprinting
- ☑ Preparation of DNA Libraries
- ☑ HACCP, GMP, GLP, iso 9001
- ☑ Australian Water Quality Guidelines
- ☑ Techniques of Hybridization & Sequencing
- ☑ Sterilization Methods, Autoclave Utilization
- ☑ Polymerase Chain Reactions & Western Blotting
- ☑ Spread Plating, Plate Count, Viable Count, MPN
- ☑ Immunological Assays (Cellular & Serological Techniques)
- ☑ Retrieving & Analyzing Nucleic Acid & Protein Sequences from Databases (i.e. GENBANK)
- ☑ Differentiations of Bacterial & Fungal Species Using Rapid Test Kits including API, Carbon Utilization Assay (BIOLOG) & Identification Using Microscope

PUBLICATIONS

Samuels, D.J., Brown, D.J.M., Stone, P.J., and Smith, L.J. "The use of phospholipid fatty acid analysis to measure impact of acid rock drainage on microbial communities in sediments." *Journal of Microbial Ecology*, due for publication April 2004.

Stone, P.J., **Samuels, D.J.**, Browne, D.J.M., and Smith, L.J. "Phospholipid fatty acid analysis of the impact of acid drainage on aquatic sediment microbiota." *Microbiology America (ISBN 1324-4272)*, 22(4): A95, 2001.

Stone, P.J., **Samuels, D.J.**, Wilkes, K.L., Browne, D.J.M., and Smith, L.J. "The Finniss River: A Natural Laboratory of Mining Impacts - Past, Present, and Future." *The Finniss River Syposium ANSTO E/748*: 19-22, 2001.

Stone, P.J., Holden, P.J., **Samuels, D.J.**, and Browne, D.J.M. "Bacteria as bio indicators of pollution: characterization of the impact of acid mine drainage on microflora using phospholipid fatty acid analysis." *ABA 2000: Proceedings 15th American Biotechnology Conference*, 47, 2000.

Stone, P.J., **Samuels, D.J.**, Holden, P.J., Browne, D.J.M., Kennedy, R.A., Wilkes, K.L., and Smith, L.J. "Phospholipid Fatty Acid Analysis as a Measure of Impact of Acid Rock Drainage on Microbial Communities in Sediment and Comparison With Other Measures." *ANSTO C616: Proceedings of the Third Brukunga Workshop: Quantifying the degree of ecological detriment in the Dawesley Creek/Bremer River System*, 43-46, 2000.

PRESENTATIONS

"Microbial Measures of Impact of Acid Rock Drainage on Waterways," WAMMO: 99 Water Management in Metallurgical Operations, 1999

PROFESSIONAL DEVELOPMENT

University of New York	Microbial Communities Characterization (1999 – 2003)
DNA Labs	DNA Fingerprinting (1999)
	Paternity Tests (1999)
	Southern Blotting (1999)
	PCR Analysis (1999)
	Gel Electrophoresis (1999)
CSIRO	Enumeration of Yeasts & Molds in Foods (1999)
New Jersey Community College	Project Management
Military Officer's Academy, Israel	Logistic Management & Leadership
St John's Ambulance	First Aid Certificate

TECHNOLOGY SKILLSET (ADVANCED USER)

TOOLS:	MS Suite: Word 2000, Excel 2000, PowerPoint, Outlook, Project, Access; Netscape, Internet Explorer, Composer, Front Page, Adobe Photoshop, Ulead Photoimpact,
OTHER TOOLS:	Minitab, Canoco for Window, Primer, SPSS, Medline, Cambridge Scientific, Biblioscape5
PLATFORMS/OS:	PC, Macintosh, Windows 95, 98, 2000 & Dos 7

REFERENCES AVAILABLE UPON REQUEST

Part III

LETTERS

Chapter 10

Do I Really Need a Cover Letter?

Do you really need to send a cover letter with your résumé? The answer is a resounding "yes!" The cover letter serves an important purpose. It is not simply a quick letter that you throw together to get your résumé out in the mail. It is an important tool that, at the very least, informs a hiring manager who you are and why you are sending your résumé. At best, it is an effective selling tool that will make a hiring manager *want* to read your résumé and pick up the phone to schedule an interview.

All of your job-hunting correspondence should include some type of letter. "Cover letter" is a broad term that refers to a number of different letters that are a part of the job search. This includes the cover letter that is *always* sent with a résumé, thank you letters, networking letters, job acceptance letters, and even resignation letters. This correspondence is more than simply a formality. Not only are these letters a common courtesy, but they can also be used to progress your candidacy or rekindle an old application. This chapter will focus on letters used in the job search process, beginning with the letter that accompanies the résumé. Other letters will be addressed in the following chapter. Of special concern will be issues of particular interest to new graduates and those entering the workforce for the first time.

The Résumé Cover Letter

This is the communication most often thought of when people hear the term "cover letter." A cover letter should always accompany a résumé. From the practical point of view, the letter informs the hiring manager who you are and why you are writing. Do not assume that the person reading your résumé will automatically know which position you are applying for, even if you are responding to a job posting. Even if you think your background and skills are an obvious perfect match for a job, do not leave it up to the reader to make that connection for you. It is up to you to inform your reader of your purpose.

This does not mean that your cover letter is simply an introduction to your résumé, as in, "Please see the attached résumé for your consideration in regards to the electrical engineering position listed in the Sunday edition of the *Daily Times*." Hiring managers have seen too many of these types of letters. Your cover must convey much more than informing the reader that your résumé is enclosed (or attached, if you are sending your résumé via e-mail).

Your cover letter should be used as an additional sales tool. This is not to say that it should be a repeat of your résumé in prose form. Instead, it should sell your best qualities in a brief manner, making the reader want to read your résumé. Think of your cover letter as a movie trailer or teaser. Show your audience some of the most exciting and enticing things that you have to offer, and make your reader want to see the whole picture.

As with résumé writing, there are no hard and fast rules; however, the cover letter needs to accomplish a few things. Here is a list of some basics that should be included in your letter:

Your name and contact information Sounds obvious, but if you include only your signature at the bottom of the letter (and some candidates have even forgotten to sign their names), a potential employer may not have any way of contacting you. Résumés do get detached from the cover letters. Be sure all your contact information is included. The best solution is to use the same heading as in your résumé. This will ensure a professional and consistent look to your correspondence. (You will also want to use the same header for all additional correspondence. Your information may be kept on file, and it will speak well for you if all your letters are uniform in appearance. Employers appreciate attention to detail.)

Who you are and what you do (or hope to do) You may assume that the reader knows which job you are applying for, particularly if you are responding to an online posting or a classified listing in the newspaper. This is a dangerous assumption and could well land your résumé in the recycle bin. Introduce yourself and inform your reader of your reason for writing.

Why you are writing What is your purpose for sending your résumé? You want to get an interview! If you are sending a résumé to a networking contact, you are writing to have your résumé forwarded to someone else who can grant you an interview. The goal of sending your résumé is to sell yourself so that you will be invited to meet (or in some cases, speak on the phone or videoconference) with someone who has the power to offer you a job. Rather than simply stating "Thank you for your time and consideration," ask for an interview or at the very least state that your purpose is to gain an interview.

Where your résumé is Inform your reader that your résumé is either enclosed, if sending a hard copy, or attached, if sending an e-mail and the company accepts attachments; otherwise, inform your reader that your résumé is pasted below. While your cover letter is more than an introduction to your résumé, you still need to convey that the résumé is available for reading; otherwise, you would not be writing.

Your signature Do not forget to sign your name. Sounds obvious, but more than one candidate has overlooked this important detail. Forgetting makes you look sloppy. Sign your name in blue or black ink. (Some experts will argue for one color or another—black is generally more professional. Blue automatically shows the reader that the signature is not a "stamp." This is not really an issue for a cover letter.) Do not use other colors. Sure, purple may be fun, and yes, it will stand out but not in the way that you want it to.

At the close of your letter, space down four lines and type your name to match the way it appears in your header. Sign between the typed name and the close of your letter.

An enclosure notation Two lines below your typed name indicate that there is an enclosure or enclosures. Even though you have already informed the reader that your résumé is included in the correspondence, use the enclosure notation. If sending an attachment, indicate that instead. If your résumé is pasted in an e-mail, it is okay to eliminate this notation.

Now that you know the bare minimum, it is time to review the real meat of your cover letter: what you have to offer a prospective employer. As with your résumé, your focus in the letter has to be what you can offer the employer rather than what you are hoping to gain. It may be okay for a new graduate to include that he or she has always wanted to pursue a career in social work due to a sense of wanting to give back to the world. But this needs to be followed up, and quickly, with what that student can offer the employer. It can be okay to express enthusiasm for a position, as long as you can demonstrate how that enthusiasm can be to the employer's advantage. Your job is to sell yourself to the employer. Following the sale, you need to keep your promises (if you hope to be able to continue selling yourself as you progress through your career).

If you find the idea of "sales" intimidating or off-putting, think of it this way: Approach everything you do in your job campaign as if you were the employer. What is it that you would be looking for? What qualities do you want to see? Then think about how you can best relate what you have to offer to what the employer needs.

Imagine you just found the most amazing cell phone you had ever used. It came with every feature you could imagine, was reliable, had a guarantee, and fit within your budget. Would you tell your friends about it? Probably. Would you think that you were selling the product? Not likely. You were just doing your friends a favor by telling them about it.

In your job search, you are the product. In your cover letter, you are telling an employer or recruiter about the great product.

The difference between how you sell yourself in your résumé and how you sell yourself in your cover letter is the purpose and the delivery. The purpose of your résumé is to present your benefits to an employer in a document that, while tailored to your desired position, is not tailored to individual companies or specific positions. Your cover letter, on the other hand, is ideally addressed to a specific person with hiring power at a specific company. If possible, you will have researched the company or, if responding to a blind ad (one that does not list the hiring company), researched the industry. This research allows you to tailor your cover letter to that specific field. Through your research, you may be able to address how your qualifications can fill a need at the company. If responding to an advertisement, you can address how your qualifications are the perfect match for the requirements listed in the ad. Except for a direct mailing campaign, just as you would not send the same letter to all of your friends (okay, those Christmas letters may be the exception), you will not send the exact cover letter for each position you apply for. This is both the beauty and the difficulty of cover letters.

The beauty is that you can address your qualifications that are perfect for the position that may not be as readily visible in your résumé, such as specialized skills or experience. You can also give an employer an idea of your personality. Keep in mind that you do not want to repeat verbatim information on your résumé in your cover letter. You want to reword the information or summarize multiple points on your résumé while still quantifying your achievements where possible.

The difficulty with the individualized cover letter is that you will be writing a new, or mostly new, letter for each position you apply for. Those who do not like to write may find this daunting. There are a few tips, however, that make this process easier. First, keep in mind that you probably will not have to change the entire letter. Obviously, you will change the contact name and company, and address the position to which you are applying or for which you would like to be considered. But once you have a basic format, you can make appropriate changes to the body of the letter, which is where you highlight your qualifications—the meat of the letter.

Just as with the résumé, a cover letter will rarely be longer than one page. Three to four concise paragraphs are about as long as it needs to be. Longer cover letters are generally reserved for those with extensive experience, those changing careers, and those in highly technical fields. None of the examples in this book exceed one page.

How do you write this stuff? Let us turn to the pros. Your cover letter has two important distinctions: One, it is a marketing document designed to sell a product (you); two, it is a business document that, while giving a glimpse of your personality, needs to remain professional. It therefore stands to reason that lessons from those who sell, and those who write for business, can teach all of us a little something about composing an effective letter.

Selling Yourself

Ah, advertisers. They try to suck us in within a matter of seconds. Sound familiar? Hiring managers typically spend less than 30 seconds reviewing a cover letter or résumé—unless it grabs their attention enough so that they read on. The average television commercial is 30 seconds long. What about print? How long do you spend looking at an ad in a magazine before flipping the page? Or reading a bulletin board along the freeway (assuming you are not stuck in rush hour traffic)? Those who write ad copy have to get a message across quickly. That means sharp, succinct, to-the-point writing.

What are you really selling? Yes, you are selling yourself and all that you have to offer: Your skills, your experience, your attitude, and your personality. But think about it for a moment. Is that what you are *really* selling? Take the example of a health club membership. What is it that members are buying when they join the club? Access to classes and a large variety of strength training and cardio equipment? Sure, at the outset it looks like this is what you buy when you sign that one-year contract. In reality, health clubs are selling a desire: a desire to be thin, a desire to be muscular, a desire to be healthier. This is what a health club is really selling, not the fancy equipment and wide range of classes.

When you are selling yourself to an employer, think about what you are really selling. What is the employer buying? An employee who shows up to work, does the job, and leaves? Or a person who can come to work and identify and solve problems—someone who can fill the need of the company to make money. To do that, the company needs employees who can save money, make money, or save time, which in turn saves money. Identify a need and offer a solution, which is the benefit to the employer. Who can find hidden costs and eliminate them? Who is great at sales? Does this company need someone efficient? When you identify a specific need and show how you can meet that need, you become someone who will be a benefit to the company, not merely just another employee.

Think about how you can sell technical skills, for example. You can list all the technical skills that you have, such as software, hardware, and computer networking. This is like listing the features of the cell phone mentioned earlier. Or you can demonstrate how your knowledge of accounting software allowed you to introduce a better program at your summer position as an intern, thereby reducing time spent creating reports by 40 percent. The first method is simply a list of features. The second method demonstrates the benefit gained from putting those features (your knowledge) to work.

Marcia Yudkin, in *Pursuading on Paper* (Penguin Books, 1996), summarizes it well when she writes, "Benefits motivate, while features merely inform." What makes you different? Refer to everything you learned about yourself from your assessments. Pull together your accomplishments from your résumé, and show in your cover letter why you are a benefit to the company—because you can accomplish X, Y, and Z. Go beyond simply stating your features.

Know your audience Whom are you writing to? What would this person care about? When writing your letters, imagine that you are an employee of the company. What would you like to know about? This is what you need to put in your letter. What is the atmosphere in the company? Is it corporate or a small, family-owned business? How you would address a hiring manager of a Fortune 500 company is very different from how you would address the CEO of a mid-sized private company.

Who will be reading your letter? Will it be someone in human resources or the head of the department? If you are writing to human resources, for example, be sure to write in "plain" English rather than using a lot of technical jargon. If you are writing to a senior scientist, you will need to demonstrate your knowledge of the terminology used in your field, or you may come off looking inept. You must write a personalized letter every time, keeping your audience in mind.

Back up your claims So, you say you are good at obtaining contracts. Great. Now prove it. When writing your letters, do not simply state what you are good at. Show it. Give examples. Mine your past and come up with every possible example you can think of where you used the skills you claim to have. Make a list, and then choose the best ones to include in your letter. If you have a lot to choose from, keep the list so you can use different examples with each subsequent letter you send to a company.

Write professionally Remember that your letters are much different from your résumé. You will not use the telegraphic style that you did in your résumé. You must write complete sentences. Use words instead of abbreviations. Use the active voice and sprinkle your letters with action verbs. Keep your correspondence brief and to the point. Do not include irrelevant information. Use a tone that exudes professionalism, not amateurism. Avoid using clichés and slang, and avoid any references to political or religious beliefs.

What Makes a Letter?

Following the header and company contact information, your letter has three primary components: the introduction, the body, and the closing. Each has a distinct purpose.

The opening of your letter is where you want to hook your reader in, just as an advertisement's goal is to grab the reader's attention. How can you hook your reader immediately, while still conveying the important information such as the job for which you are applying or the type of job you would like to find? One handy trick is to use a "RE:" line or similar header between the company contact information and the opening paragraph. Don't begin your letter with the tired line of, "Please see the enclosed résumé in response to your advertisement for the position of X listed on January 1st of the *Daily News*." Yawn. Not much of an attention-grabber is it? Using the "RE:" line, you can include the position title at the top of your letter and instead focus on selling yourself in your opening paragraph. See the examples in this book of how writers use the opening paragraph to entice the reader.

Once you have your reader's attention, you have the opportunity to hit 'em hard with what you can offer a prospective employer. The body of your letter will focus on your accomplishments. This is where you will review your résumé and company research. You do not want to repeat word-for-word what your résumé says; find a way to reword your accomplishments, or introduce new ones related to the specific position you are aiming for. Because you will have done some company research, you can gear your letter toward the needs of that company. Target the body of your letter and demonstrate that you are familiar with the company and that you are the right person for the job. Again, review the samples in this book to see how the body of the letter is focused on showing what the candidate can offer. The idea here is that what you have done in the past is a reflection of what you will do in the future—show off your abilities!

The conclusion of your letter is where you explicitly state why you are writing—to gain an interview. Ask for the interview. Rather than using "I look forward to hearing from you," try something along the lines of "I will be contacting you within the next week to see when we can meet." Is it more aggressive? Yes. Do you want the interview? If you prefer something a little more subdued, even a closing along the lines of "I look forward to speaking with you about what I can bring to the position" is better than the overused lines of the past. When composing your conclusion, take into consideration your personality and the position. If you say you will be contacting the person in the next week, you need to make the call. (This approach also gives you legitimate reason to bypass the person answering the phone, because you can now say that so-and-so is expecting your call.) See the examples for more ideas on closing paragraphs.

Layout

There are three basic layouts to use when writing your letter: the paragraph style, bulleted lists, or the "T" layout, also known as an executive layout.

The paragraph style is exactly how it sounds. Each part of the letter is written in paragraph form. Just because you are using this form, however, does not give you license to ramble on. Keep your sentences short, but vary the length of each just a little. Keep your paragraphs short as well. Remember to keep your reader in mind. If your job were to screen applicants, reading tens or even hundreds of cover letters per week, would you take the time to wade through a lengthy letter? Screeners look for any reason to put your application in the rejection pile. Do not make it easy for them.

Cover letters using a bulleted list typically open and close with a paragraph style; the body of the letter is presented in bullets. Again, do not make the mistake of copying bulleted points directly from your résumé and pasting them into your cover letter. Hiring managers do not need or want to read your information twice.

The "T" or executive format takes its name from the design of the layout. In this format, the body of the letter is presented in two columns: Your Requirements and My Qualifications. This letter is best used for responses to ads placed by employers or recruiters. (See the example of this style on page 198.) When using this format, it is necessary that your qualifications meet, or preferably exceed, the employer's requirements. Otherwise your shortfalls will be glaringly obvious. As a new graduate, it may be difficult to meet all the requirements of a position. Be careful when using this format.

If you do not meet all the requirements, does this mean that you should not apply for the position? If you meet most of the requirements, go ahead and apply for the job, but choose the paragraph or bullet style letter. Employers realize that they will likely not find someone who fits the exact description; they are listing their wish list. If, however, you fall short by quite a bit, look for something that more closely matches your profile.

The actual writing process

Before you begin, make some notes about what you want to cover. Which of your accomplishments best sell you for the particular job you are applying for? What aspects of your personality do you want to express? As with résumé writing, if you are feeling stuck, you can use a few tricks to get the writing going. Free writing can help you get going. Instead of trying to craft the perfect letter the first time, just start writing. You can edit later. For now, write ideas as they come to you. It may also be helpful to take some time after you have written your first draft of a letter. Even leaving the writing for a few hours or over night can give your mind a chance to rest. You never know when the right wording may come to you: while you are brushing your teeth, watching a movie, or going for a run.

It may also be helpful to start with the easier parts of the letter first. There is no rule saying you have to write the letter in the order that it is read. If the closing line comes more naturally to you, start with that. Sometimes it helps get ideas flowing just to fill in the name of the addressee and company.

One of the more difficult parts of the letter to write will be the body, where you will do the hardest "selling." This section will highlight the specific accomplishments and skills that you offer an employer. There is a common phrase used by creative writers: "Show, don't tell." For example, rather than telling a reader that the main character is angry, the writer might show it by having the character throw a plate at a wall. The action does the "talking" and is much more engaging for the reader. Similarly, when presenting your accomplishments and skills, focus on the showing. Rather than telling your reader that you work well with others, show how you led your project team to an A+ grade by acting as project manager. As with your résumé, focus on using action verbs.

No matter what format you decide to use for your cover letter, keep your writing tight and concise. Wherever possible, cut, cut, and cut some more. Take this example from the local news: "Over the next year, one in three people over the age of 65 will suffer a fall." In other words, "One third of those over 65 will fall next year." Seventeen words are cut down to 10. Whenever possible, use one word instead of two or more. For example, instead of writing "in an accurate manner," write "accurately." Also focus on shorter words instead of longer ones. Instead of "utilize," say "use." Do not try to impress your reader by scouring the thesaurus for words that you think will make you look smarter. You will only end up with a jumble of words that confuses your reader, if your reader stays with your letter long enough to get confused. Because your letter is more likely to be skimmed rather than read through thoroughly (at least the first time), you will lose your reader in a matter of seconds if you opt for lengthy, perplexing declarations.

Tone

Your résumé does not give a hiring manager much insight into who you are as a person, what your personality is like, or why you are corresponding with him or her. Your cover letter, on the other hand, is an opportunity to show that you are a real person. While it is important to remember that your cover letter is still a business document you should use this opportunity to give a glimpse of who you are; and the beauty of this is that you are in total control of what you let the reader see. How you present yourself and what you show your reader will be up to you; however, there are some things to keep in mind.

Both your personality and the position for which you are applying will factor into the tone you use in your cover letter. Someone applying for a demanding sales position would be wise to use a more aggressive tone in their letter than someone applying for a social services position in a long-term healthcare facility. You can use these factors to your advantage by determining what you want your reader to know about you.

Again, the primary focus is on how you can meet your reader's needs. What can you demonstrate through your personality and attitude that can help put the polish on your sales pitch? Take the time to experiment with how you write your letter and how you approach your prospective employer. Ask a few friends to read the letter; what impression do they get from your presentation? Take notes and make adjustments until your readers are left with the impression you want to leave.

Types of Cover Letters

How you write your letter and which format you choose will be determined in part by the type of letter you are writing. The following is a list of some situations you may find yourself responding to in your letters.

Responding to an advertisement

This letter is what is typically thought of when responding to a newspaper classified advertisement, but it also refers to online job postings and similar postings found through government agencies such as the job service where you are instructed to contact the company directly rather than go through the agency.

When responding to a posting, read the advertisement carefully for hints about what the employer is seeking. The listing is likely to have keywords scattered throughout. Use these keywords when composing your letter, but be careful not to repeat the ad word for word. Use your own voice.

The "T" letter format is often useful when replying to a job posting, because the requirements of the job are listed in the ad. However, be wary of using this format if you do not meet all the requirements. You want to highlight your qualifications that match rather than point out where you are weak. If you do not meet all the requirements listed, this will be obvious in the "T" format. Instead, opt for a paragraph or bullet style letter.

If a contact name is not listed in the ad, call the company and do some research, unless the ad specifies "no calls." Always respect this request; if you do not, you may lose out on an interview even before you submit a résumé. Otherwise, try and get a contact name so that you can address your letter appropriately. People like to be acknowledged, and taking the time to find this information can work in your favor by showing your attention to detail and willingness to take the extra step.

Before composing your letter, do some research on the company. Many companies now have websites. You can also check with your local reference librarian. He or she can direct you to resources that track company information. If the targeted business is a public company, you can also check the EDGAR database on the U.S. Securities and Exchange Commission website at http://www.sec.gov/edgar/searchedgar/webusers. htm. You may also want to try Hoover's online at http://www.hoovers.com, and, of course, try Google at http://www.google.com and type the name of the company you are looking for or the name of the field you are investigating followed by the word "companies." If you happen to know someone who works at your target company, do some networking, and, if appropriate, use your contact's name in your letter.

Once you have done your company research, you should have a better feel for the atmosphere of the business. Write in a tone that reflects company policy. Were you able to find the company's mission statement? If so, direct your letter to show how you can support that mission. Has the company recently won an award, been featured in an article, or been involved in a major business deal? While it may not be appropriate to gush or be overly congratulatory, mentioning the achievement could work to your advantage. It will demonstrate that you are "up" on what is going on with the company, which can only work in your favor.

"Blind" advertisements

The blind ad is nearly identical to any other job posting, except for one minor detail—it does not say who the hiring company is. This poses a few problems. One, if you are currently employed and do not want your employer to know you are looking, you could inadvertently send your résumé to your current employer. Two, you are unable to research the company. Three, you may wonder what the company is hiding when they place a blind ad and decide not to apply, even if it looks like a good fit. This could be a mistake.

Many companies place blind ads because they do not want to be inundated with phone calls or drop-ins. Smaller companies may not have the time or staff to deal with the influx when they list company information. Others may place a blind ad simply to test the market or to build their résumé files.

If you find a blind ad that seems to be a good fit, send in your résumé and cover letter. You may be able to determine the name of the company or at least find out if the ad was placed by your employer. Blind ads will most likely use a post office box number for receiving résumés. A call to the post office may lead you to the name of the company. When you call, ask for the name of the company renting the box. If you are given a "no," you can then ask if your current employer is the name of the company renting the box. You should at least be able to get that much information.

You will also run across job postings on the Internet that provide minimal company information. If there is no company website listed, you may be able to get some clues from the e-mail address. For example, if you are directed to send a résumé to hr@possiblecompanyname.com, go to the web and type possiblecompanyname.com and see if anything comes up. Whether or not you decide to apply to a posting online that provides little or no company information is up to you. Use your best judgment.

A few more words about searching online. The Internet delivers many promises through job boards and large résumé banks. It can be tempting (and so much easier) to post your résumé in a job bank or take advantage of one of the services that posts your résumé on numerous job banks. Keep in mind that these job banks host millions—yes, millions—of résumés. The competition is fierce. There is no guarantee. As enticing as the commercials are for this method of attaining employment, it is not the final solution to the ongoing problem of finding work. This is not to say that you should avoid the Internet; it is in your best interest to take advantage of all methods available for finding your dream job.

When using the Internet for your job search, you may want to consider using a separate e-mail address strictly for your job search. Hotmail, Yahoo!, and others provide free e-mail addresses that you can access from any computer that has an Internet connection. This will help you keep better track of your job search and also ensure that the information you post online will not lead someone to your personal e-mail.

There are bogus listings on the Internet. Remember to never give out important personal information such as your social security number when applying to listings online. You may also decide to remove your personal contact information for listings that are questionable, providing only your "job search" e-mail address.

Because you may be unable to obtain any company information, you will have to use your best judgment when composing your letter if you opt to apply to a vague online listing. Instead of speaking to specific company needs, address the needs of the industry, stressing how you are able to meet them.

Responding to recruiter's ads

Letters to recruiter's ads will be very similar to letters written to other job postings, with two exceptions. Whereas in almost all other situations you want to avoid listing salary information, it is necessary to inform a recruiter of your salary requirements. For someone new to the workforce, it may be necessary to do some research. Again, check with a reference librarian. A librarian can direct you to salary information resources based on your field. You can also do salary research online. Monster.com's Salary Center allows you to search by field. The Occupational Handbook Online also lists general salary information by job type at http://www.bls.gov/oco/. You can also find salary information through the following sites:

http://www.Collegegrad.com
http://www.CollegeRecruiter.com
http://www.CampusCareerCenter.com
http://www.Job-Hunt.org

When providing salary information to recruiters, list a range rather than a specific number. You do not want to place yourself too high or too low—this is why your research is so important.

The other piece of information you need to provide to recruiters is whether or not you are willing to relocate. Some recruiters place national ads. You need to let them know if you are willing to move and if you have any special considerations in regard to relocating.

Keep in mind that recruiters work for the employer, not for you. Be respectful of their time and knowledge. Do not pretend to know more about job hunting than a recruiter, and always use professionalism when contacting and working with a recruiter. But do not rely on a recruiter to find you a job.

Cold call letters to employers

You have done your research and found the perfect company. Problem is, they are not hiring at the moment. Should you give up and look elsewhere? No! Should you slap together a cover letter and send your résumé asking the company to keep your information on file in the event that something opens up? Not exactly. Through your research, you found either an area of the company that is perfect for you, or better yet you identified a need that you can fill.

When sending a cold call letter, go above and beyond every other candidate that simply asks to be kept on file. Use the advice in this book and show an employer who you are and what you have to offer. Because you are not responding to a specific ad, the subject line may not be appropriate for this type of letter (although this is not to say it can never work). Make it clear who you are and what you do. Rather than writing, "I am a *title* seeking a position in *department*," say something along the lines of "I am a *title* who can offer . . ." and go into the rest of your letter outlining what you bring to the table. Say, "I can solve this problem for you."

Just as in other types of letters, address your letter to a specific person. You may find that there are multiple people within a company to whom you can send your letter. How do you decide? Send a letter to each person on your list. You

never know which department may have an opportunity, and you cannot count on your résumé being circulated throughout the company.

Cold call letters to recruiters

Cold call letters to recruiters are similar to cold call letters to companies. Before writing your letters, however, you need to do some research. Recruiters specialize, and you should approach one that works in your field. Otherwise you are simply wasting their time and your efforts. Also pay attention to what career level recruiters work with; many choose only to place candidates for jobs over $100,000. And as already mentioned, remember that recruiters work for the employer, not for you.

When writing to recruiters, just as when writing to companies, you need to make it clear who you are and what you do. You also need to clarify specifics related to the type of job you are seeking. Sales, for example, covers a broad range; recruiters need detailed information from you as far as what you are willing to accept. You will also need to include a salary range that you are seeking and if you are willing to relocate and to where. For more information on recruiters, refer to http://www.TheRecruiterNetwork.com.

Direct mail campaigns

This type of letter campaign is less focused than a cold call letter to a company in that you are sending hundreds of letters to potential employers. Aside from the contact information, these letters are not geared specifically to each company, because that would be too time consuming for your purpose.

In the direct mail campaign, you create a cover letter introducing yourself and the type of position you are seeking. You then show why you are qualified for this type of employment before sending it to as many companies that hold potential for what you are seeking. This approach is time consuming, requires some research, and is not as likely to produce the desired results as are targeted letters. Many people who read these letters recognize when the writer has not put in the effort to target the letter to the specific company. But then again, you never know when you might get a lead, so use your discretion when exploring this method.

Broadcast letters

This type of letter is rarely used for anyone below the executive level. It can also be effective for career changers and those who have not worked in a number of years but have previous work experience. The format of the broadcast letter combines the cover letter and résumé into one document and is sent in place of both. It is longer than a typical cover letter and sent to a few specifically selected companies. Because this type of letter is generally not recommended for a recent graduate, it is not covered in greater detail here.

Letters following referral

If you have been referred to a position or company by someone working in the company or by someone with contacts in the business, you need to mention this in your letter. When you introduce yourself, mention that so-and-so suggested you contact your reader. If appropriate, mention any specifics from the conversation with your referral and any insider information you have been provided with. If you have ever heard that it is rude to "name drop," this is not the time to follow that advice.

Follow-up letters

The follow-up letter is sent after you submit your application materials and before you hear anything from the company. If, after a reasonable amount of time, you have not heard anything about your candidacy, you may send a follow-up letter. This type of letter could also be used if you have or have not heard back but notice that the position you applied for is listed again. It could be that the company hired someone and it did not work out, that they decided not to fill the position at the original time, or any other number of reasons.

Your follow-up letter is yet another chance to put your name in front of the hiring committee. Address the letter to the same person you sent your original materials, but *also list the position title of that person*. It could be that you never heard anything because the person doing the hiring was promoted or is no longer with the company. In the letter, state that you are following-up the correspondence you sent on such-and-such a date regarding the position. Follow the format similar to that of your original cover letter. In the first paragraph, remind the person of who you are and the position you are seeking. Follow this by more examples of your qualifications, achievements, and education. Do not use the same wording as you did in your previous correspondence.

When composing new letters, use the "save as" function when creating new letters based on the old ones. This way you can track what you have already sent to an employer and eliminate the risk of sending the same wording twice. In the closing, state that you are still interested in the position and ask for an interview.

If you were referred by a company employee, send a follow-up letter to this person as well. Thank the referral again for the information they provided about the company and position. Inform your referral that you sent your application materials on such-and-such a date and that you are following-up on the status of your candidacy. Follow this by reminding him or her of your qualifications. End the letter by stating that you are still interested in the position, and ask your contact for information about the status of the position.

Sponsor letter

A sponsor letter is not written by you but by a professional in your field who writes one of his or her contacts on your behalf. These letters can be especially useful in getting your foot in the door for an interview; they do not guarantee you a job offer. It is up to you to make the best impression at an interview and act as professionally as you would in any other situation. Because your sponsor is putting his or her reputation on the line when speaking for you, it is in your best interest to do all you can to live up to the recommendation.

Always send a thank you letter to the person who wrote a sponsor letter on your behalf, regardless of whether or not you were given an interview and regardless of the outcome. This person took time out from a busy schedule to do you a favor.

E-mailing cover letters

Letters that are e-mailed take a different approach than do letters that are mailed or faxed. With the prolific use of e-mail these days, it is generally considered acceptable to e-mail your letters. They get to the recipient fast (which can be very useful when writing thank you letters) and allow the reader to respond easily as well.

When submitting your résumé by e-mail, you need to follow a few guidelines. First and foremost, do not send your résumé only as an attachment, unless the company specifically requests this method. Most businesses are wary

of viruses and worms and will forward any messages with attachments directly into the junk e-mail folder for deletion. That said, if no guidelines are given, you may want to consider pasting your résumé (see the information on creating your ASCII résumé on page 210) into the body of the e-mail and also attaching the "pretty" version as an attachment. In your letter, inform the reader that your résumé is pasted below and also attached. Another possibility is to upload your résumé onto a web page and send the URL in addition to pasting your résumé in the e-mail. One word of caution if doing this—whatever link you send to a potential employer, make sure that it contains only your résumé and any additional information that specifically supports you as a serious candidate. Do not send a link to your personal web page that includes pictures of you with your dog and boyfriend, a detailed account of your recent skiing vacation in Utah, and, oh yeah, your résumé.

Whatever you decide, when sending your résumé by e-mail, always paste the ASCII version of it in the body of the e-mail, even if you opt to give the employer additional methods of viewing your credentials.

You will not send an attachment of your cover letter, for the reasons already noted. Nor will you copy and paste your cover letter into the e-mail. Rather, you will take the most important elements of your hard copy cover letter and create a much shorter version that you will use in your e-mail correspondence. The basics remain the same: You will introduce yourself, state your most hard-hitting qualifications, and ask for an interview. Did you notice something missing in this last list? How will the employer know what position you are seeking? When e-mailing, you will use the subject line of the e-mail to state your desired position as well as throw in a very succinct tag line about your qualifications. Remember the discussion of how advertisers write to grab your attention immediately? Here you will use the same concept to write a one-liner about who you are and what you do. For example, an engineering graduate's subject line could read:

Cum Laude grad seeks entry level civil eng. position

The subject line essentially replaces the "RE:" line discussed earlier. This allows you to jump right in immediately on your introduction and qualifications. Because e-mail is a "fast" medium, you want to write a short letter. The other reason for writing a short letter is that you want your best highlights to be viewable when the recipient opens the message. If the reader has to scroll through the message to find out who you are, what you have done, and why you are writing, your message is more likely to be deleted.

Aim for about four to five lines for your e-mail cover letter. The first line will be your introduction. Using the example of the engineer, it could read, "Could your office use a Civil Engineering graduate with a proven history of leading projects to completion and under budget?" This will be followed by an example or two of your qualifications. "As project leader, I led our five-member team to develop a $500,000 parking lot design for XYZ company that not only received a grade A, but was also used by the client." After listing another qualification or two, end your letter by stating that your résumé is pasted below and ask for an interview. Then remember, of course, to paste your résumé below.

As with any cover letter, you still want to address your e-mail to a specific person. If possible, find the e-mail address of the person with the hiring power rather than sending your résumé to the human resources or an administrative generic e-mail address. Browse through the company website; this may lead you to the address. If you know the name of your desired contact but not his or her e-mail address, call and say you need to send some information to so-and-so and could you please have the e-mail address. If you do not know a contact name or e-mail, try to obtain the desired information.

Many companies have forms on their websites specifically for uploading your résumé. These systems are often automated and will send you an automated response when you have successfully uploaded your information. By all means, use this form; however, if you also have a referral or contact name (or names), send a separate e-mail to those persons as well. While your résumé sits in the automated system, you could hear something immediately when sending it to a direct contact within the company.

Insert your contact information—all of it—following the cover letter portion of your e-mail. This includes your name, address, telephone number(s), and e-mail address. Just because you are e-mailing does not mean that you should provide only an e-mail address as a way for an employer to contact you, unless you do not want to be contacted. And as previously mentioned, it is a good idea to set-up an e-mail account specifically for your job search. Not only does this help you track your contacts better, but it also eliminates the use of a "cutesy" e-mail address that you think is incredibly clever but an employer may find offensive or childish.

Following your cover letter, copy and paste your résumé into the e-mail, but delete your header. You do not need to list your contact information twice, because your cover letter and résumé are now one document instead of two. If you attach your résumé as well, do not alter that version. Should it be printed and separated from your e-mail, you want the employer to know how to contact you.

Chapter 11

Other Types of Letters

Your written correspondence with a potential employer does not end with the cover letter that you send with your résumé. Nor does your contact with networking associates end with a phone call. Your job search and subsequent career is filled with written correspondence. Letter writing is a fact of business life. With the tips presented here, and a little practice, you can become an expert letter writer.

When it comes to your job search, letter writing can be used as a powerful tool. As discussed, these letters can take the form of hard copy or e-mail. Whichever methods you employ (and it will probably be both), you want to take advantage of letter writing. It is yet another way to put your name in front of an employer's eyes. Letters are also a method to remind an employer of your qualifications and the reasons why you are the person for the job. The following is an overview of some of the letters you may find yourself writing (note that some are not optional!). Much of what is written here is common sense. But if you are caught up in the angst of looking for a job, or if you have not thought much about it before, some reminders follow to keep in mind as you develop your job search and subsequent career.

Networking letters

Networking letters are very similar to networking phone calls, except in written form. For those who are extremely shy, writing a letter to a networking contact before making a phone call can help ease nerves. Your contact has an idea that you will be calling (because you will have told him or her) and can be prepared for your call. The letter helps reduce the fear of "cold calling" your contacts.

The letter can also be a useful tool if you are unable to contact a network associate by phone. People are very busy; if you find yourself continually running into voice mail, the letter can be a useful alternative.

When writing your networking letters, observe the same courtesies in the letter as you would in a phone call. Respect the reader's time. Rarely will you need to write a letter longer than one page. Following some niceties, such as mentioning the last time you saw the contact or mentioning something you have in common, get to the point. You are currently looking for a job, and because your contact is an expert in the field/has a large contact base/whatever is appropriate, you are writing to inquire if the contact may have any suggestions for you in your search or if he/she would be willing to provide information, pass your name along, and so on as is appropriate for your situation. *Do not ask for an interview or for a job!* This is not the point of contacting your network. Your purpose is to gain information, conduct an informational interview, and perhaps gain a lead, but you must be careful in how you approach your reader. If you are unsure of your wording, have a friend or relative read the letter to give you an impression. Review the information on networking provided in this book. At the end of your letter, ask if you can meet to discuss your job search or for an informational interview.

Thank you to a networking contact

Whenever you have contact with someone in your networking circle who is directly related to your job search and career, send that person a thank you letter. Thank him or her for the time and effort put into helping you and for any information that you took away from the conversation (or e-mail or letter).

As you will do for a follow-up thank you letter after an interview, you may want to highlight a few areas in your letter as a result of your communications with this person. If you were given an immediate lead, or if the contact agreed to read and critique or forward your résumé, be sure to say a thank you for this as well. If the conversation led a certain way, or did not go as you planned, you can use this opportunity to reiterate points or make new ones. As with all your job search correspondence, this is another opportunity to sell your wares. Although you

are not asking for a job, you do want to make sure you are presenting as much positive information about yourself as possible so that the contact can act appropriately on your behalf.

After the Interview: More than "Just" a Thank You
Thank you letter following an interview

You survived the interview! Take a deep breath, and start thinking about your thank you letter.

This one is a biggie, and it is not optional. During the interview, you will have brought a pad of paper and pen with you (see more on this in the chapters on interviewing). If it is not awkward to do so, take notes during the interview. This will make you appear professional and interested in the job. Make notes of things you want to mention or address in your follow-up letter. Upon leaving the interview, take a few moments to jot down a few more reminders. Do this before you start your car or hop on the bus to go home. While you may think you will not forget anything, chances are you might, so do not skip this step.

Immediately upon arriving home, fire up your computer (or head to the library if you do not have a computer) and start composing a thank you letter to the person or persons with whom you just interviewed. If you met more than one person, address a separate letter to each one, using different wording and stressing different points for each one. For example, if one interviewer seemed concerned about your lack of work experience, address those fears in your letter, showing why your experience qualifies you for the position. If another seemed concerned that you lack the necessary technical skills to do the job, address those fears in the letter to that person by showing how you learn quickly. In other words, customize your letters. Just as you customize your initial cover letters when submitting your résumé, you need to customize the thank you letter as well. A "canned" letter that you send to every contact will be obvious and will leave a negative last impression. You want the employer to be even more impressed with you following an interview, not less. As with the other letters, keep it brief, but respect the valuable tool you have in front of you.

The thank you letter can serve many purposes. First and foremost, it is proper business etiquette, and it will set you apart from other candidates who choose to skip this step (and an alarmingly high number do). Second, it is yet another chance to make an impression on the employer and show why you are the ideal person for the job.

In your letter, first thank the interviewer for taking the time to meet you and reiterate your interest in the position. Then, as with your original cover letter, address the points that show that you are the person for the job. The direction of the interview will determine what you decide to focus on in your thank you letter. You may want to reemphasize your experience and skills in a particular area that was mentioned. Or, if you forgot to mention important information or an opportunity to discuss it never arose, this is the place to do so. Perhaps the conversation moved toward some mutual interests. You may want to mention this to jog the person's memory, just in case. Remember, people tend to hire those who are similar to themselves.

Perhaps the interviewer specifically mentioned some areas of concern (this is quite likely and can occur in almost any interview). Use your thank you letter to address those concerns. Is the interviewer concerned about your ability to work on a team? Show how you

worked with other volunteers on a local community project. Did the interviewer express concerns over your lack of technical skills? Show the employer that you completed your senior project using the latest and greatest design software. Whatever the issue, mention it in your letter and show how you do in fact have the necessary skills. For example, you could write, "You mentioned concerns about my ability to work on a team. Let me assure you that I possess the necessary skills to work with other members on a project. For example, I recently served on a volunteer committee to develop plans for a local park. Not only did I work with several other members of the community, but I also conducted extensive research regarding the costs associated with the project." This not only addresses the employer's fear (that you lack the ability to work on a team), but it also conveniently ties in another of your skills—the ability to conduct research.

Did you forget to mention something in the interview, or did the conversation not allow for a natural place to discuss specific experience you wanted to mention? Use the letter to show that you have that experience. As you did in your original cover letter, highlight your experience using strong action verbs and writing in the active voice. You can present the missed information using a paragraph or bullet style—just be sure to include the information.

Now that you know more about the job, you may decide that you need to introduce additional information about yourself that is not on your résumé. Use your thank you letter as a selling tool to show how you have just the skills to address the requirements mentioned by the interviewer. Remember, the interviewer is looking for someone to solve a problem; that is, he or she needs a person to do a specific job, and until someone is hired, there exists a problem.

How can you solve this problem? Show that you can come into the workplace and make an immediate difference because of your background/skills/education that supports the goals of the position.

After you have composed your letter, print a copy and review it for errors. If necessary, find a second pair of eyes to proof it for you. When you are satisfied with the letter, which needs to be finished and sent within 24 hours, send the letter as either a hard copy, or, if doing so seems appropriate (such as in a technical field, for example), send it by e-mail. If you choose to use e-mail, remember to keep your letter short and to the point, just as you would with an e-mailed cover letter.

By sending your letter immediately, you keep your name in front of the person with the hiring power. You remind that person of your qualifications and have yet another chance to sell yourself for the position. And you make a good impression by demonstrating your professionalism, drive, and attention to detail.

Acceptance letter

Congratulations! You aced the interview with flying colors. You have been offered a job and have discussed all the particulars. Now you need to put it in writing.

Even if the interviewers tell you a formal job offer is in the mail, it is still a good idea for you to write your own letter thanking the company for the position, expressing your enthusiasm about working there, and outlining the details of employment as you understand them. It will often take the company a few days to compile your offer letter; you can put together a quick letter and get it in the mail immediately. Then, should any discrepancies in the understanding of the terms occur, you will be able to discuss these immediately before you sign the formal acceptance letter or agreement.

Letters to other employers

If you have interviewed with other companies and have not received a response, it is common courtesy to send a letter to them, explaining that you have accepted a position elsewhere. If you were in the running, this allows the company to focus their time and efforts elsewhere. Thank them for their time and let them know you enjoyed meeting them. You want to maintain and build as many positive relationships as you can in your job search and throughout your career. You could face a layoff or leave your accepted position for a variety of reasons; if you project a positive and professional image to those you meet along the way, you will be much better off if you find yourself looking for employment again down the road.

Thank you letter following a rejection

You did everything correctly, but you still received that letter or phone call stating that you were not chosen for the position. This will happen. Not every job is for you, and not every interview will result in a job offer.

However, you can still use a thank you letter to your advantage. First, you do not want to burn any bridges. Second, if you are still interested in the company, you can express this in your letter. Third, you never know if the person who takes the job will work out, so if you are a close second, you have yet another chance to put your name in front of the hiring committee and project a positive image.

Thank the interviewer(s) for the time invested in meeting you. Express your best wishes for the company, and, if appropriate, state that you are still interested in working with the company. You may want to ask that your information be kept on file in the event of future openings.

Maintaining your professionalism on all levels is important. You never know what might happen in the future. You could be referred to another opportunity by the people who turned you down. Interviewers have been known to send their "second choices" to their network contacts. Just because you are not an exact match for one position does not mean that the people who have "rejected" you do not know of the perfect opportunity somewhere else. Keep those contacts open!

COLD CALL
COVER LETTERS

Abygael Brown

98 Ben Franklin Drive • Cherry Hill, New Jersey 07896 • abrown@aol.com • Work: (555) 333–3333

February 28, 2004

Attention: Doris Macka
Manager
Just It Clothing Warehouse
82 Christopher Street
New York, NY 10014

Dear Ms. Macka,

It is with great interest that I am forwarding my résumé for consideration as a Sales Assistant within your organization. Combining my previous experience within customer-centered environments with strong interpersonal and communication abilities, I am confident that you will quickly realize my ability to make major contributions to your organization. Therefore, I ask you to consider the following in addition to my enclosed résumé:

- Possess a great work ethic and superb team skills.

- Proven experience in customer service positions, including customer relations, cash handling, and point of sale operation.

- Ability to close major sale opportunities due to strong relationship building and presentation skills.

- Significant experience operating cash registers and other computerized equipment within stores.

- Excellent communication and interpersonal skills; takes initiative in managing client relationships and developing effective working relationships with clients.

- Ability to adapt quickly in new and changing business, social, and cultural environments.

My record of schoolwork, employment, and volunteer activities demonstrates attributes that make me a valuable employee. In all of my employment and volunteer positions, I have maintained an excellent record of being on time, prepared, and eager to take on new responsibilities.

My résumé is enclosed to provide you with details of my skills and accomplishments, but I am certain that a personal interview would more fully reveal my desire and ability to contribute to your organization. Thank you for your time and consideration, and do not hesitate to contact me if you have any questions. I look forward to speaking with you soon.

Sincerely,

Abygael Brown
Enclosed

GREGORY JOHN GARSON

9000 59th Street, Flatland, Texas 79000   *gg95@hotmail.com*   **(800) 555-0000**

P. O. Box 986, Green River, Texas 76000   **(543) 866-9900**

March 31, 2005

Karen M. Black
DAVID WELLS INC.
P.O. Box 9900
Border Town, Texas 72400

RE: **Summer 2004 Internship**

Dear Ms. Black:

I am very interested in applying for and receiving an **internship with David Wells, Inc.**, and have enclosed my résumé for your review and consideration. Having interned several summers for financial organizations and worked for my father, a representative and role model at David Wells, Inc. in Green River, I am no stranger to the arena. Plus, this first-hand observation of the financial industry has solidified my choice of careers, making me a sincere candidate for this internship.

I am concurrently working on **a master of science in family financial planning** while completing coursework for a **bachelor of business administration in finance** from Superior University. My goal is to earn a master's degree so that I may sit for the Certified Financial Planner (CFP) exam in spring of 2005.

Through exposure to the daily business operations of my father's David Wells office, I have learned:

- that David Wells is paramount in providing individuals with the investments, services, and information they need to achieve their financial goals.

- that meeting customer needs in a professional manner through personal contact is primary to success in the financial industry, and support your efforts to keep contacts face-to-face as opposed to utilizing impersonal Internet services.

- that David Wells rewards representatives who are self-motivated, profit-oriented achievers, decisive, and able to implement actions to benefit both the organization and its clients.

I am confident that I will be able to surpass expectations and make substantial contributions to your organization, and hope to begin my career as a member of a team such as that at David Wells.

A drive to succeed combined with my knowledge and previous experience make me a strong candidate for an internship at David Wells, Inc. Please do not hesitate to contact me should you desire additional information. I will be available for this internship from mid-May through mid-August of this year. I would welcome an interview at your convenience to further discuss my qualifications and prospects for serving your company.

Thank you for your time and consideration.

Sincerely,

Gregory John Garson

Enclosure: Résumé

Mary J. Hamilton

234 W 3rd Avenue • Marysville, California 95999
Home: 535-344-0555 • Cell: 535-511-9988 • E-mail: mjh@isp.com

March 15, 2003

Charles Martin
Director of Internships
Bear Creek Orchards
2564 Orange Drive
Oregon City, Oregon 96354

Dear Mr. Martin:

I am currently interested in an internship that involves learning about orchard production and management and would like to work for a company that specializes in agriculture production. I would welcome the opportunity to speak with you directly regarding internship opportunities within your company.

I am currently enrolled at California State University in Chico and will complete my Bachelor of Science in Agricultural Business in the spring of 2004. My record of school work, involvement in a sorority, and volunteer activities demonstrate attributes that make me a valuable employee. Included in my list of talents are:

- **Leadership Skills:** As a member of Kappa Sigma Delta I have held the following leadership roles: Fundraiser Chair, Secretary, Rookie Educator, and Vice President.

- **Reliability and Work Ethic:** In all my leadership roles and volunteer activities, I have maintained an excellent record of being on time, prepared, and eager to take on new responsibilities. I am very goal oriented and am able to get things done in a timely manner.

- **Community Involvement:** I have volunteered for such programs as Community Challenge, the Boys and Girls Club, Children's Miracle Network, and the Humane Society. I enjoy helping others and continually look for ways to help make my community a better place to live.

Please see the attached resume for a more detailed description of my skills and abilities. I look forward to speaking with you about the opportunity to intern with your company this summer. I can be reached at the above phone numbers. Please call me at your earliest convenience. Thank you for your time.

Sincerely,

Mary J. Hamilton

Enclosure

EVELYN MORRIS

556 Summit Drive • Englewood, NJ 07053 • (201) 577-9286 • Morris30@aol.com

January 6, 2003

Ms. Suzanne Reynolds
Director, Social Services
Borrin Correctional Institution
2299 Central Avenue
Englewood, NJ 07053

Dear Ms. Reynolds:

Becoming a social worker has been a lifelong dream of mine, and I have taken the first step toward fulfilling this dream. In May, I will graduate with a bachelor's degree. As part of my educational training, I am seeking an internship at the Borrin Correctional Institution to further develop my clinical social work skills while applying my training to benefit others.

Currently, I am completing a clinical internship at the Borrin Families in Crisis Center. This experience has not only taught me valuable lessons about human life, but has also reinforced my interest in employment in a correctional environment following graduation. My future plans include pursuing a master's degree in clinical social work.

Complementing my education in social work are both employment and volunteer experiences that relate to my career interests while adding to my skill development in this profession. Such experiences over the past several years have included employment as a medical assistant at a physician practice, providing support services to families of children with cancer at a community hospital, and volunteering at a crisis-counseling center. In addition, my professors and supervisor at the Borrin Families in Crisis Center have frequently commented on my natural aptitude for a career in social work.

Highly self-motivated with an energetic style, I am eager to learn new skills and enhance my education while contributing to your organization. My strengths also include communications, maturity, and the ability to relate effectively with individuals at all levels and cultural backgrounds as demonstrated throughout my prior career in business.

I look forward to discussing an internship opportunity at your institution and appreciate your consideration.

Sincerely,

Evelyn Morris

Rachel Smith

98 Ben Franklin Drive   Home: (609) 666–1111
Cherry Hill, New Jersey 07896   rachelsmith@aol.com   Home Fax: (609) 666–7777

February 24, 2004

HR Assistant
Human Resources
American Wildlife Sanctuary
New Jersey Parkway
NEW JERSEY NY 07896

Dear Sir/Madam,

RE: WILDLIFE ATTENDANT – PART TIME

It is with great interest that I am forwarding my résumé for consideration as a Wildlife Attendant within your organization. Combining my veterinary work experience with a long standing interest in wildlife and animal studies, I am confident that I possess the skills and—most importantly—the dedication and commitment to care for and raise the young farm animals in your petting zoo. Please consider the following in addition to my enclosed résumé:

- Compassionate and sensitive to the needs and emotions of animals.

- Proven experience implementing the proper care for various animals while completing work experience at the City & Country Veterinary Clinic and the Cherry Hill Veterinary Clinic. Included food preparation, cleaning of enclosures, treating minor injuries, ear cleaning, dog walking, and hydrobaths.

- Outstanding communication and people-to-people interaction skills, with the ability to connect with all people at all levels with confidence.

- Significant experience in customer service positions, including customer relations, cash handling, and point of sale operation.

- Excellent planning, time-management, and business writing skills as Treasurer/Secretary for Adventurers Scout Association. Involves also planning and coordinating unit activities and camps for the group.

Currently studying a Level 1 Nutritional Adviser Program (Animal Nutrition) at Cherry Hill State High School, I am hoping to do further studies and work experience within the wildlife and animal field, enabling me to embark upon a career within this industry. I believe I have the necessary personal and social qualities, as well as the relevant experience, to do this important work.

My résumé is enclosed to provide you with details of my skills and accomplishments, but I am certain that a personal interview would more fully reveal my desire and ability to contribute to your organization. Thank you for your time and consideration, and do not hesitate to contact me if you have any questions. I look forward to speaking with you soon.

Sincerely,

Rachel Smith
Enclosed

DIRECT MAIL
COVER LETTERS

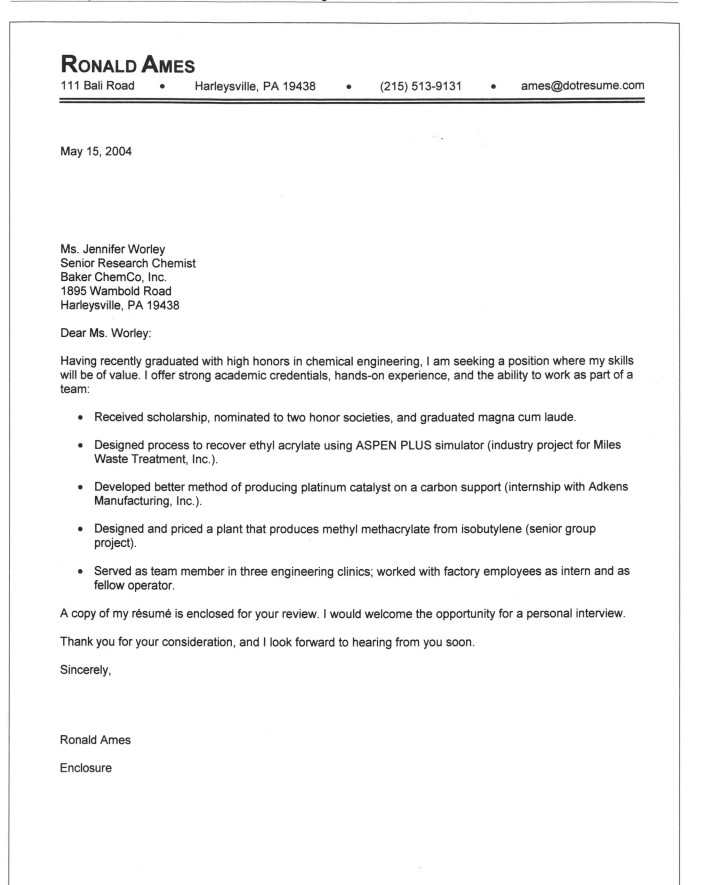

RONALD AMES

111 Bali Road   •   Harleysville, PA 19438   •   (215) 513-9131   •   ames@dotresume.com

May 15, 2004

Ms. Jennifer Worley
Senior Research Chemist
Baker ChemCo, Inc.
1895 Wambold Road
Harleysville, PA 19438

Dear Ms. Worley:

Having recently graduated with high honors in chemical engineering, I am seeking a position where my skills will be of value. I offer strong academic credentials, hands-on experience, and the ability to work as part of a team:

- Received scholarship, nominated to two honor societies, and graduated magna cum laude.

- Designed process to recover ethyl acrylate using ASPEN PLUS simulator (industry project for Miles Waste Treatment, Inc.).

- Developed better method of producing platinum catalyst on a carbon support (internship with Adkens Manufacturing, Inc.).

- Designed and priced a plant that produces methyl methacrylate from isobutylene (senior group project).

- Served as team member in three engineering clinics; worked with factory employees as intern and as fellow operator.

A copy of my résumé is enclosed for your review. I would welcome the opportunity for a personal interview.

Thank you for your consideration, and I look forward to hearing from you soon.

Sincerely,

Ronald Ames

Enclosure

BEA K. BILLINGSLY
5555 55TH STREET
FLATLAND, TEXAS 79000
BKBILL5533@HOTMAIL.COM

(555) 555-5555

August 25, 2004

Brad Collingsworth
Superintendent
Flatland ISD
2222 88th Street
Flatland, Texas 79000

"Be the change you want to see in the world."
~~ **Mahatma Gandhi**

Dear Superintendent Collingsworth:

As graduation from Flatland University with a ***BS in interdisciplinary studies*** approaches (12/04), I begin searching for an ***elementary school teaching position***. I am excited by the prospect of modeling character and citizenship to my students and hope to help mold some of them into adults who can change the world. Idealistic? Maybe. Nevertheless, I believe one person can make a difference somewhere, somehow. The enclosed résumé reflects a ***hard-working achiever*** ready to face difficult challenges.

The following beneficial ***skills and personal characteristics*** further strengthen my candidacy for a teaching position in your school district:

PERSONAL TRAITS
- An ***energetic, enthusiastic, and positive teacher*** fosters students who are ***motivated and excited to learn***.
- A ***sense of humor*** eases stress and ***improves performance under pressure***.
- ***Honesty, loyalty, and commitment*** exude a ***strong work ethic*** and ultimately reflect ***school distinction***.
- ***Creativity enhances lesson plans and problem solving***.

INTERPERSONAL/COMMUNICATION SKILLS
- ***A cheerful, positive attitude and supportive style strengthen parent, student, and peer relationships***.
- ***Respect for differences*** enables ***successful interaction with a diverse population*** at appropriate levels.
- Communication that is ***caring, yet direct, concise, and assertive*** ensures ***positive outcomes***.
- ***Attentiveness, perceptiveness, and sensitivity*** allow ***accurate assessments of and responses to*** student needs.
- Openness to and ***acceptance of change*** allows for ***smooth transitions***.

LEADERSHIP SKILLS
- Ownership ***of responsibility and accountability*** demonstrates ***leadership*** to peers and students alike.
- ***Time management, planning, and coordination*** contribute to ***teaching excellence and successful events***.
- ***Team spirit and high expectations*** motivate a class to reach ***measurable goals***.
- Ease and ***experience in dealing with difficult people*** represents a ***take-charge person who can handle adversity***.

I am eager to speak with you in person to investigate your needs and answer any of your questions. Thank you for your time and consideration.

Sincerely,

Bea K. Billingsly

Enclosure: Résumé

RHODA BLAIN

4 Hilltop Circle, Medford, NJ 03333
(home) 856.555.5555 • (cell) 609.777.7777 • rblain@aol.com

(Date)

(Employer Name & Address)

Re: Graduate Assistantship

Dear Employer: (insert name if you know it)

Can you use a highly energetic, highly positive, highly productive graduate student for your graduate assistantship?

I am a graduate student in the Masters Program here at Trenton University, majoring in School Psychology. I expect to graduate in May of 2004 and anticipate starting the EDS Program in the Fall. I have extensive experience in secretarial/administrative work, and in work with children, and believe I would be a good candidate for your opening.

I have worked 25-40 hours / week as a secretary for a busy private psychological practice for the last 2 years. I have done this while maintaining a full course load, and a strong GPA (3.87). I fulfill a very hands-on position where I have handled the administrative needs of 3 doctors including scheduling, receptionist, reports, phone work, and scoring tests.

I also have extensive experience with children. I started as a teenager with babysitting for several families on my street. More recently, I have worked with children who have behavioral and emotional difficulties, in a school setting and also in a partial care facility.

I am a dedicated professional who would welcome a personal interview and hope you will call me at your earliest convenience. Thank you for your consideration.

Sincerely,

Rhoda Blain

SARAH E. BOURNE

1463 North Mesquite Trail • Austin, Texas 78721
Residence: 812.555.1234 • Cell: 917.123.4589 • sebourne@yahoo.com

Legal Assistant / Paralegal dedicated to providing superior support to legal staff

September 18, 2003

Jonathan McEwan
McEwan & Beckwith, LLP
98234 High Street
Austin, Texas 12345

Dear Mr. McEwan:

I recently completed paralegal training and one year's experience in a residential real estate practice. I am now seeking to broaden my skills in litigation or family law. The enclosed résumé details my education, experience, and skills.

Taking initiative has always been a strength of mine. I understand responsibility, hold an intense work ethic, and strive to be my best in any situation. During my past experiences, I made strong contributions to my work and received positive feedback from my supervisors as well as clients.

> *"Sarah's dedication, integrity, and loyalty were truly exceptional. Excellent interpersonal skills, unfailing good humor, honesty, and concern for feelings of others."* Professor Jobin, Supervisor, Texas Christian University

With the combination of experiences outlined in my résumé, I am confident that I have developed a professional resourcefulness and personal diversity that will enable me to become a capable member of your firm. Your consideration of my qualifications will be appreciated.

Sincerely,

Sarah E. Bourne

Enclosure

TONY DEMARCO

12 Butterfield Court • West Hampton, New York 11933 • (631) 446-3201
tdemarco@optonline.net

Dear Sir or Madam:

In August 2003 I will graduate from the State University of New York at Stony Brook with a **Bachelor of Science in Cytotechnology, with a minor in Biology**. I am seeking to pursue my long-term personal and professional goal of a challenging career as a **Cytotechnologist** *within a hospital environment so that I may screen both gynecological and non-gynecological specimens.* Let me briefly highlight the skills, values, and contributions I will bring to your healthcare facility including:

- Dedicated commitment to a long and successful career as a **Cytotechnologist.**

- Excellent attention to detail, time-management, troubleshooting, interpersonal and communication skills, developed through experience at **Good Samaritan Hospital as a Cytology Specimen Preparation Assistant**.

- Ability to perform independently, or as part of a team, building cooperative working relationships among physicians management and support staff in order to meet goals and achieve successful results.

- An energetic, hard-working, and self-motivated work ethic, coupled with a flexible approach to assignments.

Since a résumé can neither fully detail all my skills and accomplishments, nor predict my potential to your **Cytology Department**, I would welcome a personal interview to further explore the merging of my *education, experience, ambition,* and *enthusiasm* with your facility's objectives.

Very truly yours,

TONY DEMARCO

Enclosure

Sarah T. Freeman

3030 Marigold Dr., Crystal, Texas 75000 (000) 999-9999
sfreeman59@yahoo.com

March 31, 2005

Dr. Simon Proctor
Dean of Admissions
Silverstone Institute of International Studies
P.O. Box 9930
Metro, Texas 79000

*"Politics should be the part-time profession of every citizen who
would protect the rights and privileges of free people and who
would preserve what is good and fruitful in our national heritage."*
-- Lucille Ball (1911-1989), US actress, producer

RE: GRADUATE SCHOOL ADMISSION

Dear Dr. Proctor:

My academic success, maturity, and a **strong interest in global affairs** augment a **BA in politics** (GPA 3.5) from Saint Gregory's College of California (May 2004). Current career goals center on attaining a master's degree from Silverstone Institute of International Studies. The enclosed résumé reflects an **intelligent, dedicated** individual who sincerely desires acceptance into your master's program.

The following **characteristics and skills** further exhibit **strong candidacy** for admission:

Interpersonal / Communication Skills
- Integrate easily into team environments using personable, helpful, and energetic demeanor.
- Employ attentive listening and perceptiveness in understanding others.
- Develop trust and rapport with diverse populations through respect for differences.
- Present self articulately, demonstrating and rephrasing for various learning styles.
- Possess English grammar proficiency. Bilingual: English / Spanish.

Leadership Qualities
- Organize time and plan proactively to avoid inefficiency.
- Benefit from an astute mind and ability to focus on tasks until completion.
- Prioritize tasks for positive outcomes.
- Take initiative and assume responsibility, motivating and leading others.
- Solve problems decisively. Effectively cope with stress and time pressure.
- Incorporate integrity, diligence, and stamina into all endeavors.

I am **confident** that my **determination** coupled with a **desire to succeed** will help me **fulfill the requirements of graduate school.** I look forward to hearing from you in the near future regarding my admissions status. In the meantime, thank you for your time and consideration.

Sincerely,

Sarah T. Freeman

Enclosure: Résumé

JODY KELIN

Home Address:	*Cellular:* 609.123.4567	*School Address:*
12 Meadowbrook Drive	*Home:* 732.987.6543	*15 Medford Court*
Lakewood, NJ 01234	*E-mail:* *jkelin@rutgers.edu*	*Newtown, NJ 66666*

(Date)

(Employer Name & Address)

Re: (state specific position such as: "IT professional")

Dear Employer: (insert name if you know it)

Can you use an entrepreneurial IT professional, who has demonstrated good technical solutions, the ability to consult well with clients, and consistently initiates effective new ideas in the workplace?

I started up my own business in high school, providing technical consulting and support to small businesses and individuals. I believe my strong technical skills, together with a keen ability to relate well to others, contributed to the success of my reputation in this venture. Further education and training in college have enriched both my knowledge base and technical abilities. I am enthusiastic about applying this expertise in an exciting IT environment. Some additional highlights of my background include:

- ❑ Experience providing an extensive variety of technical help including troubleshooting, technical support, networking, building PCs, increased security for wireless networks
- ❑ Worked 30 hours per week in a sales management / technical support position while carrying a full-time college course load
- ❑ Won numerous service or recognition awards from two different employers, such as Sales Associate of the Month (10 times)
- ❑ Well organized, dedicated, strong work ethic

I am a dedicated professional who would welcome a personal interview to discuss what I can do for you. I hope you will call me at your earliest convenience. Thank you for your consideration.

Sincerely,

Jody Kelin

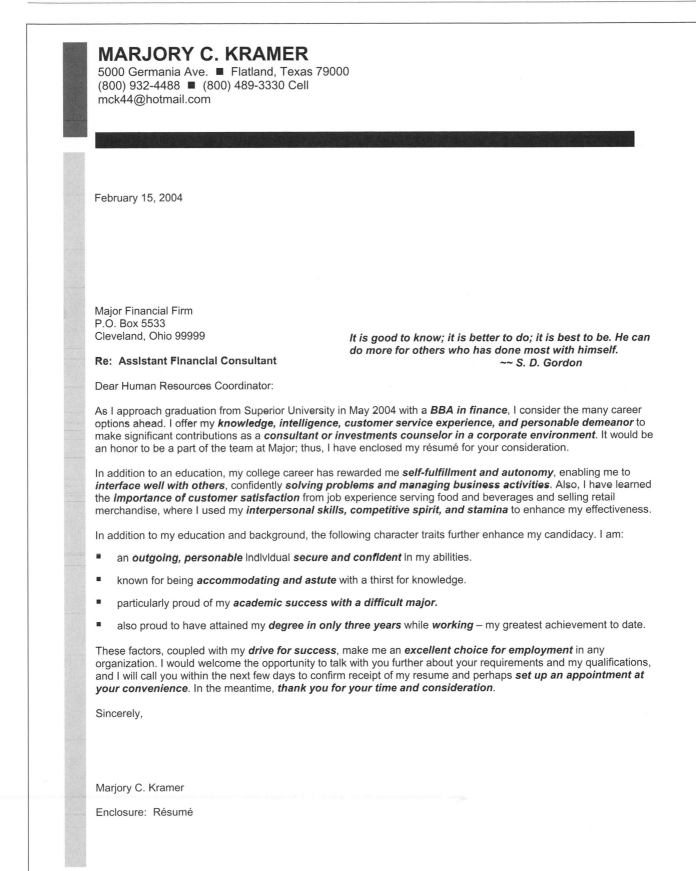

MARJORY C. KRAMER
5000 Germania Ave. ■ Flatland, Texas 79000
(800) 932-4488 ■ (800) 489-3330 Cell
mck44@hotmail.com

February 15, 2004

Major Financial Firm
P.O. Box 5533
Cleveland, Ohio 99999

*It is good to know; it is better to do; it is best to be. He can
do more for others who has done most with himself.*
~~ S. D. Gordon

Re: Assistant Financial Consultant

Dear Human Resources Coordinator:

As I approach graduation from Superior University in May 2004 with a **BBA in finance**, I consider the many career options ahead. I offer my **knowledge, intelligence, customer service experience, and personable demeanor** to make significant contributions as a **consultant or investments counselor in a corporate environment**. It would be an honor to be a part of the team at Major; thus, I have enclosed my résumé for your consideration.

In addition to an education, my college career has rewarded me **self-fulfillment and autonomy**, enabling me to **interface well with others**, confidently **solving problems and managing business activities**. Also, I have learned the **Importance of customer satisfaction** from job experience serving food and beverages and selling retail merchandise, where I used my **interpersonal skills, competitive spirit, and stamina** to enhance my effectiveness.

In addition to my education and background, the following character traits further enhance my candidacy. I am:

- an **outgoing, personable** Individual **secure and confident** in my abilities.

- known for being **accommodating and astute** with a thirst for knowledge.

- particularly proud of my **academic success with a difficult major.**

- also proud to have attained my **degree in only three years** while **working** – my greatest achievement to date.

These factors, coupled with my **drive for success**, make me an **excellent choice for employment** in any organization. I would welcome the opportunity to talk with you further about your requirements and my qualifications, and I will call you within the next few days to confirm receipt of my resume and perhaps **set up an appointment at your convenience**. In the meantime, **thank you for your time and consideration**.

Sincerely,

Marjory C. Kramer

Enclosure: Résumé

BRADLEY ROUND

Apartment 4, 204 George St.
Columbia, MD 21045

E-mail: rounder@hotmail.com

Moblie: 410 666 555
Residence: 410 444 2111

June 15, 2004

Mr. John Maxfield
Human Resources Director
Maxfield, McGrath & Howard, Solicitors
145 Main Street
Columbia, MD 21045

Re: Law Clerkship

Dear Mr. Maxfield:

Currently studying for my Bachelor of Laws at the University of Maryland, I am perhaps unique in terms of the type of student normally applying for Law Clerkship opportunities. Far from being a drain on resources while I learn, I believe my "real life" work experience in the telecommunications sector brings with it a degree of maturity and self-sufficiency that distinguishes me from my student peers.

I don't have to be taught the importance of client satisfaction; that is why my research is consistent, accurate, credible, and "best practice"—to minimize errors and boost the reputation of the company I serve. I don't have to be trained on the realities of business and how "time is money." I understand that only too well and apply it by finding the best solution to a problem that will achieve the client's needs.

Please feel free to review my résumé attached. As you will see, I currently enjoy a distinction average in my Bachelor of Laws studies, and a GPA of 4.3. The diversity of the academic project experiences I have highlighted shows uniformity of results, and the ability to mediate and find solutions despite the multitude of challenges presented.

My experience is no doubt a little different to many graduates. I have traveled internationally, enjoyed opportunities to challenge my technical know-how, trained and directed teams, and led projects that had "hopes riding on them" to cement the company's reputation. Yes, I am different, but it is that very difference that I believe will allow me to continue to learn, advance my professional knowledge, and hopefully establish my career in law in the years to come.

Being community-minded, you will note in my résumé that I am an active participant in sporting clubs, and also volunteer in community legal services, and in marine rescue work.

Naturally I would welcome the opportunity to meet, and discuss a clerkship opportunity with you in more detail. I can be contacted at the details listed above and will make myself available at any time convenient to you.

Thank you for considering my candidacy. I look forward to speaking with you soon.

Sincerely,

Bradley Round

JEFFREY M. RUSSELL

456 Parkstone Place • Dallas, Texas 75007
(972) 222-2222 • JMRussell@hotmail.com • Cell (972) 222-3333

February 18, 2004

Simon Hartford
Director of Human Resources
Pacific Enterprises, Inc.
56 Enfield Place
Phoenix, Arizona 99841

Dear Mr. Hartford,

It is with great interest that I am forwarding my résumé for consideration as International Business Analyst within your organization. With a sound understanding of accounting and management techniques for major corporations, combined with outstanding cross-cultural communication skills, I will bring a unique blend of creative, strategic, and management talents of significant value to your organization. Please consider the following in addition to my résumé:

- Completed Bachelor of Management (2003) and Accounting and Financial Diploma (2001).
- Diverse educational background, including International Marketing & Management, Tourism, Electronic Commerce, and Multimedia Design.
- Effectively managed complex projects and provided troubleshooting skills to resolve difficult issues, ensuring adherence to targets.
- Outstanding communication and interpersonal skills, with expertise in developing and maintaining strong and productive working relationships with clients and staff at all levels.
- Ability to work independently as well as collaboratively to meet company objectives.
- Extensive international experience acquired while working in Malaysia and traveling extensively throughout Australia, Malaysia, Vietnam, and North America.

Throughout my professional and academic careers, I have consistently driven myself to meet challenges and achieve goals. I thrive in challenging and results-oriented environments, and it is these qualities that attract me to a highly competitive and exciting career in international business.

As a highly motivated, results-driven individual, I have a strong desire to exceed expectations and deliver the extra effort necessary to achieve company goals. With my strong management skills in accounting, marketing, and international business, combined with a diverse technical background in computers and software applications, I am confident in my ability to make a strong positive contribution to your organization.

I would welcome the opportunity to discuss how my credentials and expertise can benefit your company and address the unique challenges of this position. I will contact your office next week to arrange a mutually convenient time for us to meet. In the interim, I thank you for reviewing this letter and the accompanying material.

Sincerely,

Jeffrey Russell
Encl.

DAVID JOHN SAMUELS

22 McDonald Street, New York, NY 10014
Home: (000) 333–3333 · djsamuels@hotmail.com

Date

Company Personnel
Company Department
Company Name
Department
Address
Suburb, State, Postal Code

Dear _____,

It is with great interest that I am forwarding my curriculum vitae for consideration as [Position Description] within your organization. With considerable strengths in statistical analysis of various data types, particularly in the use of multivariate methods, combined with finely honed interpersonal and communication skills, I am confident that my qualifications and experience will be of great benefit to your organization. Please consider the following in addition to my curriculum vitae:

- Excellent analytical and report writing skills, with several publications in top international scientific journals. PhD thesis research accepted for publication in the journal *Microbial Ecology* in March 2004 and was presented at ANSTO, UNY, and several scientific conferences.
- Extensive experience in conducting Gas-Chromatography-Mass Spectrometry (GC-MS) analysis and interpreting GC-MS data.
- Strong comprehension of statistical techniques and methods, contributing to scientific research and to the development of risk assessment methods for ANSTO.
- Proven leadership, team management, and organizational skills. Successfully completed military officer academy training and served as a logistic support officer in an infantry unit and subsequently moving to an inspection and training position.
- Extremely self-motivated with the initiative to achieve results, working effectively in diverse independent or team environments in order to meet company objectives.
- Advanced computer skills in MS Word, Excel, and PowerPoint and numerous other packages.

Throughout my professional and academic careers, I have consistently driven myself to meet challenges and achieve goals. As a highly motivated, results-driven individual, I offer your organization decisive leadership, dedication, and a commitment to excellence. Any task or project I undertake is consistently completed to the best of my ability. With focus, drive, determination, and acute attention to detail, I am confident in my ability to make a strong positive contribution to your organization.

Thank you for your time and consideration of my application. I look forward to discussing in detail with you the ways in which I can bring significant value to your organization, and I invite you to contact me, at your convenience, at the above number.

Yours Sincerely,

David Samuels
Enclosed

KEVIN STRONG

5555 Cattle Road, Ranchland, Texas 79000
222-222-2222 (Cell) ☎ 999-999-9999 (Home)
kstrong880@yahoo.com

August 31, 2004

Mr. Brad Crawford
Owner/Operator
Rejuvenation
5599 IH 35
San Antonio, Texas 78000

*What lies behind us and what lies before us are
tiny matters compared to what lies within us.*
~~ Ralph Waldo Emerson

Dear Mr. Crawford:

As I relocate to San Antonio after receiving a **BS in exercise sports science and a minor in health** from Success University, I anticipate the start of a professional career in my field. As a **take-charge leader with a dynamic and energetic style**, I am confident that I will be an asset to your fitness center, and have enclosed my résumé for your review.

Positive feedback from internship and personal trainer endeavors has reinforced my career decision. As you will discover, I am a very personable individual who is able to determine and act on what motivates others. The following **personal attributes and highly developed skills** further confirm credibility as a personal trainer:

PERSONAL CHARACTERISTICS
* Self-motivation, a competitive spirit, a positive attitude, and persistence ensure steady results.
* High standards and a quest for excellence promote success and quality of service.
* Ability to easily interact with others and support team objectives strengthens peer / public relations.
* Flexibility and openness to new ideas foster introduction of new and innovative procedures.

COMMUNICATION AND INTERPERSONAL SKILLS
* Appropriate interpersonal styles and communication techniques gain client trust and rapport.
* Perceptiveness and attentiveness allow understanding of and direct response to customer needs.
* A tolerance of diversity and ability to relate at multiple levels enables success in building strong client/trainer relationships.
* A genuine concern for the emotional and physical well being of others reflects sincerity and contributes to building a solid customer base.

LEADERSHIP QUALITIES
* Integrity, loyalty, diligence, and stamina earn respect and reflect distinction.
* Responsibility and accountability demonstrate leadership and character.
* Time management and organization skills lend themselves to larger client loads and effective events planning.

I am **confident** that my expertise will be an asset to your company's goals and objectives, and I anticipate a **mutually beneficial meeting** with you at your convenience. Excellent references are at your disposal. **Thank you for your consideration**.

Sincerely,

Kevin Strong

Enclosure: Résumé

KANCHANA PERERA

124 Melville Road
Rocklin, CA 95677

E-mail: kanchi@rockman.com

Telephone: (916) 600 0323
Mobile: (916) 622 8071

June 15, 2004

Mr. Larry Vincent
Human Resources Manager
BE Corporation Limited
124 Little Street
Rocklin, CA 95677

Re: Graduate Appointments

Dear Mr. Vincent:

With my Masters in Professional Accounting from Rocklin University of Technology now complete, I respectfully offer my candidacy as an accounting professional offering more than the "average" graduate.

Aided through "real world" accounting and bookkeeping experiences with a large restaurant chain, a small importer/retailer, and a not-for-profit charitable foundation, I have been exposed to a full spectrum of accounting activities—from a national cash-based, high-turnover operation, through to a primarily ad hoc manual system in dire need of attention and computerization.

In each of these roles, I have been praised for my quick ability to identify data anomalies, establish priorities, follow-through each problem to resolution, and analyze methods for improvement—and do so quickly, effectively, and within time constraints.

My résumé attached, will provide you with the details.

You will see that supporting my Masters studies is a Bachelor of Business majoring in accounting and management from Rocklin University, and a Diploma in Business from Fairfield Institute of Business & Technology. I've noted some project highlights for you to garner a better understanding of the depth of my knowledge.

Chronicled also, is my employment with the "Quicker Pasta" restaurant chain as an Accounts Assistant reporting directly to the Financial Controller, where I oversee all bank/sales reconciliations and accounts payable functions for 14 outlets across the state. Working solo on these accounts has been a rare opportunity to expand my professional expertise, and it has been gratifying that my employers have regularly praised my efforts.

However, I'm keen to begin my career in earnest. I see the position you offer as a dual-opportunity in which I can continue to perfect my craft over the long-term and can contribute towards ensuring your accounting function is responsive to your needs, professionally maintained, and accurate so that it aids management decision-making over the short-, medium-, and long-term.

I would appreciate the opportunity to meet with you to discuss the role of (name) in more detail, and can make myself available at a mutually convenient time. Thank you for your consideration. I look forward to meeting with you soon.

Sincerely

Kanchana Perera

RESPONSE TO ADVERTISING COVER LETTERS

JONATHAN BENTLEY, E.I.T.

100 Central Rd.   555-111-1212 (home)
Middletown, MT 55555   JBentley@email.com   555-222-3434 (cell)

August 31, 2004

David Messing
Enterprising Engineers
1000 Waterford Way
Middletown, MT 55555

Dear Mr. Messing:

I can support your company's goals with experience in many aspects of engineering training. I've worked on projects involving complex structural issues, transportation design, and water control. As you will see from my attached résumé, I meet or exceed your listed requirements for the position of Structural Engineer I as published in the August 2004 edition of *Emerging Engineers*.

Your Needs:	**My Qualifications**:
▪ Experience with CAD software	▪ Proficient in AutoCAD, WaterCAD, SewerCad and Flowmaster
▪ Project management experience	▪ Led four-member team in development of complex parking lot design for city
▪ Supervisory experience	▪ Supervised up to 150 employees in high-stress environment, maintaining 100% safety record
▪ Ability to think under pressure	▪ Over four years' experience managing wildfire crews requiring immediate action in dangerous, unpredictable conditions
▪ B.S. degree in civil or structural engineering	▪ Bachelor of Science degree in Civil Engineering with emphasis in structures

My résumé is only a summary of the qualifications I can offer your organization. I will be calling in the next few days to see if we might schedule an interview.

Thank you for your time and consideration.

Sincerely,

Jonathan Bentley

Enclosure

TARA LAWRENCE COLE

90-34 Brownstown Circle • East Islip, New York 11796 • (631) 843-8385 • TLC@Healthmatters.net

May 2004

Long Island Health Care System
Human Resources Department
555 Suffolk Avenue
Brentwood, NY 11717

Re: HCMTG7

Dear Human Resources Administrator:

In response to your open position announcement in *Newsday* for a health care management trainee, I have enclosed my résumé for your review and consideration. Ideally, this position will allow me to further my understanding of the health care system while allowing me to contribute to the management and improvement of day-to-day facility operations.

I offer a Bachelor of Science degree in Health Care Management, along with valuable internship experience gained at Prince of Peace Nursing Home. During this time, I had the opportunity to work closely with other health care professionals to ensure quality resident care, regulatory compliance, and workflow efficiencies.

Prior experience includes positions as a Certified Lifeguard and Teacher Assistant. In these capacities, I proved myself as a caring and responsible person who can be depended upon to manage multiple activities while ensuring the well-being of others. Combined, I am confident I would be an asset to your health care management team.

If you feel there is a mutual interest, I would welcome the opportunity to interview for a suitable position, as I am eager to join a progressive health care facility such as yours. Thank you for your review and consideration. I look forward to hearing from you soon.

Sincerely,

Tara Lawrence Cole

RAYFORD COLLINGSWORTH
8888 Pine Street, Plains, Texas 79400

(800) 999-5555
rcollingsworth87@nts-online.net

March 31, 2005

Mr. Abbot Caster
Director
Texas Legislative Council
P. O. Box 5599
Austin, Texas 79999

...an ordinary person who is motivated, enthusiastic, who has dreams, and who works hard; who has the ability to laugh, to think, to cry; and who can give the gift of belief to other people can accomplish anything.
Unknown

RE: Political Scientist

Dear Mr. Caster:

As a recent Major University graduate holding ***a bachelor of arts in political science (pre-law),*** I am seeking employment in my field. I am particularly interested in the Political Scientist position found posted on your website, and have enclosed my résumé for your review. You will find that my qualifications are a perfect match to the requirements for this position.

A well-rounded individual with a history in sales, teaching, and business ownership, I have developed the networking and public relations skills necessary for success in the political arena. Furthermore, I offer the following ***additional reasons to take a closer look at my credentials.*** My background demonstrates:

- ***enthusiasm, motivation, resourcefulness, and an optimistic attitude for achieving excellence.***

- ***professional integrity and highest ethical and service standards that reflect distinction.***

- ***assertive communication style and effective interpersonal skills for building rapport and trust.***

- ***a team mindset and personable demeanor that enhances peer relationships.***

- ***understanding of diverse populations instrumental in developing strong business and associate relationships.***

- ***creative thinking and idea generation for brainstorming and planning strategies.***

- ***ability to define problems, assess long- and short-term solution implications, and implement action.***

These skills and character traits, coupled with my ***experience and a drive to succeed,*** will ***benefit the goals and objectives*** of the Texas Legislative Council. I would welcome the opportunity for a personal interview at your convenience, and look forward to hearing from you soon to set up a meeting. Excellent references are at your disposal upon request.

Thank you for your consideration.

Sincerely,

Rayford Collingsworth

Enclosure: Résumé

Cara J. Fielding

266 Garfield Avenue
Lansdale, PA 19446

Phone: (215) 361-6133   caraf@dotresume.com

May 21, 2004

Mr. James Wilson
Barkley Creative Group
276 Second Avenue
Collegeville, PA 19426

Re: Junior Account Executive

Dear Mr. Wilson:

Having just completed my bachelor's degree with a major in public relations, I am seeking employment as a junior account executive. The position you advertised appears to be an excellent fit for my background. I offer hands-on experience, the ability to work as part of a team, and solid academic credentials.

Some highlights of my qualifications include the following:

- Helped garner more than $13 million for account during PR agency internship.
- Worked successfully as team member during internship and in three class projects.
- Graduated with 3.5 GPA; worked full-time while carrying full course load.

I have top-notch communication skills with experience conducting training; giving presentations; and writing press releases, articles, and research reports. My internship supervisor described my research skills and professionalism as exemplary and remarked on my ability to work through unfamiliar tasks with little hand-holding.

A copy of my résumé is enclosed for your review. I welcome the opportunity for a personal interview at your earliest convenience.

Thank you for your consideration. I look forward to hearing from you soon.

Sincerely,

Cara J. Fielding

Enclosure

Chapter 12

Special Considerations

For someone new to the job market, it can be difficult to determine what to include on both the résumé and cover letter. You may feel that you have no experience to include, and your work experience could be non-existent or very limited.

I Put All My Best Information in the Résumé. What Do I Say in the Cover Letter?

When composing your cover letter, keep its purpose in mind: The cover letter is written to a specific position and asks for an interview. While you will probably not make many, if any, changes to your résumé each time you send it out, your cover letters will be different each time. Maintaining the right focus will help you determine what to include in the letter. The type of letter will also help you focus: Are you writing to a recruiter or to a blind advertisement? What you know of your audience will also help you focus your letter. Finally, your company research will guide you toward a direction appropriate for that particular opening or desired opening.

Just as you did when writing your résumé, review everything you learned about yourself through your assessments. What are your core values? What is your personality profile? What are your best skills? Why are you drawn to this profession? Put all this information in front of you, and review which aspects from your assessments are best suited to this particular position at this particular company. These are the areas you want to highlight in your cover letter.

Are you still feeling as though you are repeating exactly what is on your résumé? If you are feeling absolutely stuck, use the same information in the body of your letter, *but word it differently*. Look for information that you can summarize in one sentence instead of the two or three bulleted points you have on your résumé. Did you work summer jobs in sales? How much did you contribute to the bottom line overall? Were you repeatedly in leadership roles on school projects? Instead of listing each project, combine your experience in one pack-it-with-a-punch sentence. And if all else fails, focus hard on presenting your best accomplishments in a new way, but be wary of overusing your thesaurus.

As someone new to the working world, you will be focusing on your educational background, volunteer activities, summer or part-time jobs, and any clubs or memberships that may be applicable. Review your background in all of these areas to see which should be stressed in the letter you are composing.

How Long Should My Letters Be?

Generally speaking, aim for one page for all your correspondence. Of course, some circumstances may warrant more than one page, but if you find yourself going over the "limit," first review your letter for anything that can be cut.

Does everything you have written support your goal? If not, cut it out. Are you using wordy phrasing? For example, "due to the fact that" can be rewritten as "because." Look for any wording that can be rephrased. If you do find that you need more than one page, use discretion.

Are you one of those students who, on occasion, adjusted margin or font sizes to reach the minimum page requirement on a paper? Everyone adjusts these settings on occasion for various reasons. However, if you are trying to squish a very long letter onto one page and decide to use this option, be forewarned. Just as you want your résumé to have enough white space on the page to make it easier on the eye, so too do you want your cover letter to have adequate white space. Too many words will immediately turn off most readers and land your résumé in the reject pile before it is even read.

In general, aim for one-inch margins all around. You can adjust the top and bottom margins to as little as a half inch if necessary, but try not to reduce your right and left margins. Never use a font smaller than a 10 point. A range of 10 to 12 is acceptable. Anything smaller or larger makes you look amateurish. Watch for fancy fonts. Some print much larger or smaller than a typical font. When in doubt, err on the conservative side when it comes to fonts. And just as in your résumé, avoid mixing multiple fonts in the same letter. The exception is the header—you want to use the same header as you did on your résumé. Then use the same or a very similar font in the body of your letter that you used in the bulk of your résumé.

I've Been Staring at a Blank Page for Hours. Now What?

Writing a cover letter, or any type of letter, can be intimidating at first. The good news is that the more you do it, the better you will get. If you are really stuck, try a few of these tips to help you get going.

Freewriting This method has been mentioned throughout this book. In this technique, you put the pen to paper (or fingers to keyboard) and just start writing. It does not matter what comes out; you can pull out the good stuff later. Just start writing, making notes on the points you want to make. As you write, more ideas will come to you as you go along. Try to ignore that internal voice that wants everything to come out perfectly the first time. This is just a time to help you put your thoughts on paper. Some you will use, and some will go in the trash. The point of this exercise is to get your brain moving and to get something out on the page—this in and of itself may help reduce many anxieties because you will be taking action rather than just worrying. When you are done, review what you have and pull out the best material. You can then go through your letter point by point, rewording as necessary. Remember that it may take a few drafts before you get your wording just the way you want it.

Record your letter   If you are more comfortable communicating orally than in writing, you may want to record yourself talking about what you want to say in your letter. You can then play it back and type it into your computer. When you are done, rearrange and reword as needed.

Review the samples provided   Read through the samples provided in this book. While you do not want to use anything word-for-word because it will not be your own "voice," you may find something that is close to what you want to say or that sparks an idea for the perfect wording.

Hiring a professional   Some people simply feel that they cannot write a letter of the quality they want or need. If you choose to use a professional, find a member of a professional organization. You will also want to research any credentials held by the professional you choose. Refer to Appendix II for more information on professional organizations and certifications. See Appendix I for information on the professionals who contributed their fine work to this book.

Chapter 13

Common Mistakes and How to Avoid Them

Knowing what not to do in a cover letter is just as important as knowing what to do. The tips provided here are not necessarily comprehensive. Much of this is common sense, but a review is never a bad thing. You have a lot on your mind when compiling a job search. The following is a list of common errors and reminders when it comes to writing letters.

Misspelling recipient's name   This is a common problem that occurs more than it should and can put you out of the running. Those who review cover letters and résumés are often looking for any reason to disqualify a candidate, particularly when they have hundreds of letters to read. When conducting your research, be sure to inquire how to spell the recipient's name. If you are unsure whether the recipient is male or female, inquire as to gender as well. Sometimes you will find that only an initial and last name are provided in a job posting. Unless the advertisement specifically states "no phone calls please," call to find out the first name; even though you

will not address the person by first name only, it will speak well for you to include the full name with the address information. You will then address the recipient as Mr. or Ms. *last name*, followed by a *colon* as you begin your letter.

Using Sir or Madam   There is no reason to use one of these salutations. Ideally, you will have the name of a person to whom to address your letter. If you do not know, and there is absolutely no way to find out, do not use either sir or madam, because you do not know the gender of the person you are addressing. Acceptable salutations include Dear *Hiring Manager, Hiring Executive,* or *Hiring Committee.* You may also opt to leave off the salutation and use the "RE" subject line in its place, thereby avoiding the situation altogether.

Forgetting to change company name or addressee when sending direct mail letters   It has happened more than once: A writer uses the "save as" function or copies and pastes wording from an earlier letter to create a new one. Without carefully reviewing the letter, the writer forgets to change the company information or the contact name. Oops! This is one sure way to get your letter tossed into the recycle bin.

When conducting a direct mail campaign, learn to use the mail merge function in your word processing program. This will allow you to write a letter with functions that will let you create your addresses and salutations in a separate document. You can then merge the two, eliminating the risk of sending out a letter with the wrong information. If you are using the "save as" function to create a new letter from an old one, be sure to review the letter thoroughly before sending it out. Do not rely on your eyes reading from the computer screen. Print the letter and review the hard copy.

Including personal information   Some information should never be included in a cover letter or in your résumé. Do not discuss your marital status, race, religious preferences, sexual orientation, or anything of the sort. Nor should you mention that you own five cats unless you are applying for a position in animal care. Only include information directly related to the job. Leave your personal life out of it.

Including information on why you lost your last job or that you are under qualified   If you left a job on not-so-good terms or were fired, do not include this in your cover letter! Some people feel the need to explain situations that need no explanation unless it comes up in the interview. Even if you had a bad experience, focus only on the positives in your letter. You do not need to inform a prospective employer that, even though you were fired from your last job, you have now seen the errors of your ways and are ready for more responsibility.

Instead, highlight the skills and experiences that will support your candidacy, not put you in a bad light. In the job-hunting process, you are the only person who can sell yourself; avoid actions that will break the sale before your résumé is even read.

Similarly, do not inform the employer of where you are lacking. If you are applying for a position for which you are mostly qualified but lack one or two skills, do not inform the reader that you are not fully qualified. Instead, focus on those areas where you do meet the requirements and sell those in the best way you know how.

Selling an unrelated history   For those of you seeking a position not related to previous jobs or unrelated to your degree, focus only on those skills and experiences that are transferable to the position being sought. Do not go on and on about your extensive sales records while working in retail when you are seeking a job in physical therapy. Instead, focus on the people skills you developed while working with the public.

Writing in too casual a manner   One purpose of your cover letter is to let the reader see that you are in fact human and to allow some of your personality to shine through in the letter. However, this is not the place to be overly casual; this is still a business document. Remember that you are not writing to your best friend; you are writing to your potential boss. Mind your manners and keep it professional.

Writing in third person   Third person is when you write about yourself as he or she. "Robert earned his degree at the University of Utah in 2004." This is too formal and awkward of a way to compose your letters and is not recommended.

Using inappropriate humor It can be very tempting to attempt humor in your letter. You may think that this will endear you to your reader or allow your lighthearted personality to become evident. The problem with including humor in your letter is that humor is very difficult to write. You run the risk of being misunderstood, viewed as unprofessional, or as a clueless job hunter who does not know what is appropriate. Including lines such as "plays well with others" or "holds godlike status among peers" will only be viewed as amateurish. Save moderate humor for in-person meetings, and then use it with discretion.

Gearing letter towards what you want Hopefully the point has been hammered home that you want to gear your correspondence toward what you can offer an employer, not what you hope to gain from a position. In case the point has been missed, here is one more reminder. Do not include a list of things you hope to gain from the position, and definitely avoid the cliché of "seeking an entry-level position with room for advancement" or anything close to this.

Including salary or benefit requests Salary requirements should rarely be mentioned in a cover letter. Some job postings ask that you include your current salary or salary requirements. You can sidestep this by saying something along the lines of "As for salary, I am sure you offer a competitive wage for this market." You do run the risk of not having your résumé read because you did not give a specific number, but this is rarely the case if you present yourself well. If you feel you must provide a dollar amount, provide a range rather than a specific number. Be sure to research typical salaries for your field and for the local market. Salary information can be found at the following websites: http://www.abbott-langer.com, http://www.bls.gov/bls/wages.htm, and http://salary.monster.com. Ideally, the issue of salary will not be raised until you have been given a job offer. Wait until then to discuss it, and let the employer be the first to initiate the money discussion.

Similarly, do not mention anything about benefits or perks you would like to have included in a job offer. This is not the place. The only time you should include salary requirements in your letters is when you are writing to a recruiter. He or she needs to know what your requirements are to place you appropriately.

Using garish paper or paper that does not match or compliment the résumé All of your correspondence to a company probably will end up in the same file. Use the same header for all of your correspondence for continuity. When you use quality paper that is the same or is complimentary, you show that you are a professional and pay attention to details and how you present yourself. Avoid using bright colors. Of course, there are some exceptions, but a general rule is to err on the conservative side using white, off-white, or light gray. Those in creative fields, such as graphic arts or some design jobs, for example, can be more experimental in their presentations. Everyone should avoid using poor-quality paper.

Using completely different font from that of résumé/too many fonts/etc. It is preferable to use the same font as you do in your résumé to create a uniform look. If you choose to use a different font, use one similar in appearance. For example, if you use a serif font in your résumé, use a serif font for your correspondence. Avoid mixing many fonts. At the most, you may have a different style in your heading than you do for the body of the letter. Other than that, do not add fonts to the mix. It will be distracting to your reader and take away from the message you are trying to present.

You also want to use enhancements sparingly. This includes **bold**, underlining, ALL CAPS, and *italics*. When used appropriately, these enhancements can add emphasis to important points. If used too much, your reader is left wondering what is most important. These enhancements can be visually distracting and take away from the message if over used.

Remember, you want your words to convey your meaning instead of relying on gimmicks. It is possible to write an effective letter without using any enhancements. If you find yourself relying on these tools to emphasize your points, consider rewriting the letter. Ask a trusted friend to read the letter for you and provide suggestions. Review the samples provided in this book. You will notice many letters that do not use text enhancements at all.

Using an inappropriate style
Pay attention to the style of letter you choose to write. If you are under qualified for a position, do not use the "T" style letter, as this will only have the opposite effect of what you are trying to do by highlighting where you are lacking as opposed to showing how you match the requirements point by point.

A paragraph letter may be more appropriate than a bulleted list in some instances, particularly if you are aiming for a friendlier approach in your letter. Use your discretion, and have someone else read your letter if you are in doubt. Review the samples provided to get a feel for how each style is most effectively used.

Misspellings or grammatical errors
Any errors in your letter can automatically put you out of the running. *Print* your letter before sending it. Proof it, proof it again, and proof it one more time. Review Chapter Nine for an overview of spelling, grammar, and commonly misused words.

Also review the section on writing in the active voice. You want all of your communications to be written this way. The passive voice is much less effective and results in wordiness. Using the active voice therefore serves you in two ways: It makes your writing more effective and keeps your sentences shorter.

Chapter 14

Putting It Out There

This is a true story: A woman walked into a retail store located in a mall and asked if the company was hiring. She was told that she would need to submit a résumé. The woman then sat on a bench in the middle of the mall, hand wrote a résumé on a piece of notebook paper, and brought it back in. Obviously, she did not get called back for an interview.

While the preceding is an extreme example, many presentation mistakes are made by job seekers. You have worked hard putting your résumé and cover letter together. So why would you want to fold it up, stuff it into a small envelope, and send it out, hoping it will look as good when it arrives as it did when coming off the printer?

When sending your hard copy résumé, treat it with care. If you do not treat it with care, why should the person on the other end? Use quality paper and mail it in a full-size envelope so it can go flat, particularly if you know the résumé will be scanned. There are many good résumé papers out there. Choose a paper weight of some substance, but do not go as far as card stock or cardboard. If possible, choose a paper that has matching envelopes, and use the same paper for your cover letter. Some stationery comes with matching folders as well to help keep damage to a minimum. This is probably as far as you want to go. You do not need to bullet-proof your résumé or send it in a fancy folder; further, if your résumé is going to be scanned, you do not want to make the person on the other end have to remove your résumé from some elaborate binder.

There was a time when people sent résumés out on neon paper or some other attention-grabbing stationery in the hopes that this would help get their résumé noticed. This practice likely will get your résumé noticed—and tossed. Garish paper will only make you look less professional. There are few cases where a piece of attractive stationery will help, but as a general rule, conservative is better. Even some of the fancier marble-effect paper borders are garish. Typically, a nice white or off-white paper will suffice. For those seeking more conservative positions, choose a bright white or light gray paper. Others may want to lean toward ivory. If your paper has a watermark, hold it up to the light to figure out which side is "correct." (You will be able to read the correct side.) This is the side you want to print on.

Try to avoid the temptation to send your résumé in a fancy package, using a gimmick, or attaching your résumé to a box of chocolates and addressing it to the CEO. Antics like these will more often than not make you look foolish. Those in creative fields may get away with a nontraditional résumé or delivery, such as a brochure or clever marketing package, but these are few and far between.

If possible, print your résumé and letters using a laser printer. This will ensure the best print. Inkjet printers can smear or the lettering can flake off once the paper is dry (especially if the paper is folded). Mail a copy of your résumé to yourself before sending it to employers. This will give you an idea of what your résumé looks like after it has gone through the mail, and you can then make any necessary adjustments.

To Staple or Not to Staple

The jury is still out on this one, but the recommendation from this camp is to use a paper clip instead of a staple. This keeps your pages looking nicer, and again, if the résumé is going to be scanned, it is much easier to remove a paper clip than a staple. Do not worry—the paper clip won't cost you much extra in postage.

One thing you must keep in mind is that the paper clip can come off. What does this mean for you? *You must put your name and page number on subsequent pages of your résumé and letters if they are longer than one page.* You do not need to repeat the entire header of your first page; your name and page number will suffice.

Electronic and Scannable Résumés

Putting your résumé out there electronically can occur a few ways. Your résumé could end up in an electronic database even if you send a hard copy. Many companies scan résumés into a computer system, at which point the system "looks" for keywords. If you have enough of the correct keywords in your résumé, it might be read by a human being. Keywords for scannable résumés can be grouped together in a keyword list or scattered throughout the résumé within the text. If your résumé is sent electronically, it will go through the scanning process automatically.

Sometimes you do not know if your résumé will be scanned. Try to find out by contacting the company. If it is scanned, you want to include as many keywords as possible, and if sending a hard copy, you want to address some formatting issues. All résumés that are scanned should be written in a traditional font such as Times New Roman or Ariel. Because scanned résumés are then converted by a computer system into an ASCII format, it is best to keep your scannable résumé simple, or you may want to submit an ASCII format résumé in the first place (see what follows). If you are unsure if the résumé will be scanned, you can send two hard copies: one of the "pretty" version to be read by a human and a second, simplified version that can be scanned.

If you did not use an objective in your hard copy résumé, add one for your scannable résumé. You want to name the job title that you are after. Use a simple font, and keep your font sizes between 10 and 14 (up to size 20 is okay for your name). The rule is that you want to use a font where none of the letters touch each other. Because of this, avoid using underlining, as this can confuse the reading system. Underlining touches letters that fall below the line, such as p, g, j, etc. Italics is generally okay as long as you use a simple font. Avoid using decorative fonts. All caps are okay in replace of fancy headers. Also avoid any fancy bullet